GW00544990

A SUDDEN CLASH OF THUNDER

BHAGWAN SHREE
RAJNEESH

talks on Zen stories
and answers questions

A
SUDDEN
CLASH
OF
THUNDER

compilation and editing
MA YOGA ANURAG

design
SWAMI ANAND YATRI

RAJNEESH FOUNDATION

Published by Ma Yoga Laxmi
Rajneesh Foundation
Shree Rajneesh Ashram
17 Koregaon Park
Poona — 411 001 India

First Edition December 1977

Printed by
K. P. Puthran at the Tata Press Ltd.,
414, Veer Savarkar Marg, Prabhadevi,
Bombay 400 070.

Acknowledgement is given to the following for the
stories reproduced in this book:
ZEN BUDDHISM — Peter Pauper Press
ZEN: POEMS, PRAYERS, SERMONS, ANECDOTES,
INTERVIEWS —
ed. Lucien Stryk and Takashi Ikemoto — Anchor
Printed in India

Printed in India

CONTENTS

INTRODUCTION

This is a book of fragrances. Fresh, heady, sensuous, awakening—
they are instantly in commune with the centre of one's being. This
communion is not intellectual for fragrances are not concerned with
intellect.

A fragrance, like Truth, simply is. It cannot be dissected or affected in
any way by the knives of intellect. A fragrance need not be understood,
cannot be understood. Yet its truth is absolute, is irrefutable, is undeniable.

You are in a position to savour slowly each fragrance of this book. Do
so. Enjoy its simplicity, its profundity, its directness. And remember
that regardless of how heady these fragrances are, their source is infinitely more intriguing, more alive, more beautiful, more sensuous,
more inspiring.

The source of these fragrances is Bhagwan Shree Rajneesh.

I wish I could tell you who Bhagwan is or what he is. However, in order
to do that I would have to know it myself—which I don't.

I could say that he is an Enlightened human being, but that would just
be using words that I myself don't understand.

He is simply beyond my comprehension. Part of what he is I can see and
register in the pigeonholes of my computer-mind. However, I don't
know what to do with the rest of what I see. This alone is disconcerting
enough for my logical, rational, modern Western psychologist mentality.
And to make comprehension even more difficult, a part of me knows
with absolute certainty that he exists on and is functioning on additional
levels which are totally invisible and unknown to me. He seems to exist
on levels of consciousness that were uncharted seas for Freud, Jung,
Adler and the other "fathers of modern psychology".

As a psychotherapist of the Human Potential Movement, I have always
been convinced that man is a flower that is just beginning to blossom.
I have been uplifted and inspired by Carl Rogers, Abraham Maslow,
Fritz Perls, Wilhelm Reich and many others who have pioneered the

Growth Movement. They helped me see my own life more clearly, which allowed me in turn to help others see their lives more clearly.

As I used the available psychological theories and techniques to aid my own growth, I realized that each of them, although extremely valuable, had its upper limits. I felt like someone climbing a staircase which ended at a certain floor, but where I knew there were still many floors above me. The staircase had been invaluable in getting me as high as I was, but since it went no higher it obviously couldn't help me get to the upper floors.

I began searching for a staircase that would take me farther upstairs.

I had rejected traditional religion years ago. It was not only useless and cowardly, it was downright detrimental. Yoga was something I had been practising for years and had benefited from its effects on my body and psyche. However, I felt that its approach to man's spiritual development was dusty, antiquated and not in touch with the problems of modern Western man.

Other Eastern philosophies also attracted me, but none spoke directly to my inner core. Zen appealed to me, even inspired me. I liked its cleanness, its briskness and its brusqueness. Its simplicity seemed honest and true.

However, Zen also had something unattainable in it. Something vague and absurd. Something distant. I knew I could never stick to the Zen path even though I often considered it. What kept me from Zen was not a lack of determination on my part or lack of authenticity in Zen. Rather it was the suspicion that Zen was developed in a different day and age and that there must be faster, more effective techniques than those used by traditional Zen masters.

Luckily, before this became anything like a dilemma, one of Bhagwan's books was put in my hands. After only a page or two I was convinced in some unknown way that the author knew, really *knew* what he was talking about.

Why I was so immediately convinced I can't say. But my inner core was touched. I simply had to see this man.

INTRODUCTION

I came to Poona. And stayed. There was no place else to go. Nothing else to do. I, a sceptic by nature, was overwhelmingly convinced.

(Now I lead therapy groups in the ashram which is rapidly becoming one of the world's largest growth centres. In addition to both traditional and unconventional forms of meditation, seekers can also participate in Encounter, Primal Therapy, Massage, Marathons, Tai Chi Chuan, Karate, Rolfing, Hypnotherapy, Sufi Dancing, African Dancing, Soma, movement and music groups, spontaneity groups, endurance groups, Gestalt Therapy, Centring, Alexander Technique, Psychic Healing and Vipassana. New groups are being added continuously. Each participant's progress through the groups is personally guided by Bhagwan.)

Each morning Bhagwan talks to us of Truth. For an hour and a half his words speak fragrances of Truth and his presence exudes Truth. I am now more convinced than ever that he is Enlightened, that he is Awakened. Even so, there is nothing I can say to convince anyone else. Nor do I want to try.

If you are open to Truth you will recognize it. As you read this book you will discover no new truths. Rather, you will have the impression that Bhagwan is saying things that you already knew but hadn't quite been able to formulate. He speaks to that part of you that actually *does* know, has always known, the Truth.

Helping the disciple get closer to this Truth is the task of an Enlightened master. To do this he must come down to the disciple's level. He must speak the disciple's language, figuratively and literally.

Every Enlightened master has had his own style, his own way of expressing the Truth. But the style used was not necessarily a personal style of the master's. No. It was a reflection of what was needed at that time, in that place to interpret Truth to the disciples.

Whether a master speaks of self discipline, of love, of awareness or surrender—of service, of prayer or meditation, he uses it as a device, as a bridge between the disciple and the Truth. And it must be a bridge that the disciple can accept and tred upon.

INTRODUCTION

The Truth remains the same. But through the ages masters who have interpreted it have used different devices, different bridges, different languages. Seekers living in later ages and different cultures have often confused the masters' bridges with the Truth those bridges were trying to reach. They have compared the bridges, found them vastly different in many cases, and incorrectly concluded that each master was teaching something different.

Bhagwan Shree Rajneesh is an Enlightened master who not only builds innovative, appropriate bridges for his modern-day disciples, but who also renovates those bridges used in the past, again making it clear which is bridge, which is Truth, and how the bridge can help its user come closer to the Truth.

Bhagwan cleans up these old bridges, tears down the false and superfluous additions that have accumulated through the centuries, and recreates them in their original clarity and purpose. The result is beautiful.

In this book this living master recreates all of the Truth and Beauty of the old Zen masters. But he does it in such a way that today's seeker immediately recognizes the timelessness and infinitness of Truth.

Each chapter is a direct transcription of one of Bhagwan's morning talks here at the Poona ashram. Five chapters are concerned with the restoration and renovation of some especially beautiful Zen bridges to Truth. In the other five chapters he answers disciples' questions, either about the Zen approach or about their spiritual growth in general.

Although this book quivers with the fragrances of life and truth, it remains nevertheless a book. And as a mirror is not the mountain it reflects—this book can only reflect in an insufficient way the beauty, the love, the knowing emptiness of Bhagwan Shree Rajneesh.

SWAMI ANAND SANTOSH

A SUDDEN CLASH OF THUNDER

is a collection of ten spontaneous talks
given by Bhagwan Shree Rajneesh
on Zen alternating with questions & answers
at Shree Rajneesh Ashram
from august eleventh to twentieth 1976

CHAPTER 1

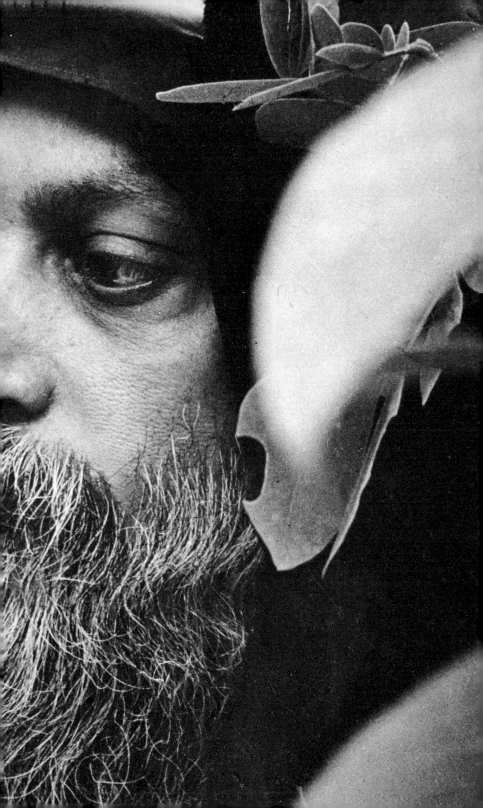

BUTEI, the Emperor of Ryo, sent for Fu-daishi to explain the Diamond Sutra. On the appointed day Fu-daishi came to the palace, mounted the platform, rapped on the table before him, then descended and, still not speaking, left.

Butei sat motionless for some minutes, whereupon Shiko, who had seen all that had happened, went up to him and said, "May I be so bold, sir, as to ask whether you understood?"

The Emperor shook his head sadly.

"What a pity," said Shiko. "Fu-daishi has never been more eloquent."

A SUDDEN CLASH OF THUNDER
eleventh august 1976

TRUTH IS. It simply is. Nothing can be said about it. And all that can be said about it will falsify it.

There is no need for any explanation. Unexplained, utterly immediate, truth *is*. It surrounds you. It is within you, without you. There is no need to come to any conclusion about it. It is already concluded! You *are* in it. You cannot be without it. There is no way to lose it. There is no way to become distracted from it. You may be fast asleep, unaware, but still you are in it.

So those who know truth know well that philosophy is not going to help. The more you try to know about truth, the more you become asleep. The very effort to know leads you astray. Truth can be felt but cannot be known. When I say it can be felt, I mean you can be present to it, it can be present to you. There is a possibility of a meeting. There is a possibility of becoming one with it. But there is no way to know it.

Truth cannot be objectified. You cannot put it *there* and see it. You cannot hold it in your hand and see it. You cannot examine it from the outside—only from the inside, only by becoming one with it, can you feel it. Feeling is the only knowledge possible. Hence, those who know say: Love is the way.

Knowledge is a sort of ignorance. The word 'ignorance' is very beautiful. Split it in two—it becomes 'ignor-ance'. Truth can be ignored. That's what ignorance is; otherwise, truth is already present. Ignorance is nothing but ignoring the truth which is already there. And a man of knowledge becomes more ignorant, because the more he thinks he knows, the more he becomes capable of ignoring that which is. Lost in his theories, dogmas, creeds, scriptures, he no longer has any eyes to look at the reality. Lost in words, verbalizations, his vision is clouded. He cannot see that which is.

The more you are clouded by your thinking, the more you are a mind, the more you will be able to ignore the truth. Nothing like knowledge is needed—only innocence, a childlike innocence. Vulnerable, open . . . . Not *trying* to know. In the very effort to know, there is violence. In the very effort to know, you have trespassed reality. In the very effort to know, you have become a voyeur. You have attacked reality, you are trying to rape reality.

That's why I continuously say science is a rape on reality. The word 'science' comes from a root which means 'to know'. Science is knowledge. Religion is not knowledge. Religion is love. The word 'religion' comes from a root which means binding together— falling into love, becoming one.

Truth is felt. It is a lived experience. So whatsoever can be said about truth will be untrue. Just because it has been said, it becomes untrue.

All that has been said up to now, and all that will be said in the future, has nothing to do with truth. There is no way of expressing it. Truth is very elusive. You cannot catch hold of it in words. You cannot catch hold of it through the mind. Mind goes on missing it, because the very functioning of the mind is anti-truth. The functioning of the mind is non-existential: it functions in that which is not, either in the past or in the future. The past is no more, the future not yet, and the mind only functions either in the past or in the future. In the present there is no mind.

If you *are* herenow, suddenly you have slipped out of the mind. How can you think herenow? Thinking will take you away from the herenow. A single thought, and you are thousands of miles away from here and now. In the here and now there is no possibility, there is no space for thinking to arise.

Mind functions in the non-existential, in the fictitious, in the imaginary. Mind is a faculty of dreaming—it is a dream faculty! Truth is not known by mind; that's why I say it is not known at all. Truth is felt by the heart, by your totality; by *you,* not by your head; by you as an organic unity. When you know truth, you know by the head and by the toes; you know by your bones and by your guts; you know by your heart and by your blood; you know it by your breathing—just by your very being. Truth is known by being.

That is the meaning when I say truth is felt. It is an experience.

I have heard:

> A monk asked Joshu: "What is the Buddha?"
> "The one in the hall."
> The monk said, "The one in the hall is a statue, a lump of mud."
> Joshu said, "That's so."
> "What is the Buddha, then?" asked the monk again.
> "The one in the hall," said Joshu.

Now what is this Joshu trying to do? He is saying: "Your question is absurd. Because you are asking an absurd question, I am answering it in an absurd way. Your question is stupid, and there can be no intelligent answer to a stupid question." He is trying to show to this monk that the very question: What is the Buddha? is nonsense, because there is no way to say anything about the Buddha. It is an awakening. It is an experience. It happens within you. You cannot read it through the scriptures, and you cannot ask those who have come to know it. The only way is: you have to go to it; you have to allow it to happen.

In the Buddhist terminology 'Buddha' is equivalent to 'truth'. They don't talk much about truth; they talk much more about

Buddha. That too is significant, because when *you* become a Buddha—'Buddha' means when you become Awakened—truth is, so why talk about truth? Just ask what awakening is. Just ask what awareness is—because when you are aware, truth is there; when you are not aware, truth is not there.

So the basic and real question is about awareness. But that, too, cannot be asked and solved. One has to become aware—there is no other way.

A disciple asked a Zen master, "If someone were to ask me a hundred years from now what I thought was your deepest understanding, what should I say?"

The master replied, "Tell him I said: This is it!"

Now what type of answer is this?—This is it! He indicated to the immediate reality: This.

Vedanta, the greatest philosophical effort in India, talks about 'That': *Tatwamasi* Swetketu—That art thou, Swetketu. Zen people talk about 'this'. Certainly their understanding is deeper—because 'that' is again in the future, far away; 'this' is present. This is that. This shore is the other shore. This life is the only life, and this moment is eternity.

If you can live *this* moment, if you can be here *this* moment, then everything takes care of itself. Then you need not be anxious. Then there is no need to ask—before you ask, the answer is delivered. The answer has been always there, but we are not aware. So the whole effort of Zen is how to bring awareness to you.

Man is as if asleep. Man lives in a stupor—moves, works, is born, lives and dies, but almost fast asleep, snoring. Man's mind is very dull. Mind is dullness. Mind has no intelligence in it. There has never been an intelligent mind. I don't mean that there have never been intelligent people; there have been intelligent people, but there has never been an intelligent mind. Intelligence is something that comes when mind is dropped. Mind is never original, never radical. Mind is always orthodox. Mind is always repetitive, mechanical; it functions like a robot. It goes on repeating the same thing again and again. It is like a computer: whatsoever you feed into it, it goes on chewing it again and again.

6

Have you watched your own mind and its functioning? Nothing new ever happens to it. Nothing new can happen to it. And because of it you remain oblivious of all that is happening all around you; you go on ignoring it. You are too much attached to this mediocre, stupid instrument. It is good to use it; it is good as a reservoir, as memory; it is good to keep records—but it is not a way to see into reality. It has no eyes.

Mind is blind like a bat. It has no eyes. Mind can never be intelligent—only no-mind is intelligent. Only no-mind is original and radical. Only no-mind is revolutionary—revolution in action.

This mind gives you a sort of stupor. Burdened by the memories of the past, burdened by the projections of the future, you go on living—at the minimum. You don't live at the maximum. Your flame remains very dim. Once you start dropping thoughts, the dust that you have collected in the past, the flame arises—clean, clear, alive, young. Your whole life becomes a flame, and a flame without any smoke. That is what awareness is.

Consciousness without thinking: that's what awareness is. Being alert and with no thought. Try it! whenever you see thinking gathering, disperse it! pull yourself out of it! Look at the trees with no screens of thinking between you and the trees. Listen to the chirping of the birds with no chirping of the mind inside. Look at the sun rising and feel that inside you also a sun of consciousness is rising . . . but don't think about it, don't assert, don't state, don't say. Simply be. And, by and by, you will start feeling glimpses of awareness, sudden glimpses of awareness—as if a fresh breeze has entered into your room which was getting stale and dead; as if a ray of light has entered into the dark night of your soul; as if, suddenly, life has called you *back*.

YOU HAVE heard the story of Lazarus—that is a story of man as such. It is said Lazarus died. Jesus loved him very much. His sisters informed Jesus; by the time the news reached him, Lazarus had been dead for four days. Jesus came running. Everybody was crying and weeping, and he said, "Don't weep, don't cry! Let me call him back to life!"

Nobody could believe him. Lazarus is dead! And the sisters of

Lazarus said, "He is now stinking—he cannot come back. His body is deteriorating."

But Jesus went to the grave where the body was preserved for him to come. The stone was pulled aside. In the dark cave Jesus called out, "Lazarus, come out!" And it is said he came out.

It may not have happened that way; it may be just a parable—but it is a beautiful parable about man. When I look into your eyes, that's all I can say: "Lazarus, come out!" You are dead and stinking. You are not yet alive. You are born, but you need to be reborn. Your first birth has not been of much help. It has brought you to a certain extent, but that is not enough. You have to go a little further. The birth that has already happened to you is only physical—you need a spiritual birth.

It is said: One professor of Jerusalem university went to see Jesus. Of course, he went in the night. His name was Nicodemus; he was a very rich, respectable man, a great scholar, well known in the Jewish world. He was afraid to go to Jesus in the daylight, because what will people think? He was known to be a great, learned man, wise—what will they think? that he has gone to this carpenter's son to ask something? He was older than Jesus—could almost have been Jesus' father. No, it was not possible for him to go in the daylight. Cunning and clever, he went in the night when there was nobody else. And Jesus asked him, "Why didn't you come in the day?"

He said, "I was afraid."

Jesus must have laughed. He said, "Nicodemus, for what have you come? What do you want of me?"

He said, "I would like to know how I can know God, how I can know the truth."

Jesus said, "You will have to be reborn."

Nicodemus could not understand. Jokingly he said, "What do you mean? Have I to enter again into a woman's womb? Are you joking or something? Are you kidding or something?"

Jesus said, "No, I mean it—I mean what I say. You have to be reborn. You are such a coward. This is not life. You don't have any courage. You will have to be reborn! You will have to become a new man, because only that new man can come to truth and realize

8

it. Even to see me you have come in the night. How will you be able to go and see the truth? How will you encounter God? You will have to go naked. You will have to go in deep humility. You will have to drop all your respectability, all your scholarship. You will have to drop your ego—that's what to be reborn means."

The first birth is only a physical birth; don't be satisfied with it. It is necessary but not enough. A second birth is needed. The first birth was through your mother and father; the second birth is going to be out of the mind. You have to slip out of the mind and that will be your rebirth—you will be reborn.

And, for the first time, trees will be greener than they are, and flowers will be more beautiful than they are, and life will be more alive than you have ever known it, because you can know it only to the extent that you are alive. You cannot know life if you are not alive. Whatsoever you are, you know life only up to that extent.

Mind, and mind's hold on you, is the imprisonment. Get rid of the mind. The question is not how to know truth; the question is how to get rid of the mind, how to get rid of this constant ignoring, this ignorance; how to be just here naked, throbbing, streaming, flowing, overflowing, and meeting the truth that has already been there, that has always been there.

Somebody asked a very famous Chinese poet, Yang Wang-li:

"Now what is poetry?"

He said, "If you say it is simply a matter of words, I will say a good poet gets rid of words. If you say it is simply a matter of meaning, I will say a good poet gets rid of meaning. 'But,' you ask, 'without words and without meaning, where is the poetry?' To this I reply: Get rid of words and get rid of meaning, and there is still poetry."

In fact, only then is there poetry. When words are no more there, when meaning is no more there, then suddenly poetry erupts, explodes. Poetry is a flowering of your being, and religion is more like poetry than like philosophy.

Philosophy tries to explain things—never succeeds. At the most, it can succeed only in explaining away things, but it never succeeds in explaining them. Religion makes no effort to explain life.

9

It tries to live it. Religion does not take life as a problem to be solved—it takes life as a mystery to be lived. Religion is not *curious* about life. Religion is in awe, in tremendous wonder about life.

Just our *being* here is such a miracle. It cannot be explained why I am here, why you are here. Why these trees are here, why these stars are here. Why at all this universe exists, and goes on peopling itself with trees and birds and people. Why in the first place it is there, there is no way to know. It simply is there. But it inspires awe! It fills the heart with wonder. It is unbelievably true—it is incredible! It is absurd, but tremendously beautiful.

Why it is there, there is no way to say—but it is there. And religion says: Don't waste your time for the why. It *is* there: delight in it! Celebrate it! Be lost into it! And let it be lost into you. Meet it! Let the meeting be like two lovers entering into each other. Let it be an orgasmic experience.

But religion in the West has a very wrong connotation. It has almost reached to a point where the very word 'religion' creates a repulsion, where the very word 'religion' reminds one of dead churches and dead priests. It reminds one of serious looking people, long faces. It has lost the capacity to dance, to sing, to celebrate. And when a religion has lost the capacity to dance, to celebrate, to sing, to love, just to be, then it is no more religion— it is a corpse, it is theology. Theology is dead religion.

In the West theology has overpowered religion. When theology overpowers religion, then religion is nothing but philosophy. And the philosophy is also not very philosophic—because philosophy can exist only through doubt, and theology bases itself on faith. So it is impotent philosophy, not even philosophy in the real sense.

Religion is not based on belief or faith: religion is based on awe, religion is based on wonder. Religion is based on the mysterious that is your surround. To feel it, to be aware of it, to see it, open your eyes and drop the dust of the ages. Clean your mirror! and see what beauty surrounds you, what tremendous grandeur goes on knocking at your doors. Why are you sitting with closed eyes? Why are you sitting with such long faces? Why can't you dance? and why can't you laugh?

Nietzsche is right: God is dead . . . because theologians have killed Him. God can be alive only when a lover is dancing. When a theologian is trying to find arguments to prove God, He is dead. God is alive when two persons fall in love—then God is throbbing and kicking. God is alive when you look at a flower and you cannot move from there—something overpowers you, overwhelms you. When you look at the stars and you are one with the mystery, and your boat starts sailing towards the other shore, then God is alive. When you sing a song—it may be meaningless, it may be just la-la-la—it may not have any meaning, but God is alive in that sheer expression of joy.

God is alive when you are alive. If you are not alive, how can your God be alive? Your God is yours. If you are dead, your God is dead; if you are alive, your God is alive. Your God cannot be more than you, because your God is your innermost core of being. So if you want to know what God is, become more alive. If you want to know what God is, become more divine. If you want to know what God is, then don't try to know—try to feel. He comes through the door of the heart.

God is such a mystery—or call it life, or existence—life is such a mystery that even if you enter into the innermost shrine of it you will not be able to believe it. It is unbelievably true. It is incredible.

I was reading a poem of Leopold Staff. Listen to it:

The Bridge

I didn't believe,
Standing on the bank of a river
Which was wide and swift,
That I would cross that bridge
Plaited from thin, fragile reeds
Fastened with bast.
I walked delicately as a butterfly
And heavily as an elephant,
I walked surely as a dancer
And wavered as a blind man.
I didn't believe that I would cross that bridge,

11

And now that I am standing on the other side,
I don't believe I crossed it.

Even when you have known God, you will not be able to believe
that you have known Him. That is what I mean when I say God is
a mystery. Unknown, He remains unknowable. Known also, He
remains unknowable. Unseen, He is a mystery; seen He becomes
an even greater mystery. It is not a problem that you can solve.
It is bigger than you. You can dissolve into it—you cannot solve it.

I have heard that Wittgenstein, a great Western philosopher,
who comes nearest to the Zen attitude, used to say that he did not
solve philosophical problems—he dissolved them. And he used
to say: "We leave things as they are but perhaps for the first time
we come to see them as they are." Nothing can be done about
things as they are. All that can be done is to help you to see them
as they are. "We leave things as they are but perhaps for the first
time we come to see them as they are."

And again: "Philosophy simply puts everything before us, and
neither explains nor deduces anything—since everything lies open
to view, there is nothing to explain."

Yes, life is a mystery, and there is nothing to explain—because
everything is just open, it is just in front of you. Encounter it!
Meet it! Be courageous! That is the whole standpoint of Zen.

NOW LET ME help you to enter into this beautiful story. I will
not explain it. I can just seduce you to enter into it. I can
simply allure you to enter into it. I can only persuade you to
have a taste of it.

Butei, the Emperor of Ryo, sent for Fu-daishi
to explain the Diamond Sutra.

Now the Diamond Sutra is really a Kohinoor; it is one of the most
significant utterances ever uttered on this earth. Buddha's sayings
in the Diamond Sutra are the most precious. But the basic thing
in the Diamond Sutra is that nothing can be explained, that life
is utterly unexplainable; that life is such that all explanations fall
short, that all philosophies prove very narrow. The sky of life is

so vast that there is no way to confine it in any hypothesis or doctrine.

Buddha himself never used to talk about metaphysical problems. He made a list of ten or twelve problems, and before he entered a town or a city his disciples would go and declare in the town: "Don't ask about these twelve problems because he will not answer." Not that he cannot answer—if *he* cannot answer then who will answer?—but that these problems are unanswerable. They are better left not touched; better they are left alone.

Nobody should ask about God. Buddha would not say God is; he would not say God is not—because he said both are irrelevant. To say God is, is as irrelevant as to say God is not—because that which is, is beyond the positive and the negative. That which is, it is beyond the minus and the plus. That which is cannot be said 'is' and cannot be said 'is not'. It is *far* beyond both. That which is, it is beyond dichotomy, it is beyond dialectics, it is beyond duality. 'Is' and 'is not' create a duality. Existence is one, organically one; it comprehends both.

Questions like this, Buddha would say, please don't ask.

This Emperor Butei asked another Buddha, Fu-daishi, a Zen master, to come to his palace and explain to him the Diamond Sutra. Buddhists long too much to understand what this Diamond Sutra is. It is utterly absurd. It is difficult to understand, because it has nothing explained in it. Those are utterances of tremendous value, but no philosophy is woven around them, no system is created. Those are atomic utterances. And the substratum of them all is that nothing can be said. Just like Lao Tzu's *Tao Te King:* The Tao that can be uttered is no longer Tao. The truth that is said is no longer truth. Truth said becomes untrue—*said* and it becomes false. Now what to do? How to understand?

The Emperor must have been reading the Diamond Sutra. And there is *no* other way than to ask some Enlightened person— because the Diamond Sutra, or scriptures like that, are utterly illogical. Unless you can find someone who has become awakened you cannot sort it out, you cannot figure it out. It will be very confusing to you. You can go on repeating it, you can even enjoy the music of your repetition, the rhythm, but you will never be able

13

to penetrate into the mystery. The mystery can be explained only by an alive person.

> *On the appointed day Fu-daishi came to the palace, mounted the platform, rapped on the table before him, then descended and, still not speaking, left.*

This was his discourse on the Diamond Sutra. He did a great job! What did he say by doing this?

First thing: that truth can be explained only in action; words are not enough. If the Emperor had watched rightly the way Fu-daishi walked, *there* was the commentary on the Diamond Sutra. The grandeur, the dignity, the beauty, the grace, the way he walked— there was the commentary on the Diamond Sutra. He must have walked like Buddha—he *was* a Buddha. He must have carried a milieu of Buddhahood around him. He must have brought a different type of universe with him into the palace — a dimension *alive.* His door was open: if the Emperor had had any eyes, he would have seen that Buddha himself had come. It was not Fu-daishi, it was Buddha walking again on the earth—in another form, under another name. The container may have been different, but the content was exactly the same.

Fu-daishi walked, *mounted the platform, rapped on the table before him* . . . why did he rap on the table before him? He must have seen the Emperor fast asleep. He must have seen him dozing. Just to make him a little alert, just to shock him! . . . *then descended* . . . he did well! What more can you do? When a person is asleep, that's all that can be done: you can *shout* at him, you can *knock* at his door. *He rapped on the table* . . . what *else* can you do? Then gracefully he must have descended . . . *and, still not speaking, left.* Because if he had spoken on the Diamond Sutra he would have proved that he himself had not understood it.

On the Diamond Sutra it is impossible to speak: it is the *very* truth. No, it would have been profane. It would have been a sacrilege! It would not have been right. Only silence can be the commentary. Had the Emperor had any ears to listen to silence, he would have understood.

. . . and, still not speaking, left. Why did he leave so suddenly? —because more is not possible. You cannot forcibly give the truth to somebody who is not ready. He did whatsoever he could; now there was no point in lingering any longer.

And that suddenly leaving the Emperor was also another shock. He must have jolted the Emperor to his very roots. He came like a cyclone, almost uprooted the tree of Butei! The Emperor could not have even dreamt that such a *rude* behaviour. . . . He was doing it out of tremendous compassion, but to the Emperor it must have looked rude, uncivil, unmannerly.

And in a country like Japan where people are obsessed with manners, where their faces have all become false, where everybody is carrying a mask! For centuries the Japanese have been the most false people in the world, always smiling. The Emperor must have been shocked; he could not have believed what happened . . . and so suddenly comes Fu-daishi!

And he must have waited for so long for this appointed time. And he must have longed for so long that he would say something, that he would enlighten him, he would help him to know. And here comes this man: walks, mounts on the platform — leaves without uttering a single word!

Butei sat motionless for some minutes. . .

He must have been completely incapable of figuring it out. Fu-daishi had shocked him out of his wits! But had he been a little aware, that interval would have opened a new dimension for him. Fu-daishi has invited him, he waits there, seeing that the Emperor is completely asleep — even shouting is not going to help. Even if you call "Lazarus, come out!" he will not listen.

He left. The Emperor was shocked. For a few minutes he sat motionless

> *. . .whereupon Shiko, who had seen all that had happened, went up to him and said, "May I be so bold, sir, as to ask whether you understood?"*

Now to ask this even of an ordinary man is dangerous. And to ask an emperor: "Sir, whether you understood . . . ?"

Now this man, Shiko, is a man of tremendous understanding — must have been. He has understood the significance of the gesture of Fu-daishi. He must have seen the glory that walked; he must have seen the light that shone in silence. He must have seen those eyes overflowing with compassion. He must have felt the grace that came like a breeze — cool, calm, serene. He must have felt sorry for the Emperor also.

> *"May I be so bold, sir, as to ask whether you understood?"*
> *The Emperor shook his head sadly.*

He has not been able to understand. He is sad. He must have become even sadder because of this man, Shiko. Now he can see that something *has* happened; now he can *feel* that some opportunity has passed his door, that some momentous interval was available to him, and he has missed.

> *The Emperor shook his head sadly.*

Many people have been doing that down the centuries. A Buddha comes, a Jesus comes, a Krishna, a Zarathustra — very few, very rarely. Shiko's are very few — those who understand. Butei exists as the mass; Butei is the many; Butei is the majority, the crowd. Buddha comes and walks; he brings another world into this world. He brings tremendous beauty, but you cannot see, you cannot feel.

Jesus goes on saying to his disciples: "If you have ears, listen! If you have eyes, see!" Truth was standing before them. God Himself was standing before them. God has come many times to the earth — He *cares* for it! In many forms He has been seeking you. Never think for a moment that you are uncared for.

It is not only that you are seeking God — God is also seeking you in many, many ways. Sometimes as a Krishna with his flute, sometimes as a Buddha with his silence, sometimes as a Jesus with his revolutionary approach to life — in millions of ways God has been extending his hand towards you, groping for you. Sometimes your hand has even touched His hand — but you don't understand. Sometimes even a glimmer, a tremor has gone through your spine, but you don't understand. On the contrary, you explain it somehow.

16

A WOMAN came to me a few years ago. She sat just in front of me holding my feet, crying. It was a beautiful moment. Somehow, she had been able to feel me. But then she became afraid; then I could see — suddenly she left my feet, recoiled backwards. I asked her, "What has happened? Something was going deep in you — why have you withdrawn yourself?"

She said, "I am a professor in a university and I teach psychology — this must have been a relapse, a regression. I must have regressed towards my childhood; you must have worked like a father-figure. No, this is nothing. Yes, something happened, but it was a relapse into childhood. Yes, something happened, but it was nothing but a sort of hypnosis. Your eyes got hold of me." Now she has explained it away.

Something was on the way, something was *really* going to happen. One moment more and she would have been a totally different woman, and there would have been no possibility of her falling back. She would have crossed the point of no return. But just before it, she recoiled back, became afraid. And, of course, she was intelligent — as intelligence goes — a well-educated woman, capable of rationalizations. She immediately produced a rationalization: "It may be a sort of hypnosis, or a relapse into childhood, or you must have reminded me of my dead father." Now that which was happening has been cut.

Many times God has reached you, and many times you have withdrawn yourself. Many times He has walked with you and you have not recognized Him. Many times He has shouted at you: "Lazarus, come out!" and you won't listen. Or you think: "He must be calling somebody else — Lazarus is not my name." Let me tell you: Lazarus is *your* name!

And don't think about this story just as a story. That's what Buddha has done, that's what Bodhidharma has done, that's what Lao Tzu and Chuang Tzu have done: they have shouted at you, they have taken you by your hands and shaken you. Very few understand. In most of the cases people become angry, they become annoyed, because you are disturbing their sleep. They are sleeping and having beautiful dreams, golden dreams, sweet dreams, and you are disturbing their sleep.

17

That's why they had to kill Jesus, murder Mansoor, poison Socrates — these people were great disturbers. They were disturbing your sleep.

> *"May I be so bold, sir,"* asked Shiko, *"as to ask whether you understood?"*

Now this is a very meaningful question. People go on believing that they understand — and this *very* idea that they understand keeps their ignorance intact. The first step to be taken towards understanding is to understand that you don't understand, to recognize and realize your ignorance, to realize in deep humility that you have been ignoring the truth.

I was reading a small story:

Four frogs sat upon a log that lay floating on the edge of a river. Suddenly the log was caught by the current and swept slowly down the stream. The frogs were delighted and absorbed, for never before had they sailed.

At length the first frog spoke, and said, "This is indeed a most marvellous log. It moves as if alive. No such log was ever known before."

Then the second frog spoke, and said, "Nay, my friend, the log is like other logs, and does not move. It is the river, that is walking to the sea, and carries us and the log with it."

And the third frog spoke, and said, "It is neither the log nor the river that moves. The moving is in our thinking. For without thought nothing moves."

And the three frogs began to wrangle about what was really moving. The quarrel grew hotter and louder, but they could not agree.

Then they turned to the fourth frog, who up to this time had been listening attentively but holding his peace, and they asked his opinion.

And the fourth frog said, "Each of you is right and none of you is wrong. The moving is in the log and the water and our thinking also, but if you look still deeper then nothing has moved, because nothing can move and there is nowhere to move."

And the three frogs became very angry, for none of them was willing to admit that his was not the whole truth and that the other two were not wholly wrong; and they were not ready to think that they didn't know, and this fourth foolish frog — he knows? It was against their egos.

Then the strange thing happened — this has always been happening: the three frogs got together and pushed the fourth frog off the log into the river.

It is very difficult to see; when truth knocks at your door, it is very difficult to open the door and receive the guest, and welcome the guest — because when truth knocks at your door, suddenly you become aware that you have been living up to now with lies, that up to now you have been untrue, that all your declarations were false and all your dogmas were false. When truth comes face to face with you, suddenly your whole life is nullified. Your whole past has been just a darkness. It is too much for the ego to accept. It is better to deny the truth, it is better to close the door, and say that truth never knocked at your door. It is better to say that there has been never a Buddha, never a Jesus, never a Krishna. It is better to say that to save your own face.

It is very difficult to understand that you don't understand. It is very humiliating. And think of an emperor: emperors have been thinking that they know everything; they have even been trying that they are the representatives of God on earth, the very incarnations of God on earth. They have power — power blinds the eyes. It is very difficult to see that you are ignorant when you have money, respect, power. When others think that you know, it is very difficult.

Shiko's fear was relevant.

> *"May I be so bold, sir, as to ask whether you understood?"*
> *The Emperor shook his head sadly . . .*

but the Emperor must have been a humble person — maybe blind, but still humble; may not have seen what had happened, what had transpired; may not have seen what Fu-daishi had

19

brought as a gift, but he was not arrogant, not very egoistic. There is a possibility for him. He was sad that he could not understand; he was not annoyed.

Remember: anger and sadness are two aspects of the same energy. These are the two alternatives. Either the Emperor could have been angry, or sad. Angry — then he would have killed Fu-daishi; then Fu-daishi would have been thrown into the prison, poisoned, murdered, crucified. But he was sad. Then there is a hope.

Sadness has something beautiful in it, because sadness can become creative. Anger is always destructive. If he had been an angry person he would have thought that Fu-daishi had insulted him. But he thought: "I have missed an opportunity." If you can be that humble then more possibilities open for you.

The Emperor is not very far off the mark. Sooner or later, he will enter on the path.

> *"What a pity," said Shiko. "Fu-daishi has never been more eloquent."*

Rapping on the table, shouting so hard and so loud, walking with such intense grace — bringing Buddha to the palace: yes, Fu-daishi has never been more eloquent. He has *said* that which can be said. He created the situation in which there was every possibility that the Emperor could have seen. Whatsoever he could do, he had done. You cannot find any fault with Fu-daishi. More cannot be done. In fact, he had already gone out of the way to do it.

In the first place, it is very difficult for a man like Fu-daishi to come to the palace. Emperors should go — but he must have been of tremendous compassion: he came to the palace. A disciple should go to the master; but sometimes it has happened that a master has come to the disciple — out of sheer compassion and love. Then, he came with his full flame, he came naked. He had never been so aflame, he had never revealed his being so totally as on that day.

And then. . . there are stories: Once Buddha came and sat silently. There are other stories of other Zen masters: They came. They stood on the platform, looked around, left the platform, not saying a single word. But Fu-daishi is the only one who rapped on the table, who shouted loudly, who tried to shake the Emperor out of

20

his stupor. Yes, Shiko is right: "Fu-daishi has never been more eloquent."

In that moment a transfiguration was possible.

Chao-pien says:

> *A sudden clash of thunder. . .*
> *The mind-doors burst open,*
> *And lo! there sitteth the old man*
> *In all his homeliness.*

Fu-daishi created a sudden clash of thunder. If the Emperor had really been ready to receive this tremendous compassion, this grace, this gift, then the mind-doors must have opened, burst open . . . *and lo! there sitteth the old man.*

You are already that which you are seeking. That which you are seeking is already sitting inside you, it has already entered you. It has been there before you ever were: *And lo! there sitteth the old man in all his homeliness.*

But the Emperor missed.

I AM shouting to you every day, every morning. Of course, I am not rapping on the table — I am rapping on your heads! because your stupor is bigger and greater. Beating on the table won't help. Beating on the table, there is every possibility you will become angry at me — you will not even be sad. So, in different ways, in different words, I go on hammering on your head.

But remember: whatsoever I am saying is not the thing that I want to say to you. Whatsoever I am saying has nothing to do with truth, because truth cannot be said. . Whatsoever I am saying is nothing but a hammering. If you become awake, you will see the truth. This is just to create an opportunity. I am shaking you hard — and if you allow, if you don't resist, if you cooperate with me, if you are ready to go with me, if you can trust, if you are courageous, then my words can become a clash of sudden thunder.

Life is slipping by . . . each moment . . . you are missing it. Enough is enough! You have missed long; now missing it has become a habit — you will have to break this habit. The only way to be benefited by me, the only way to be blessed by me and by my presence, is to gather courage. Come out of your graves! Only your periphery is dead — you can never be dead. That is the meaning of the story of Lazarus: only the periphery can be dead; you can never be dead. Deep down, life is eternal. Burst forth! Rush out!

This is the whole effort of all the masters: to create a sudden clash of thunder so those who are fast asleep can be awakened.

> *A sudden clash of thunder. . .*
> *The mind-doors burst open,*
> *And lo! there sitteth the old man*
> *In all his homeliness.*

That old man is what Zen people mean by God. Their term is beautiful: the old man. It is your nature — ancientmost, eternal nature. It is the old man. Drop the mind! Stop thinking! Become more alert! See the trees and listen to the birds, with *no* screens of thoughts hindering the path. Meet directly! Truth is immediate, radiant, herenow. It is not that truth has to be discovered — only you have to become aware. Truth is already here.

Let me shake you, allow me to shake you out of your sleep. Don't go on thinking that you understand. You don't. Your knowledge is a way of ignoring the truth. Drop this ignorance — and ignorance cannot be dropped by accumulating more knowledge. Ignorance can be dropped only by dropping the knowledge that you have already accumulated.

Knowledge is the barrier to knowing. When knowledge is dropped, knowing flowers.

CHAPTER 2

How to stop thinking?

It sounds like me!

*What is the difference between
  looking and seeing?*

*How to avoid the perils of withdrawal
  on the path of meditation?*

Knowing . . . knowledge . . . practice.

WHEN YOU ARE NOT, GOD IS

twelfth august 1976

The first question: *I have been thinking all day of a way to ask the question: How to stop thinking?*

THINKING cannot be stopped. Not that it does not stop, but it cannot be stopped. It stops of its own accord. This distinction has to be understood, otherwise you can go mad chasing your mind.

No-mind does not arise by stopping thinking. When the thinking is no more, no-mind is. The very effort to stop will create more anxiety, it will create conflict, it will make you split. You will be in a constant turmoil within. This is not going to help.

And even if you succeed in stopping it forcibly for a few moments, it is not an achievement at all — because those few moments will be almost dead, they will not be alive. You may feel a sort of stillness, but not silence, because a forced stillness is not silence. Underneath it, deep in the unconscious, the repressed mind goes on working.

So, there is no way to stop the mind. But the mind stops — that is certain. It stops of its own accord.

So what to do? — your question is relevant. Watch — don't try to stop. There is no need to do any action against the mind. In the first place, who will do it? It will be mind fighting mind itself. You will divide your mind into two: one that is trying to boss over — the top-dog — trying to kill the other part of itself, which is absurd. It is a foolish game. It can drive you crazy. Don't try to stop the mind or the thinking — just watch it, allow it. Allow it total freedom. Let it run as fast as it wants. You don't try in any way to control it. You just be a witness. It is beautiful!

Mind is one of the most beautiful mechanisms. Science has not yet been able to create anything parallel to mind. Mind still remains the masterpiece — so complicated, so tremendously powerful, with so many potentialities. Watch it! Enjoy it!

And don't watch like an enemy, because if you look at the mind like an enemy, you cannot watch. You are already prejudiced; you are already against. You have already decided that something is wrong with the mind — you have already concluded. And whenever you look at somebody as an enemy you never look deep, you never look into the eyes. You avoid!

Watching the mind means: look at it with deep love, with deep respect, reverence — it is God's gift to you! Nothing is wrong in mind itself. Nothing is wrong in thinking itself. It is a beautiful process as other processes are. Clouds moving in the sky are beautiful — why not thoughts moving into the inner sky? Flowers coming to the trees are beautiful — why not thoughts flowering into your being. The river running to the ocean is beautiful — why not this stream of thoughts running somewhere to an unknown destiny? is it not beautiful?

Look with deep reverence. Don't be a fighter — be a lover. Watch! — the subtle nuances of the mind; the sudden turns, the beautiful turns; the sudden jumps and leaps; the games that mind goes on playing; the dreams that it weaves — the imagination, the memory; the thousand and one projections that it creates. *Watch!* Standing there, aloof, distant, not involved, by and by you will start feeling....

The deeper your watchfulness becomes, the deeper your aware-ness becomes, and gaps start arising, intervals. One thought goes and another has not come, and there is a gap. One cloud has passed, another is coming and there is a gap.

In those gaps, for the first time you will have glimpses of no-mind, you will have the taste of no-mind. Call it taste of Zen, or Tao, or Yoga. In those small intervals, suddenly the sky is clear and the sun is shining. Suddenly the world is full of mystery because all barriers are dropped. The screen on your eyes is no more there. You see clearly, you see penetratingly. The whole existence becomes transparent.

In the beginning, these will be just rare moments, few and far in between. But they will give you glimpses of what samadhi is. Small pools of silence — they will come and they will disappear. But now you know that you are on the right track — you start watching again.

When a thought passes, you watch it; when an interval passes, you watch it. Clouds are also beautiful; sunshine also is beautiful. Now you are not a chooser. Now you don't have a fixed mind: you don't say, "I would like only the intervals." That is stupid — because once you become attached to wanting only the intervals, you have decided again against thinking. And then those intervals will disappear. They happen only when you are very distant, aloof. They happen, they cannot be brought. They happen, you cannot force them to happen. They are spontaneous happenings.

Go on watching. Let thoughts come and go — wherever they want to go. Nothing is wrong! Don't try to manipulate and don't try to direct. Let thoughts move in total freedom. And then bigger intervals will be coming. You will be blessed with small satoris, mini satoris. Sometimes minutes will pass and no thought will be there; there will be no traffic — a total silence, undisturbed.

When the bigger gaps come, you will not only have clarity to see into the world — with the bigger gaps you will have a new clarity arising — you will be able to see into the inner world. With the first gaps you will see into the world: trees will be more green than they look right now. You will be surrounded by an infinite music — the music of the spheres. You will be suddenly in the presence of God — ineffable, mysterious. Touching you although you cannot grasp it. Within your reach and yet beyond. With the bigger gaps, the same will happen inside. God will not only be outside,

29

you will be suddenly surprised—He is inside also. He is not only in the seen; He is in the seer also—within and without. By and by . . . But don't get attached to that either.

Attachment is the food for the mind to continue. Non-attached witnessing is the way to stop it without any effort to stop it. And when you start enjoying those blissful moments, your capacity to retain them for longer periods arises.

Finally, eventually, one day, you become master. Then when you want to think, you think; if thought is needed, you use it; if thought is not needed, you allow it to rest. Not that mind is simply no more there: mind is there, but you can use it or not use it. Now it is your decision. Just like legs: if you want to run you use them; if you don't want to run you simply rest—legs are there. In the same way, mind is always there.

When I am talking to you I am using the mind—there is no other way to talk. When I am answering your question I am using the mind—there is no other way. I have to respond and relate, and mind is a beautiful mechanism. When I am not talking to you and I am alone, there is no mind—because it is a medium to relate through. Sitting alone it is not needed.

You have not given it a rest; hence, the mind becomes mediocre. Continuously used, tired, it goes on and on and on. Day it works; night it works. In the day you think; in the night you dream. Day in, day out, it goes on working. If you live for seventy or eighty years it will be continuously working.

Look at the delicacy and the endurability of the mind—so delicate! In a small head all the libraries of the world can be contained; all that has ever been written can be contained in one single mind. Tremendous is the capacity of the mind—and in such a small space! and not making much noise.

If scientists some day become capable of creating a parallel computer to mind . . . computers are there, but they are not yet minds. They are still mechanisms, they have no organic unity; they don't have any centre yet. If some day it becomes possible . . . and it *is* possible that scientists may some day be able to create minds—then you will know how much space that computer will take, and how much noise it will make.

Mind is making almost no noise; goes on working silently. And such a servant!—for seventy, eighty years. And then, too, when you are dying your body may be old but your mind remains young. Its capacity remains yet the same. Sometimes, if you have used it rightly, it even increases with your age!—because the more you know, the more you understand, the more you have experienced and lived, the more capable your mind becomes. When you die, everything in your body is ready to die—except the mind.

That's why in the East we say mind leaves the body and enters another womb, because it is not yet ready to die. The rebirth is of the mind. Once you have attained the state of samadhi, no-mind, then there will be no rebirth. Then you will simply die. And with your dying, everything will be dissolved—your body, your mind . . . only your witnessing soul will remain. That is beyond time and space. Then you become one with existence; then you are no more separate from it. The separation comes from the mind.

But there is no way to stop it forcibly — don't be violent. Move lovingly, with a deep reverence—and it will start happening of its own accord. You just watch. And don't be in a hurry.

The modern mind is in much hurry. It wants instant methods for stopping the mind. Hence, drugs have appeal. Mm?—you can force the mind to stop by using chemicals, drugs, but again you are being violent with the mechanism. It is not good. It is destructive. In this way you are not going to become a master. You may be able to stop the mind through the drugs, but then drugs will become your master—you are not going to become the master. You have simply changed your bosses, and you have changed for the worse. Now the drugs will hold power over you, they will possess you; without them you will be nowhere.

Meditation is not an effort against the mind. It is a way of understanding the mind. It is a very loving way of witnessing the mind—but, of course, one has to be very patient. This mind that you are carrying in your head has arisen over centuries, millennia. Your small mind carries the whole experience of humanity—and not only of humanity: of animals, of birds, of plants, of rocks. You

31

have passed through all those experiences. *All* that has happened up to now has happened in you also. In a very small nutshell, you carry the whole experience of existence. That's what your mind is. In fact, to say it is yours is not right: it is collective; it belongs to us all.

Modern psychology has been approaching it, particularly Jungian analysis has been approaching it, and they have started feeling something like a collective unconscious. Your mind is not yours—it belongs to us all. Our bodies are very separate; our minds are not so separate. Our bodies are clear-cutly separate; our minds overlap—and our souls are one.

Bodies separate, minds overlapping, and souls are one. I don't have a different soul and you don't have a different soul. At the very centre of existence we meet and are one. That's what God is: the meeting-point of all. Between the God and the world—'the world' means the bodies—is mind. Mind is a bridge: a bridge between the body and the soul, between the world and God. Don't try to destroy it!

Many have tried to destroy it through Yoga. That is a misuse of Yoga. Many have tried to destroy it through body posture, breathing—that too brings subtle chemical changes inside. For example: if you stand on your head in *shirshasan* — in the headstand —you can destroy the mind very easily. Because when the blood rushes too much, like a flood, into the head—when you stand on your head that's what you are trying to do. . . . The mind mechanism is very delicate; you are flooding it with blood. The delicate tissues will die.

That's why you never come across a very intelligent yogi—no. Yogis are, more or less, stupid. Their bodies are healthy—that's true—strong, but their minds are just dead. You will not see the glimmer of intelligence. You will see a very robust body, animal-like, but somehow the human has disappeared.

Standing on your head, you are forcing your blood into the head through gravitation. The head *needs* blood, but in a very, very small quantity; and very slowly, not floodlike. Against gravitation, very little blood reaches to the head. And that, too, in a very silent way. If too much blood is reaching into the head it is destructive.

32

Yoga has been used to kill the mind; breathing can be used to kill the mind. There are rhythms of breath, subtle vibrations of breath, which can be very, very drastic to the delicate mind. The mind can be destroyed through them. These are old tricks. Now the latest tricks are supplied by science: LSD, marijuana, and others. More and more sophisticated drugs will be available sooner or later.

I am not in favour of stopping the mind. I am in favour of watching it. It stops of its own accord—and *then* it is beautiful! When something happens without any violence it has a beauty of its own, it has a natural growth. You can force a flower and open it by force; you can pull the petals of a bud and open it by force—but you have destroyed the beauty of the flower. Now it is almost dead. It cannot stand your violence. The petals will be hanging loose, limp, dying. When the bud opens by its own energy, when it opens of its own accord, then those petals are alive.

The mind is your flowering — don't force it in any way. I am against all force and against all violence, and particularly violence that is directed towards yourself. Just watch—in deep prayer, love, reverence. And see what happens! Miracles happen of their own accord. There is *no* need to pull and push.

You ask: How to stop thinking? I say: Just watch, be alert. And drop this idea of stopping, otherwise it will stop the natural transformation of the mind. Drop this idea of stopping! Who are *you* to stop? At the most, enjoy.

And nothing is wrong—even if immoral thoughts, so-called immoral thoughts, pass through your mind, let them pass; nothing is wrong. You remain detached. No harm is being done. It is just fiction; you are seeing an inner movie. Allow it its own way and it will lead you, by and by, to the state of no-mind. Watching ultimately culminates in no-mind.

No-mind is not against mind: no-mind is beyond mind. No-mind does not come by killing and destroying the mind: no-mind comes when you have understood the mind so totally that thinking is no longer needed—your understanding has replaced it.

The second question: *Today, and many times, when you des-
cribed Zen masters, it sounded like me;
yet when you talked about the Emperor,
the ego, I also felt it is me. I feel this is
weird since my mind is not exactly silent.*

IT APPEARS weird but it is true—because on one level everybody is already a Zen master, on one level everybody is already
a Buddha; on another level everybody is the Emperor, the ego.

There are two planes in you: the plane of the mind, and the
plane of the no-mind. Or, let me say it in this way: the plane when
you are on the periphery of your being and the plane when you
are at the centre of your being. Every circle has a centre—you
may know it, you may not know it. You may not even suspect
that there is a centre, but there *has* to be. You are a periphery, you
are a circle: there is a centre. Without the centre you cannot be;
there is a nucleus of your being.

At that centre you are already a Buddha, a Siddha, one who
has already arrived home. On the periphery, you are in the world
—in the mind, in dreams, in desires, in anxieties, in a thousand
and one games. And you are both.

So it is possible that when I am talking about Zen masters you
can feel: "Yes, it is true!" Not only is it intellectually true—you
can feel it is existentially true. "Yes! This is what is happening
to me also." When listening to me, there are bound to be moments
when you will see that you have been for a few moments like a
Buddha—the same grace, the same awareness, the same silence;
the same world of beatitudes, of blessings, of benediction.

There will be moments, glimpses of your own centre. They
cannot be permanent; again and again you will be thrown back
to the periphery . . . and then it will look weird. Then you will
see that "I am like the Emperor: not understanding at all; stupid,
sad, frustrated; missing the meaning of life"—because you exist
on two planes: the plane of the periphery and the plane of the
centre.

But, by and by, the weirdness will disappear. By and by, you
will become capable of moving from the periphery to the centre

34

and from the centre to the periphery very smoothly—just as you walk into your house and out of your house. You don't create any dichotomy. You don't say, "I am outside the house so how can I go inside the house?" You don't say, "I am inside the house so how can I come outside the house?" It is sunny outside, it is warm, pleasant — you sit outside in the garden. Then it is becoming hotter and hotter, and you start perspiring. Now it is no longer pleasant—it is becoming uncomfortable: you simply get up and move inside the house. There it is cool; there it is not uncomfortable. Now, *there* it is pleasant. You go on moving in and out.

In the same way a man of awareness and understanding moves from the periphery to the centre, from the centre to the periphery. He never gets fixated anywhere. From the marketplace to the monastery, from *sansar* to *sannyas,* from being extrovert to being introvert—he continuously goes on moving, because *these two are his wings;* they are *not* against each other. They may be balanced in opposite directions—they have to be; if both the wings are on one side, the bird cannot fly into the sky—they have to be balancing, they have to be in opposite directions, but still they belong to the same bird, and they *serve* the same bird. Your outside and your inside are your wings.

This has to be very deeply remembered, because there is a possibility . . . the mind tends to fixate. There are people who are fixated in the marketplace; they say they cannot get out of it; they say they have no time for meditation; they say even if time is there they don't know how to meditate and they don't believe that they *can* meditate. They say they are worldly—how can they meditate? They are materialistic—how can they meditate? They say, "Unfortunately, we are extroverts—how can we go in?" They have chosen only one wing. And, of course, if frustration comes out of it, it is natural. With one wing frustration is bound to come.

Then there are people who become fed up with the world and escape out of the world, go to the monasteries and the Himalayas, become sannyasins, monks: start living alone, force a life of introversion on themselves. They close their eyes, they close all their doors and windows, they become like Leibnitz' monads —windowless—then they are bored.

In the marketplace they were fed up, they were tired, frustrated. It was getting more like a madhouse; they could not find rest. There was *too* much of relationship and not enough holiday, not enough space to be themselves. They were falling into things, losing their beings. They were becoming more and more material and less and less spiritual. They were losing their direction. They were losing the very consciousness that they *are.* They escaped. Fed up, frustrated, they escaped.

Now they are trying to live alone—a life of introversion. Sooner or later they get bored. Again they have chosen another wing, but again one wing. This is the way of a lopsided life. They have again fallen into the same fallacy on the opposite pole.

I am neither for this nor for that. I would like you to become so capable that you can remain in the marketplace and yet meditative. I would like you to relate with people, to love, to move in millions of relationships—because they enrich—and yet remain capable of closing your doors and sometimes having a holiday from all relationship . . . so that you can relate with your own being also.

Relate with others, but relate with yourself also. Love others, but love yourself also. Go out!—the world *is* beautiful, adventurous; it is a challenge, it enriches. Don't lose that opportunity! Whenever the world knocks at your door and calls you, go out! Go out fearlessly—there is nothing to lose, there is everything to gain.

But don't get lost. Don't go on and on and get lost. Sometimes come back home. Sometimes forget the world—those are the moments for meditation. Each day, if you want to become balanced, you should balance the outer and the inner. They should carry the same weight, so that inside you never become lopsided.

This is the meaning when Zen masters say: "Walk in the river, but don't allow the water to touch your feet." Be in the world, but don't be *of* the world. Be in the world, but don't allow the world to be in you. When you come home, you come home— as if the whole world has disappeared.

Hotei, a Zen master, was passing through a village. He was one of the most beautiful persons who have ever walked on earth. He was known to people as 'The Laughing Buddha'—he used to laugh continuously. But sometimes he would sit under a tree—in this village he was sitting under a tree, with closed eyes; not laughing, not even smiling; completely calm and collected.

Somebody asked: "You are not laughing, Hotei?"

He opened his eyes and he said, "I am preparing."

The questioner could not understand. He said, "What do you mean by 'preparing'?"

He said, "I have to prepare myself for laughter. I have to give myself rest. I have to go in. I have to forget the whole world so that I can come again rejuvenated and I can again laugh."

If you really want to laugh you will have to learn how to weep. If you cannot weep and if you are not capable of tears, you will become incapable of laughter. A man of laughter is also a man of tears—then a man is balanced. A man of bliss is also a man of silence. A man who is ecstatic is also a man who is centred. They both go together. And out of this togetherness of polarities a balanced being is born. And that is what the goal is.

So sometimes when I am talking about Buddhas, you may have glimpses, you may start flying into the inner world. And you will see, yes!—you know what it is. It simply fits with you in some moments. You can become a witness to it. But in some other moments it is weird. You don't know what a Buddha is. You have lost contact with your own inner centre; now you are on the periphery. You can understand a Machiavelli, but now you cannot understand a Buddha. You are both!

And I am not in any way suggesting that you choose one. I would like you to remain in the world and also to have a few holidays for yourself. Even God had to rest on the seventh day. In six days He created the world, and then the seventh day He rested—even God! Some theologians have reached to the conclusion that He must have been a Jew, because nobody else can work six days a week. He worked for six days continuously.

If you ask Hindus, they have a better conception of God and

His creativity. I also think that this concept of working six days *and* resting the seventh is a Jewish concept—the businessman's concept. Even on the seventh day, it seems, very reluctantly He would have allowed Himself a little space. Hindus have a totally different attitude. They say: God's world, His creation, is not like a profession, not like business—God's creation is like play. So each moment is both: work and worship, work and rest. That is the difference between work and play. Hindus call it *leela*—God's play. It means He is resting and at the same time He is doing.

That is the difference between a profession and a vocation. A profession is work—you get tired, then you need rest. A vocation is a play — while you are working you are also resting, your *very* work is your rest. In a profession, vacation is needed separately. In a vocation, vacation is implied in it—vocation is at the same time vacation also.

So Hindus don't have any concept that God created the world in six days and then rested. No, He has never rested—in that way. And, in that way, He has never created the world — He is still creating! And His very creativity is His rest.

Have you watched a businessman? Six days he works in the marketplace; the seventh day he comes home and starts painting. Now he says this is rest. Painting is his love, his play; it gives rest. Or he comes home and starts playing a flute. Six days he has been working and now he is again working, but this is no longer work — it is play.

God is playing. And a real man of understanding becomes godly—godly in the sense that he is in the world and yet he remains out of it; on the periphery and yet he remains mindful of his centre. Doing a thousand and one things, yet he remains a non-doer. In tremendous activities, but he is never lost. His inner light burns bright.

The third question: *What is the difference between looking and seeing?*

T HERE IS a great difference. Looking means you are looking for something; you have already some idea to look for. You come here and you say, "I am looking for Teertha"—then you have an idea. Then you look all around for where Teertha is. The idea is there already.

Looking is already prejudiced. If you are looking for God, you will never find Him—because looking means you have a certain idea already of who God is. And your idea is bound to be either Christian or Judaic or Hindu or Mohammedan. Your idea is going to be your concept—and your concept can never be higher than you. And your concept is bound to be *your* concept. Your concept is bound to be rooted in ignorance, borrowed. At the most, it is just belief; you have been conditioned for it. Then you go on looking.

A person who is looking for truth will never find it, because his eyes are already corrupted, he already has a fixed concept. He is not open. If you have come to me to *look* for something, then you already have an idea—you will miss me. Then whatsoever I say you will interpret according to your idea and it will not be my meaning, it will be your meaning. You may find yourself agreeing with me, you may find yourself not agreeing with me—but agreeing or not agreeing is not the question at all, it is not the point at all. You have missed me. You can agree, but you are agreeing with your own idea.

You say: "Yes, this man is right," because this man fits with your idea. Your idea is right so that's why this man is right. Or, you don't agree because it doesn't fit with your idea. But in both the cases your idea is more important. You will miss me.

A man who is looking for something will always be missing it.

Seeing is just clarity—open eyes, open mind, open heart. Not looking for something in particular; just ready and receptive. Whatsoever happens, you will remain alert, receptive, understanding. Conclusion is not there! Conclusion has to come: by your own eyes you will see — *and* there will be a conclusion. The conclusion is in the future. When you are *seeing,* the conclusion is not already there. When you are looking, the conclusion is already there. And we go on interpreting according to our ideas.

Just the other night I was reading a joke:

A small child is reading a pictorial book on wild life, and he becomes very intrigued with the pictures of ferocious lions. He reads whatsoever is there, but one question is not answered there so he asks his mother.

He asks his mother: "Mom, what type of love-life do lions have?"

The mother said, "Son, I don't know much about Lions because all your father's friends are Rotarians."

If you have some idea in the mind, you corrupt. Then you are not listening to what is being said—then you are listening according to yourself. Then your mind is playing an active role. When you are looking, mind is active. When you are seeing, mind is passive. That is the difference. When you are looking, mind is trying to manipulate. When you are seeing, mind is silent — just watching, available, open, with no idea in particular to enforce on reality.

Seeing is nude. And you can come to truth only when you are absolutely nude; when you have discarded *all* clothes, all philosophies, all theologies, all religions; when you have dropped all that has been given to you; when you come empty-handed, not knowing in any way. When you come with knowledge you come already corrupted. When you come in innocence, knowing that you don't know, then the doors are open—then you will be able to know. Only that person who has no knowledge is capable of knowing.

The fourth question: *I feel somewhat detached from all ex-
ternal events—even sharp physical pain.
It would be nice to think that this is the
first bud of meditative being, but it
seems more likely to be a chilling sign
of schizoid withdrawal. Could you
please say something about the perils
of withdrawal, and how to avoid them?*

IN THE search for a meditative state of mind, that peril
always exists. In the search of one's own self there is always
a danger that you may choose the inner against the outer—then
the withdrawal becomes schizoid, because you become lopsided, you lose balance.

Balance is health. To lose balance is to lose health. And
balance is sanity — to lose balance is to become insane. The fear
is always there. The danger is always there. The danger comes
because of your mind.

It is always easy for the mind to change its diseases. Somebody is mad after women; only sex is his obsession. One day or
other he will be fed up with this, tired of it all. He will start
moving to the other extreme: he will start thinking of brahmacharya—celibacy—of becoming a Catholic monk or something.

There is danger. It is as if you have been eating too much and
then one day you decide to fast. Eating too much is bad but
fasting is not better. In fact, by eating too much you are not
going to die so soon; you may become heavier, fatty, uglier, but
you will linger on, you will drag on. But by fasting, within weeks
you will disappear; you cannot survive more than three months.
Both are dangerous.

Eating too much is neurotic. Fasting is the opposite neurosis,
but still neurotic. Have a balanced diet. Eat as much as is needed
by the body; don't go on stuffing your body. But this is how it
happens. I have been watching people: whenever a society becomes very rich, fasting comes as a cult.

In India, Jains are one of the richest societies—fasting is their
cult, fasting is their religion. Now America is becoming very

rich—fasting is becoming more and more a fashion. It is difficult to find a woman who is not on a diet. People go to nature cure clinics to fast.

A poor man's religion is always of festivity, feast. Mohammedans, poor people, when their religious day comes they feast. They starve the whole year so, of course, the religious day, at least on that day, they change their clothes, new clothes, colourful, and they enjoy—at least for one day they can enjoy.

Jains feast the whole year, and when their religious days come they fast. That is logical. A poor man's festival is going to be a feast; a rich man's festival is going to be a fast. People move to the opposite extreme.

So when you start meditating, there *is* a danger that you may become too much attached to this introversion. Meditation is an introversion; it leads you to your centre. If you lose your elasticity and you become incapable of coming back to the periphery, then it is a withdrawal—and a dangerous withdrawal. It is schizoid.

Be alert! That has happened to many people. The whole history is full of such people who became schizoid.

When you are meditating, always remember that the periphery is not to be lost permanently. You have to come to the periphery again and again so the route remains clear and the path remains there. Hence my insistence to meditate but not to renounce the world. Meditate in the morning and then go to the market; meditate in the morning and then go to your office. Meditate and then make love! Don't create any dichotomy, don't create any conflict. Don't say, "Now how can I love? I am a meditator." Then you are moving in a dangerous direction; sooner or later you will lose all contact with the periphery. Then you will become frozen at the centre. And life consists of being alive—changing, moving. Life is dynamic, it is not dead.

There are two types of dead people in the world: dead on the periphery and dead on the centre. Become the third type: alive in between; go on moving from the centre to the periphery, from the periphery to the centre. They are enriching to each other; they are enhancing to each other. Just watch! If you meditate and then make love, your love will have a tremendously new depth to it. Love and then meditate and suddenly you will see: when your energy is full of love, meditation goes so deep and so easily. You simply ride on the wave—you need not make any effort. You simply float and reach higher and higher and higher. Once you understand the rhythm of the polar opposites, then there is no fear.

Remember: life is a rhythm between day and night, summer and winter. It is a continuous rhythm. Never stop anywhere! Be moving! And the bigger the swing, the deeper your experience will be.

So make it a point that you have to be continuously journeying, you have to travel. When you go to the inner centre in your meditation, enjoy it!—as if there is no periphery. Forget the periphery completely; there is no need to remember it. Don't be distracted by it. Dig deep into your own being—be enriched by it! And bring that flavour back to the periphery. Bring that fragrance back to the world. Bring that aura, that light, that grace, that dignity, that grandeur, back to the periphery.

Walk in the marketplace like a Buddha. Live in the world . . . the world is very enriching, because relationship mirrors. All relationships are mirrorlike. You see your face in the mirror of the other's being. It is very difficult to see your own face directly —you will need the other, the mirror, to see your own face. And where can you find a better mirror than the eyes of the other?.

Sometimes, look in the eyes of your enemy and you will see a facet of your being. Sometimes look in the eyes of your lover, your friend, and you will see another facet of your being. Sometimes look in a person's eyes who is indifferent to you and you will see yet another facet of your being. Collect all these faces — they are yours; aspects of your being. In different situations, with different people, in different worlds, move . . . and gather all this richness and awareness and alertness and consciousness. Then go back to the centre and take all this awareness with you, and your ecstasy in the meditation will be deeper and richer for that.

And this has to go on continuously. Pour your centre on the

periphery, and pour your periphery on the centre. Pour your love in your meditation and pour your meditation in your love.

This is what I teach. This is what I call a dynamic life. And a religious life is a dynamic life.

The fifth question: *You have reminded me again that, for me, knowing becomes knowledge, which becomes the practice of that knowledge. Even this is becoming a practice. Please comment.*

KNOWING always becomes knowledge — and you have to be alert not to allow it. One of the most delicate situations on the path of a seeker: knowing always becomes knowledge — because the moment you have known something, your mind collects it as knowledge, as experience.

Knowing is a process. Knowledge is a conclusion. When knowing dies it becomes knowledge. And if you go on gathering this knowledge, then knowing will become more and more difficult — because with knowledge, knowing never happens. Then you carry your knowledge around you. A knowledgeable person is almost hidden behind his knowledge; he loses all clarity, all perception. The world becomes *far* away; the reality loses all transparency.

The knowledgeable person is always looking through his knowledge. He projects his knowledge. His knowledge colours everything — now there is no longer any possibility of knowing. Remember: knowledge is not gathered only through scriptures — it is also gathered, and more so, through your own experience.

You love a woman, for example. You have never known a woman before, have never fallen in deep love. You fall for the first time — you are innocent, you are a virgin. You don't know what love is — your mind is open. You don't have any knowledge about love. You are spontaneous. You move into the unknown. It is mysterious.

44

Love opens doors of unknown temples, sings unknown songs into your ears and into your heart, dances with unknown tunes. And you don't know anything; you don't have any knowledge to judge by, to evaluate, to condemn, to say good or bad. It is ecstatic. You are gripped by the ineffable experience of love. You live in moments of grace.

But, by and by, you become knowledgeable — now you know what love means; now you know what the woman means; now you know the geography, the topography of love. You have become knowledgeable.

You fall in love with another woman. Now, nothing like the first experience happens — nothing like it. Dull. A repetition. As if you have gone to see the same movie again, or reading the same novel again. A little difference here and there, but not much. Now, why are you missing? Why is the same mysterious experience not gripping you? Why are you not throbbing with the unknown again? You are knowledgeable. Something so beautiful like love has become a repetition.

Knowing always becomes knowledge. So you have to be very alert: know something — the moment it becomes knowledge, drop it. Go on dying to your knowledge. Never carry it — because *no* other woman is the same. Your first woman was a totally different world; this new woman you have fallen in love with is a totally different world. It is *not* going to be the same. But if you move through knowledge it will look like the same.

Drop the knowledge. Be again innocent. Again move into the unknown — because no two persons are alike. Every person is so unique that there has never been a person like that before and there will never be again. Learn again from A B C and you will be full of wonder. And then you have learnt a deep experience: never allow any knowledge to settle.

All knowing becomes knowledge. The moment it becomes knowledge, drop it. It is just like dust gathers on the mirror; every day you have to clean it. On the mirror of your mind dust gathers, dust of experience: it becomes knowledge. Clean it. That's why every day meditation is needed. Meditation is nothing but cleaning the mirror of your mind. Clean it continuously! If you can clean

45

it every moment of your life, then there is no need to sit separately for meditation.

Remember, be alert that knowledge has not to be gathered, that you have to remain like a child — full of wonder, full of awe. Every nook and corner is mysterious, and you don't know what it is. You cannot figure it out, what this life is. Enchanted you run in this direction and that direction.

Have you watched a child running on the sea-beach? So elated! in such euphoria! collecting shells and coloured stones. Have you watched a child running in a garden to catch a butterfly? You will not run that way even if God is there; you will not run that way. You will not be so ecstatic even if God is there. You will move like a gentleman. You will not rush, you will not be mad. You will still keep your manners; you will still show that you are mature, you are not a child.

And Jesus says: "Only those who are childlike, they will be able to enter into my Kingdom of God" — only those who are childlike, only those who are still capable of wonder. Wonder is the greatest treasure in life. Once you lose wonder, you have lost your life — then you drag, but you no longer live. And knowledge kills wonder.

That is one of the most difficult problems the modern mind is facing, because knowledge has accumulated every day more and more. The twentieth century is so much burdened with knowledge. Hence religion has disappeared — because religion can exist only with wonder, with wonder-filled eyes; eyes which don't know but are ready to rush into any direction to see what is there; innocent eyes, virgin hearts. So remember to remain capable of childlike wonder.

Science grows out of doubt. Religion grows out of wonder. Between the two is philosophy; it has not yet decided — it goes on hanging between doubt and wonder. Sometimes the philosopher doubts and sometimes the philosopher wonders: he is just in between. If he doubts too much, by and by he becomes a scientist. If he wonders too much, by and by he becomes religious.

That's why philosophy is disappearing from the world — because ninety-nine percent of philosophers have become scientists. And one person — a Buber somewhere, or a Krishnamurti somewhere,

46

or a Suzuki somewhere — great minds, great penetrating intellects, they have become religious. Philosophy is almost losing its ground.

If you become too sceptical, you become scientists. If you become too childlike, you become religious. Science exists with doubt. Religion exists with wonder. If you want to be religious then create more wonder, discover more wonder. Allow your eyes to be more filled with wonder than anything else. Be *surprised* by everything that is happening. Everything is so tremendously wonderful that it is simply unbelievable how you go on living without dancing, how you go on living without becoming ecstatic. You must not be seeing what is happening all around.

Just to be is so miraculous, just to breathe is so miraculous. Just to breathe and just to be! — nothing else is needed for a religious person. To be full of wonder. And when one is full of wonder, praise arises, and praise is prayer. When you see this wonderful existence, you start praising it. In your praising, prayer arises. You say: "Holy, holy, holy!" It *is* holy. It is so beautiful and so holy.

So, THE QUESTIONER has raised a very pertinent question: "You have reminded me again that, for me, knowing becomes knowledge, which becomes the practice of that knowledge." These are the three steps. First knowing; then the knowing dies, shrinks, becomes knowledge; then knowledge also shrinks even more and becomes practice or character.

A man of character is the deadliest man in the world. He practises his knowledge; he tries to follow his knowledge. He is not spontaneous. He is continuously managing, manipulating, pushing himself this way and that; somehow holding himself together. He is not responsible — responsible in the sense of being capable of response. If you come across him, if you embrace him, he will answer it, but that answer will come out of his past experiencing — out of his character.

A man of character is predictable. Only a mechanism can be predictable. A fully conscious man is unpredictable. No astrologer can predict anything about a fully conscious man. He moves moment-to-moment, full of wonder. He acts *out* of wonder; he acts out of response to the moment. He carries no knowledge, he carries no character with him. Each moment he is new, reborn.

So these are the three steps: knowing dies; knowing becomes knowledge; knowledge becomes character. Be aware—*beware!* Don't allow your knowing to fall and to become knowledge. And never allow your knowledge to control you and to create a character for you. A character is an armour. In the armour you are jailed . . . then you can never be spontaneous. You are already in your grave—a character is a grave.

Let your knowing be there, but don't allow it to become knowledge or character. The moment it is turning into knowledge, drop it, empty your hands. Forget all about it. Move ahead! again like a child. Difficult, I know. Easy to say; difficult to be that way — but that is the only way you can attain to *satchitanand* — you can attain to truth, you can attain to consciousness, you can attain to bliss.

Yes, it is hard. One has to pay too much for it — but God is not cheap. You will have to pay with your whole being. Only when you have paid totally and you are not holding anything and you are not a miser, and you have sacrificed and surrendered yourself totally, will you attain. God comes to you when you are not; when you have become just a zero God comes to you. He is just waiting by the corner. The moment you become empty, He rushes towards you, He comes and fulfiles you.

Don't allow knowing to become knowledge and character. Then a totally different type of character will arise which will not be like the character you have seen in the world. It will be inner — a discipline which comes from the innermost core of your being. Never forced! — always spontaneous. It is not like a commandment: it is an organic growth. God is your spontaneous organic growth.

CHAPTER 3

*T*HERE WAS *a man of Wei, Tung-men Wu,
who did not grieve when his son died.*
His wife said to him:
*"No one in the world loved his son as much
as you did, why do you not grieve now he is
dead?"*
He answered:
*"I had no son, and when I had no son I did
not grieve. Now that he is dead it is the same
as it was before, when I had no son. Why
should I grieve over him?"*

WHY SHOULD I GRIEVE OVER HIM?
thirteen august 1976

THE MOST fundamental religious truth is that man is asleep — not physically, but metaphysically; not apparently, but deep down. Man lives in a deep slumber. He works, he moves, he thinks, he imagines, he dreams, but the sleep continues as a basic substratum to his life. Rare are the moments when you feel really awake, very rare; they can be counted on the fingers. If in seventy years' life you had only seven moments of awakening, that, too, will be too much.

Man lives like a robot: mechanically efficient, but with no awareness. Hence the whole problem! There are so many problems man has to face, but they are all by-products of his sleep.

So the first thing to be understood is what this sleep consists in — because Zen is an effort to become alert and awake. All religion is nothing but that: an effort to become more conscious, an effort to become more aware, an effort to bring more alertness, more attentiveness to your life.

All the religions of the world, in one way or other, emphasize that the sleep consists in deep identification or in attachment.

Man's life has two layers to it: one is that of the essential, and another is that of the accidental. The essential is never born, never dies. The accidental is born, lives and dies. The essential is eternal, timeless; the accidental is just accidental. We become too much attached to the accidental and we tend to forget the essential.

A man becomes too much attached to money — money is accidental. It has nothing to do with essential life. A man becomes too much attached to his house or to his car, or to his wife, or to her husband, to children, to relationship. Relationship is accidental; it has nothing essential in it. It is not your real being. And in this century, the twentieth century, the problem has become too deep.

There are people who call the twentieth century 'the accidental century' — they are right People are living too much identified with the non-essential: money, power, prestige, respectability. You will have to leave all that behind when you go. Even an Alexander has to go empty-handed.

I have heard:

A great mystic died. When he reached Paradise, he asked God, "Why was Jesus not born in the twentieth century?"

The Lord God started laughing and said, "Impossible! Impossible! Where would the twentieth century people ever find three wise men or a virgin?"

The twentieth century is the most accidental. By and by, man has become too much attached to 'my' and 'mine' — to possessions. And he has completely lost track of his being. He has completely lost track of 'I'. 'My' has become more important. When 'my' becomes more important then you are getting attached to the accidental. When 'I' remains more important and 'my' remains just as a servant, then you are a master, then you are not a slave — then you live in a totally different way.

That's what Zen people call the original face of man, where pure 'I' exists. This 'I' has nothing to do with the ego. Ego is nothing but the centre of all the non-essential possessions that you have. Ego is nothing but the accumulated 'my' and 'mine'— my house, my car, my prestige, my religion, my scripture, my character, my morality, my family, my heritage, my tradition. All these 'my's', all these 'mines', go on getting accumulated: they become crystallized as the ego.

When I am using the word 'I', I am using it in an absolutely non-egoistic sense. 'I' means your being.

Zen people say: Find out your face, the face you had before you were born; find out that face that you will again have when you are dead. Between birth and death, whatsoever you think is your face is accidental. You have seen it in a mirror; you have not felt it from the within—you have looked for it in the without. Do you know your original face? You know only the face your mirror shows to you. And all our relationships are just mirrors.

The husband says to the wife, "You are beautiful!" and she starts thinking she is beautiful. Somebody comes, buttresses you, says, "You are very wise, intelligent, a genius!" and you start believing in it. Or somebody condemns you, hates you, is angry about you. You don't accept what he says, but still, deep down in the unconscious it goes on accumulating. Hence the ambiguity of man.

Somebody says you are beautiful, somebody else says you are ugly—now what to do? One mirror says you are wise, another man says you are an idiot—now what to do? And you depend only on mirrors, and both are mirrors. You may not like the mirror that says you are an idiot, but it has said so, it has done its work. You may repress it, you may never bring it to your consciousness, but deep down it will remain in you that one mirror has said you are an idiot.

You trust in mirrors—then you become split because there are so many mirrors. And each mirror has its own investment. Somebody calls you wise, not because you are wise—he has his own investment. Somebody calls you an idiot, not because you are an idiot—he has his own investment. They are simply showing their likes and dislikes; they are not asserting anything about you. They may be asserting something about themselves, maybe, but they are not saying anything about you—because no mirror can show you who you are.

Mirrors can only show you your surface, your skin. You are *not* on your skin: you are very deep. You are not your body. One day the body is young; another day it becomes old. One day it is beautiful, healthy; another day it becomes crippled and paralyzed. One day you were throbbing with life; another day life has oozed out of you. *But you are not your periphery!* You are your centre.

The accidental man lives on the periphery. The essential man remains centred. This is the whole effort!

LET ME tell you one anecdote. I have heard a very beautiful Jewish story. It is tremendously significant — it is about a man:

He was always sleepy. And always ready to sleep. Everywhere. At the biggest mass meetings, at all the concerts, at every important convention, he could be seen sitting asleep.

You must have known that man because you are that. And you must have come across that man many, many times, because how can you avoid him?—it is you.

And he slept in every conceivable and inconceivable pose. He slept with his elbows in the air and his hands behind his head. He slept standing up, leaning against himself so that he should not fall down. He slept in the theatre, in the streets, in the synagogue. Wherever he went, his eyes would drip with sleep.

Had he been a Hindu he could have even slept standing on his head in *shirshasan*. I have seen Hindus sleeping that way. Many yogis become efficient in sleeping standing on their head. It is difficult, arduous; it needs great practice—but it happens.

Neighbours used to say that he had already slept through seven big fires, and once, at a really big fire, he was carried out of his bed, still asleep, and put down on the sidewalk. In

56

this way he slept for several hours until a patrol came along and took him away.

It was said that when he was standing under the wedding canopy and reciting the vows, "Thou art to me. . . ." he fell asleep at the word 'sanctified'—try to remember him—and they had to beat him over the head with brass pestles for several hours to wake him up. And he slowly said the next word and again fell asleep.

Remember your own wedding ceremony. Remember your honeymoon. Remember your marriage. *Have you ever been awake?* Have you ever missed any opportunity where you could have fallen asleep? You have always fallen asleep.

We mention all this so that you may believe the following story about our hero.

Once, when he went to sleep, he slept and slept and slept; but in his sleep it seemed to him that he heard thunder in the streets and his bed was shaking somewhat; so he thought in his sleep that it was raining outside, and as a result his sleep became still more delicious. He wrapped himself up in his quilt and in its warmth.

Do you remember how many times you have interpreted things through your sleep? Do you remember sometimes you have fixed the alarm clock, and when it goes off you start dreaming that you are in the church and the bells are ringing. A trick of the mind to avoid the alarm, to avoid the disturbance that the alarm is creating.

When he awoke he saw a strange void: his wife was no longer there, his bed was no longer there, his quilt was no longer there. He wanted to look through the window, but there was no window to look through. He wanted to run down the three flights and yell 'Help!' but there were no stairs to run on and no air to yell in. And when he wanted merely to go out of doors, he saw that there was no out of doors. Everything evaporated!

For a while he stood there in confusion unable to comprehend what had happened. But afterward he bethought himself: I will go to sleep. He saw, however, that there was no longer any earth to sleep on. Only then did he raise two fingers to his forehead and reflect: Apparently I have slept through the end of the world. Isn't that a fine how-do-you-do?

He became depressed. No more world, he thought. What will I do without a world? Where will I go to work, how will I make a living, especially now that the cost of living is so high and a dozen eggs costs a dollar twenty and who knows if they are even fresh, and besides, what will happen to the five dollars the gas company owes me? And where has my wife gone off to? Is it possible that she too has disappeared with the world, and with the thirty dollars' pay I had in my pockets? And she is not by nature the kind that disappears, he thought to himself.

You will also think that way one day if you suddenly find the world has disappeared. You don't know what else to think. You will think about the cost of eggs, the office, the wife, the money. You don't know what *else* to think about. The whole world has disappeared!—but you have become mechanical in your thinking.

And what will I do if I want to sleep? What will I stretch out on if there isn't any world? And maybe my back will ache? And who will finish the bundle of work in the shop? And suppose I want a glass of malted, where will I get it?

Eh, he thought, have you ever seen anything like it? A man should fall asleep with the world under his head and wake up without it!

This is going to happen one day or other—that's what happens to every man when he dies. Suddenly, the whole world disappears. Suddenly he is no longer part of this world; suddenly he is in another dimension. *This happens to every man who dies,* because whatsoever you have known is just the peripheral. When you die, suddenly your periphery disappears—you are thrown to your centre. And you don't know that language. And you don't know anything about the centre. It looks like void, empty. It feels like just a negation, an absence.

As our hero stood there in his underwear, wondering what to do, a thought occurred to him: To hell with it! So there isn't any world! Who needs it anyway? Disappeared is disappeared—I might as well go to the movies and kill some time. But to his astonishment he saw that, together with the world, the movies had also disappeared.

A pretty mess I've made here, thought our hero, and began smoothing his moustache. A pretty mess I've made here, falling asleep! If I hadn't slept so soundly, he taunted himself, I would have disappeared along with everything else. This way I'm unfortunate, and where will I get a malted? I love a glass in the morning. And my wife? Who knows who she's disappeared with? If it is with the presser from the top floor, I'll murder her, so help me God.

Who knows how late it is?

With these words our hero wanted to look at his watch but couldn't find it. He searched with both hands in the left and right pockets of the infinite emptiness but could find nothing to touch.

I just paid two dollars for a watch and here it's already disappeared, he thought to himself. All right. If the world went under, it went under. That I don't care about. It isn't *my* world. But the watch! Why should my watch go under? A new watch. Two dollars. It wasn't even wound.

And where will I find a glass of malted? There's nothing better in the morning than a glass of malted. And who knows if my wife. . . . . I've slept through such a terrible catastrophe, I deserve the worst. Help, help, he-e-e-lp! Where are my brains? Where were my brains before? Why didn't I keep an eye on the world and my wife? Why did I let them disappear when they were still so young?

And our hero began to beat his head against the void, but since the void was a very soft one it didn't hurt him and he remained alive to tell the story.

This is a story of human mind as such. You create a world around you of illusions. You go on getting attached to things which are

not going to be with you when you die. You go on being identified with things which are going to be taken away from you.

Hence, the Hindus call the world 'illusion'; they don't mean
by the 'world' the world that is there—they simply mean the
world that you have created out of your sleep. That world is
maya—illusion. It is a dreamworld.

Who is your wife? The very idea is foolish. Who is your
husband? Who is your child? *You are not yours*—how can anybody else be yours? Not even you are yours; not even you belong
to yourself. Have you watched sometimes that not even you
belong to yourself? You also belong to some unknown existence
you have not penetrated.

Deeper in yourself you will come to a point where even self
disappears—only a state of no-self, or call it the Supreme Self.
It is only a difference of language and terminology. Have you
not seen deep down in yourself things arising which don't belong
to you? Your desires don't belong to you, your thoughts don't
belong to you. Even your consciousness, you have not created
it—it has been given to you, it is a given fact. It is not you who
have created it—how can you create it?

You are suddenly there . . . as if it happens by magic. You
are always in the middle; you don't know the beginning. The
beginning does not belong to you, and neither does the end belong to you. Just in the middle you can create, you can go on
creating dreams. That's how a man becomes accidental.

Watch out! Become more and more essential and less and
less accidental. Always remember: Only that which is eternal
is true; only that which is going to be forever and ever is true.
That which is momentary is untrue. The momentary has to be
watched and not to be identified with.

I was reading a beautiful anecdote:

An elderly Irishman checked out of a hotel room and was
half way to the bus depot when he realized he had left his
umbrella behind. By the time he got back to the room, a newly
wed couple had already checked in. Hating to interrupt any-

60

thing, the Irishman got down on his knees and listened in at the keyhole.

"Whose lovely eyes are those, my darling?" he heard the man's voice ask.

"Yours, my love," the woman answered.

"And whose precious nose is this?" the man went on inside the room.

"Only yours," the woman replied.

"And whose beautiful lips are these?" the man continued.

"Yours!" panted the woman.

"And whose . . . ?" but the Irishman could not stand it any more.

Putting his mouth to the keyhole, he shouted, "When you get to a yellow plaid umbrella, folks, it is mine!"

This game of 'my' and 'mine' is the most absurd game—but this is the whole game of life. This earth was there before you ever came here, and this will be here when you are gone. The diamonds that you possess were there before you ever came here, and when you are gone those diamonds will remain here—and they will not even remember you. They are completely oblivious that you possess them.

This game of possessiveness is the most foolish game there is—but this is the whole game.

Gurdjieff used to say that if you start getting disidentified from things, sooner or later you will fall upon your essential being. That is the basic meaning of renunciation. Renunciation does not mean, sannyas does not mean, renouncing the world and escaping to the Himalayas or to a monastery—because if you escape from the world and go to a monastery, nothing is going to change. You carry the same mind. *Here* in the world, the house was yours, and the wife was yours; there the monastery will be yours, the religion will be yours. It will not make much difference. The 'mine' will persist. It is a mind-attitude—it has nothing to do with any outside space. It is an inner illusion, an inner dream, an inner sleep.

Renunciation means: wherever you are, there is no need to renounce the things because in the first place you never possessed them. It is foolish to talk about renunciation. It means as if you were the possessor and now you are renouncing. How can you renounce something which you never possessed? Renunciation means coming to know that you cannot possess anything. You can use, at the most, but you cannot possess. You are not going to be here forever—how can you possess? It is impossible to possess anything. You can use and you can be grateful to things that they allow themselves to be used. You should be thankful to things that they allow themselves to be used. They become means, but you cannot possess them.

Dropping the idea of ownership is renunciation. Renunciation is not dropping the possessions but possessiveness. And this is what Gurdjieff calls getting unidentified. This is what Bauls call realizing 'Ardhar Manush'—the essential man. This is what Zen people call the original face.

THERE IS a very famous Taoist story —I love it tremendously. The story is about an old Taoist farmer whose horse ran away:

That evening the neighbours gathered to commiserate with him since this was such bad luck. He said, "Maybe."

The next day the horse returned, but brought with it six wild horses, and the neighbours came exclaiming at the good fortune. He said, "Maybe."

And then the following day, his son tried to saddle and ride one of the wild horses, was thrown, and broke his leg. Again the neighbours came to offer their sympathy for the misfortune. He said, "Maybe."

The day after that, conscription officers came to the village to seize young men for the army, but because of the broken leg the farmer's son was rejected. When the neighbours came in to say how fortunate everything had turned out, he said, "Maybe."

This is the attitude of a man who understands what is accidental and what is essential. The accidental is always 'maybe'; it is a 'perhaps'. You cannot be certain about it, you *need not* be certain about it. People who become certain about the accidental are going to be frustrated sooner or later; their certainty is going to create much frustration for them. Their certainty will create expectations, and they cannot be fulfilled—because the universe is not there to fulfill your expectations. It has its own destiny. It is moving towards its own goal. It does not care about your private goals.

All private goals are against the goal of the universe itself. All private goals are against the goal of the Whole. All private goals are neurotic. The essential man comes to know, to feel, that 'I am not separate from the Whole and there is no need to seek and search for any destiny on my own. Things are happening, the world is moving—call it God—He is doing things. They are happening of their own accord. There is no need for me to make any struggle, any effort; there is no need for me to fight for anything. I can relax and be.'

The essential man is not a doer. The accidental man is a doer. The accidental man is, of course, then in anxiety, tension, stress, anguish, continuously sitting on a volcano—it can erupt any moment, because he lives in a world of uncertainty and believes as if it is certain. This creates tension in his being: he knows deep down that nothing is certain. A rich man has everything that he can have, and yet he knows deep down that he has nothing. That's what makes a rich man even poorer than a poor man.

A poor man is never so poor because still he has hopes: some day or other, destiny is going to shower blessings on him; some day or other he will be able to arrive, to achieve. He can hope. The rich man has arrived, his hopes are fulfilled—now, suddenly, he finds nothing is fulfilled. All hopes fulfilled, and yet nothing is fulfilled. He has arrived and he has not arrived at all—it has always been a dream journey. He has not moved a single inch.

A man who is successful in the world feels the pain of being a failure as nobody else can feel it. There is a proverb that says that nothing succeeds like success. I would like to tell you:

63

nothing fails like success. But you cannot know it unless you have succeeded. When all the riches are there that you have dreamt about, planned about, worked hard for, then sitting just amidst those riches is the beggar—deep inside empty, hollow; nothing inside, everything outside.

In fact, when everything is there outside, it becomes a contrast. It simply emphasizes your inner emptiness and nothingness. It simply emphasizes your inner beggarliness, poverty. A rich man knows poverty as no poor man can ever know. A successful man knows what failure is. At the top of the world, suddenly you realize that you have been behaving foolishly. You may not say so, because what is the point of saying it? You may go on pretending that you are very happy—presidents and prime ministers go on pretending they are very happy; they are not. They are just saving their faces. Now, what to say? There is no point even in saying anything—they are not true.

In the older ages, people were truer, more authentic. Buddha was a prince, he was going to be the emperor, but he realized that there is nothing in it. He could have pretended. Mahavir was a prince; he was going to be the emperor. He realized that there is nothing in it. They simply declared their realization to the world. They simply said that riches have failed, that kingdoms are not kingdoms; that if you are really seeking the kingdom, you will have to seek somewhere else, in some other direction.

In this world there is no way to arrive.

It happened:

Theodore Roosevelt, returning from Africa, received a most affectionate and exuberant greeting as his ship steamed into New York harbour. Bands were playing; soldiers, sailors and marines saluted; pretty girls greeted him as pretty girls will do. Ships in the harbour sprayed water in a festive white arc, and the people—throngs of people—shouted their welcome to him.

On the same ship, a mystic, a very old wise man, was also returning. A few old friends greeted him off in a corner, trying to be heard in the tumultuous noise. One of them said,

"We are sorry we can't welcome you home as Theodore Roosevelt is being welcomed."

To which the mystic answered as he pointed upward, "That's all right — I'm not home yet."

In this world there is no home. This world is accidental. It is illusory — just ripples on the surface, waves. And whatsoever you are doing is nothing but making card houses, or trying to sail paper boats: they are *doomed* to drown. This realization makes a man for the first time a little alert about his sleepiness, and then he starts moving more and more towards consciousness.

When things are no longer important, only consciousness becomes important. When things are no longer significant, a new search, a new door opens. Then you are not rushing towards the without: you start slipping into the within. The kingdom of God *is* within. And once you drop identifying with things, suddenly you are no longer fighting — there is no point. You start moving with the river of existence.

Arrival at home is effortless.

Bodhi has sent me a small, beautiful story; Werner Erhard likes to tell it:

> Once there was a famous medicine man in Northern Canada who was said to have enormous powers. When he waved a blanket at the northern lights they changed colour. Every time he waved his blanket, the northern lights really would change colour.
>
> One day, he lost his blanket, and the northern lights changed colour anyway. That ruined his reputation as a medicine man.

Life is also that way. No matter what you do, life only turns out the way it turns out. Struggling with life does not help at all. Struggling is simply destructive; there is no point in it. Effort is not needed. Effort is needed only in the accidental world, and even then there too it fails finally; eventually it fails. It gives you hope, but eventually it fails.

In the inner world no effort is needed. Once you start slipping

65

withinwards, you suddenly see everything is happening as it should. Life *is* perfect. There is no way to improve upon it. Then celebration starts.

When life is felt as perfect, when you suddenly see the tremendous beatitude, the tremendous glory surrounding you; when you suddenly see that *you have always been at home* — there was nowhere else to go; when you suddenly feel in your innermost core of being that you are with God and God is with you, that you are floating with the Whole, you don't have a private destiny . . . the destiny of the Whole is your destiny also, so wherever this existence is moving, you are also moving. You don't have any private goals; you are no longer idiotic.

The word 'idiot' is very beautiful. It comes from the same root as 'idiom'. It means a person who is trying to live a private life; a person who is trying to move against the Whole. A person who has his own idiom — that's what an idiot is. The whole world is going to the south: he is going to the north — that's what an idiot is.

The accidental man is idiotic. Such a vast universe, running so smoothly . . . look at the stars, look at the change of seasons; rivers running from the Himalayas to the ocean, clouds coming and showering. Watch nature — everything is running so smoothly! Why not become a part of it? Why create any conflict? Conflict creates anxiety; anxiety brings anguish.

If you have a private goal you are going to get mad. Relax! Drop out of the accidental world so you can drop into the essential world. Then one starts accepting things as they are. Then one starts loving things as they are. Then one starts cherishing things as they are. And they have always been beautiful. Once you are not fighting, not going anywhere, you can feel the music, the celestial music that is surrounding. You can see the infinite beauty, and you can feel grateful for it. It is a gift. There is no need to steal it — it is already given to you. By being alive, God has already accepted you. By being alive, He has already loved you.

If you don't like the word 'God', you can drop it. I am not a fanatic about language. You can call it 'the Existence', 'the

Unknown', 'the Truth', 'the Ultimate', 'the Absolute' — or anything. Any name will do — X, Y, Z — because it has no name. It is not particular so it cannot have any name; it is not particular so it cannot have any adjective. It is the Universal. It is That which is.

So THERE are two ways of living. One is the accidental way. The accidental way is the worldly way. The worldly way is against God, against the Whole. Then there is another way of living, another style — tremendously graceful, with no anxiety, no anguish.

I have heard:

> A botanist, a great scientist, came across a valley in the Himalayas where beautiful flowers were flowering, but there was no approach. It was very difficult to reach into the valley — thousands of feet down. And he had never heard about these flowers. He had studied about all flowers; this was some new species, undiscovered. He was enchanted, intrigued. He wanted to get those flowers but there was no way — what to do?
>
> In a desperate effort, he took his small child, tied a rope under the child's arms, and dropped the child into the valley — afraid, perspiring, trembling ... something may go amiss. And then the child reached and he picked a few flowers. And the father shouted from the top of the hill: "Are you okay, my son? Are you not afraid?"
>
> The son laughed. He said, "Why should I be afraid? — the rope is in my father's hands."

The father may be afraid, but the child is not afraid. That's what a religious man feels: The rope is in my Father's hands. Then, suddenly, all anxiety disappears.

In the accidental world you have to struggle. In the essential world you have simply to surrender. In the accidental world you have to doubt. In the essential world you simply trust — and this trust is not like belief. Belief is against doubt. Trust is simply absence of doubt — it is not against doubt. You simply feel trustful!

67

So the question is not how to believe; the question is how to change your consciousness from being accidental to essential— how to come to your centre, how to start feeling your centre again. Trust will arise—trust is an outcome, a by-product. When one comes closer to one's centre, one starts trusting more and more.

But ordinarily our whole training is how to fight. We have been trained as soldiers. As I see it there are only two types of people in the world: the soldiers and the sannyasins. The soldiers are those who have been taught to fight, to struggle against, to achieve their goals; to *force,* to be violent, to be aggressive, to coerce. And the sannyasin is one who knows that there is no need—life is already going that way: "I have just to be in tune with life. I have just to be a part of this vast orchestra. I have just to become a note in harmony with the Whole. I have to surrender." The sannyasin is not a warrior, not a soldier. He is surrendered.

Once it happened:

Mulla Nasrudin had harnessed a kitten to his broken-down Cadillac. When bystanders pointed out that this was absurd, he replied, "You-all may think so, but I got a horsewhip."

There are people who think that just by forcing, anything is possible—just a horsewhip is needed; just you have to do it a little harder. If you are not succeeding, that simply shows that you are not working hard at it—work a little harder. If you are still not succeeding, then you are not putting all your energy— put a little more energy into it. This is the logic of the accidental world.

The essential man knows that it is not a question of putting more energy, it is not a question of fighting at all. It is a question of allowing existence to happen. *Nothing is needed on your part to be done.* Only one thing: a deep trust and surrender.

But sometimes it happens, just like the waving of the blanket of the medicine man, that you wave the blanket and something happens—you think it is happening because of the waving of your blanket. Had you waited a little, it would have happened on its own. You simply wasted your energy by waving the blanket.

Sometimes it happens that you have been struggling for something yet it happens—that gives the idea to your mind that it has happened 'because of my effort.' Then you are in a vicious circle. When you fail you think 'I have not been making as much effort as needed.' When you succeed you think 'I have done as much as was needed.' But, in fact, things go on happening of their own accord; they don't happen by your effort. Sometimes it is a coincidence that they happen even when you are making an effort.

All that is beautiful, true and good, simply comes as a grace. It descends on you. And once some effort succeeds, you are in a mad mess. Then you think, now . . .

> An architect was having a difficult time with Mulla Nasrudin, a prospective home-builder. "But can't you give some idea," he pleaded, "of the general type of house you want to build, Nasrudin?"
>
> "Well," replied the Mulla hesitantly, "all I know is: it must go with an antique doorknob my wife bought the other day."

He has only an antique doorknob and he wants to make a house. Now, the only thing he knows: it must go with the antique doorknob. That's how we are working. A small effort has succeeded, so you have an antique doorknob—now you are trying to create the whole house of life accordingly. You are creating trouble for yourself. And that antique doorknob is also not because of your efforts. It is better to say that it happened in spite of your efforts. Somehow, you coincided with the universe.

This is the whole philosophy of the religious man: that 'I have nothing to do—just to celebrate, let things happen to me; just to dance and sing.' It does not mean that a religious man becomes inactive. No. He becomes *more* active, but in his action there is no effort, there is no strain, there is no violence. It is *not* that he becomes inactive, dull, lethargic. No. He radiates with energy, he overflows with energy, because all that energy that was being wasted in effort is no longer wasted. He has too much of it—he can share. But now he functions as a vehicle.

69

Now he has given his whole energy to the Whole. Now, wherever the Whole takes him, he goes. Now he is with the Whole and not against it.

Whether you go in a church or in a temple or not is irrelevant. If you are with the Whole, you are a religious person. Whether you are a Christian or a Hindu or a Mohammedan is irrelevant. If you are with the Whole, you are a religious person. And remember this with me: I am not here to convert you to become a Hindu, to become a Mohammedan, to become a Christian. All that nonsense is not for me. I am here to help you to become religious — with no adjective attached to it.

And once you start understanding this, the world takes on a totally new colour. Even sometimes when there is pain, you are understanding. Sometimes it hurts — yes, even then it is not all roses. It cannot be, but you start understanding it. In fact, you start seeing that thorns are there to protect the roses; that night is needed to help the day to be born; that death is needed to refresh life. Once you start understanding, you become positive. Then whatsoever happens, you can always look deeper into its meaning, its significance.

I was reading a poem:

> *The world is a beautiful place*
> *to be born into,*
> *if you don't mind happiness*
> *not always being*
> *so very much fun,*
> *if you don't mind a touch of hell*
> *now and then*
> *just when everything is fine —*
> *because even in heaven*
> *they don't sing*
> *all the time.*

Even a dancer needs a rest, even a singer needs a rest. Even a happy person needs rest. One cannot remain in one mood continuously — there is no need. When there are so many climates available, why get attached to one? Why not be enriched by all?

70

A man who has attained to his essential centre moves on dancing in different situations. Sometimes it is hot, sometimes it is cold; sometimes it is joy, sometimes it is sadness—but now everything brings him some message from the Whole. Everything has become a messenger.

THIS STORY, today's story, is a very simple story but very significant. And it always happens that significant things are very simple, and simple things are very significant.

> *There was a man of Wei, Tung-men Wu,*
> *who did not grieve when his son died.*
> *His wife said to him:*
> *"No one in the world loved his son as*
> *much as you did, why do you not grieve*
> *now he is dead?"*
> *He answered:*
> *"I had no son, and when I had no son*
> *I did not grieve. Now that he is dead it is*
> *the same as it was before, when I had no*
> *son. Why should I grieve over him?"*

A very simple parable, but tremendously significant, very meaningful. Enter into it layer by layer:

> *There was a man of Wei, Tung-men Wu,*
> *who did not grieve when his son died.*

It is very difficult not to grieve when somebody you loved so much has died. It is possible only if you have known something of the essential. It is possible only if you have tasted something of the deathless. It is possible only if you have transcended the accidental. He did not grieve, he was not sad. He was not weeping or crying, he was not broken. He remained just the same as he was before.

The wife was disturbed. She said:

> *"No one in the world loved his son as much*
> *as you did, why do you not grieve now he*
> *is dead?"*

71

Ordinarily, this is our logic, that if you love a person too much you will grieve too much when he is gone. The logic is fallacious; the logic has a very deep flaw in it. In fact, if you have loved a person really, when he is gone he is gone; you will not grieve much. If you have not loved the person deeply, then you will grieve very much. Try to understand this.

Your father dies, or your mother dies. If you have loved him totally while he was alive, you will be able to say goodbye to him without any grief—because you *loved* him. That experience of love was total and fulfilling; nothing is left undone; nothing is hanging over your head. Whatsoever was possible has happened; now you can accept it. What *more* was possible? Even if he had been alive, what more would have been possible? The experience is complete.

Whenever an experience is complete, you are ready to say goodbye *very* easily. But if you have not loved your father as you always wanted to, you have not been respectful towards him as you always wanted to, you will feel guilty. Now the father is gone; now there is no way to fulfill your desire—now there is no way to show your respect, your love. Now there is no way, you will feel yourself hanging in the middle, in mid-air, in a limbo. You will not be at ease; you cannot say goodbye. You will cry and weep and you will be broken, and you will say that you are broken because your father is dead, but the real thing is something else.

You are broken because now the possibility to love him, to respect him, is gone. Now there is no possibility—the doors are closed and you have missed an opportunity. The son will cry more if he has not really loved his father. If he has loved his father he will be able to accept the fact—*love is very accepting and very understanding.*

Once an experience is complete, you can get out of it very easily—you can just slip out of it as the snake slips out of his old skin. If you love a woman and you have been constantly quarrelling with her, and it never became a deep satisfaction, and she dies . . . now she will haunt you, her ghost will haunt you for your whole life. You could not do something that was

72

possible, but now it is no longer possible. Now something incomplete will always be there in the heart, hurting; it will become a wound.

This is the understanding of all the sages, that while you are loving a person, if you love him *totally* there is going to be no misery. If you love him totally, if you enjoy and delight in him totally, and the person is gone—of course, one feels a little sad, but it is not grief; one misses a little but one is capable of remaining centred, one is not distracted.

If you are in love, love totally, so nothing remains hanging. Otherwise, that hanging, incomplete experience, that unlived experience, will haunt you. These unlived experiences go on piling up and they become heavy burdens.

And the problem is that now there is no way—what to do with them? You cannot complete them because the person has disappeared. You cannot drop them because incomplete experiences cannot be dropped. It is just like a ripe fruit drops of its own accord. When it is ripe, it drops; when it is not ripe, it is difficult to drop. Whenever an experience is complete, it is a ripe fruit—it drops of its own accord. It leaves no scar behind, no wound.

The wife says: *"No one in the world loved his son as much as you did, why do you not grieve now he is dead?"*

She is giving the argument of the accidental mind. That is the argument of the accidental man: Why don't you grieve? In fact, the accidental man was not really happy while the person was alive, but he becomes very unhappy when the person is gone.

I used to know a woman who was very unhappy with the husband—almost in hell, continuously fighting, quarrelling, nagging. The husband started drinking too much, just to avoid all this. Then the fight became even more fierce, because the wife started fighting against his drinking. It led him to even more drinking. When he was only thirty-six he died—died because of too much drinking.

The woman was never happy. She lived with him for almost seven years, she was never happy. All those seven years I used to know them—they were next-door neighbours to me—and

73

always the husband would come with his miseries, and the wife would come with her miseries—I was a silent watcher. Then the husband died, and the woman became *so* sad. Months passed and she was crying and crying, and she was going mad!

One day I went to her, and there was nobody else so I told her, "Now I can be true to you: Stop this nonsense!—because you were never happy with this man. In fact, many times you have told me that if this man dies it will be good. Now he is dead; he has fulfilled your desire, so why are you crying and weeping? I can't see any point in it! Are you missing all those fights? Are you missing all that misery?—because I cannot see that you are missing the man, because there was nothing in it!"

She was shocked. She had never expected something like that from me or from anybody else. People in such situations expect sympathy. I said, "Stop this nonsense! I know that you were never happy. Now you can be happy! He is no longer there to create any trouble."

She looked at me, shocked. Her tears dried and she said, "It is shocking, but you have made me alert about one thing: I am not missing him at all. I am simply crying and weeping because I could not love him. It is *not his death*—it is my own missed experience of love. I *loved* that man, but I could not love him. We wasted the whole opportunity in quarrelling over futile things. Now I know those things mean nothing; now that he is gone, I know those things were just trivia. I can't even remember the reasons why we were fighting continuously."

If you love a person totally, and the experience is complete, has enriched you, you can say goodbye. Of course, there will be sadness but there will be no grief. And sadness is natural. It will disappear in time; it is nothing to be worried about. You will miss the person a little while—natural—but you will not be in grief.

The accidental man says if you don't cry when a person is dead, that means you never loved him. That's what the wife was trying to point out: "You loved him so much. At least you pretended to love him so much, as if nobody has ever loved his son so much. Now what has happened? There is no grief! What type of love is this?" If you ask me, I say it is because he really loved the child. Now that he is gone, he is gone!

Love is understanding. And love is so understanding that not only does it understand life, it understands death also.

He answered: *"I had no son, and when I had no son I did not grieve."*

This is the logic of the essential man. He says: "There was a moment in my life when the son was not there, and I was happy without him. I had known no grief then. Then the son came and I was happy with him. Now that he is gone, I am again in the same situation as before, before he was born. And I was not in grief then so why should I be in grief now? Again I am in the same situation: the son is not there; I am not a father again. Once I used not to be a father, then I became a father. I am again not a father. Something has happened, disappeared . . . I am left in the same way as I was before."

IT IS said about a great sage who was a prime minister: When he was appointed prime minister to a king, he was almost a beggar on the streets. But the news of his wisdom spread, rumours started coming to the palace, and the king started going to him and he was impressed. He was tremendously impressed by the man and his insight—he appointed him his prime minister.

The beggar came to the palace. The king said, "Now you can drop your robe." Beautiful clothes were ready for him. He was given a good bath; beautiful robes were given to him, ornaments—and as befits a prime minister.

Then everybody became intrigued by the fact that in one room he had something like treasure locked. And every day he used to go, unlock the door—he would go alone, he would not allow anybody inside—lock the door again, and he would remain there for at least half an hour, then come out. Everybody became suspicious: What is happening in that room? What is he having in that room? Is there some conspiracy? Is there some secret? And, of course, the king also became interested.

One day the king said, "I would like to come with you in your private room. I could not sleep last night. I continuously worried about what is there."

The prime minister said, "There is nothing. And it is not worthy of your eyes. I will not take you."

The king became even more suspicious. He said, "There seems to be some danger! I cannot allow this to happen in my palace. You will *have* to take me in!"

The prime minister said, "If you don't trust me then I will take you in—but then this is the end of my prime-ministership. Then take my resignation and come into the room. Otherwise, *trust* me and *never* ask about the room!"

But the king was really suspicious. He said, "Okay, you give your resignation but I am coming into the room."

With his whole court they entered. There was nothing . . . his old robe. Just the old robe hanging on a nail in the room. They looked around: there was nothing—the room was empty. They said, "Why do you come here?"

He said, "Just to see this robe—to remind me that once I was a beggar, and any day I will be a beggar again. Just to remind me so that I don't get too much attached to this prime-ministership."

He dropped out of his dress, took his robe. The king started weeping and crying; he said, "Don't go!" But he said, "Now, enough is enough. You could not trust me, and when there is no trust there is no point in my being here. I must go."

But he left the palace the same way he had entered one day. Those ten, twelve years he remained the prime minister meant nothing; that was just an accident.

This is what this man is saying: "I had no son, and when I had no son I did not grieve. I never missed this son when he was not there. When I was not a father, I never missed him, so why now should I miss him? Again the same situation has come back: now that he is dead, it is the same as it was before when I had no son. Why should I grieve over him?"

This is the way to *watch* life. Whatsoever is accidental . . . you are living in a big house, in a palace. Remember that if this palace is taken away from you, there is no point in becoming depressed. Once you were living outside the palace, so again you are under the sky. You become very respectable, and then something happens . . . you are condemned by the society. What is the point to be worried about it? One day you were not famous at all and you were happy—again you can be happy.

One day you were not in this world! When you were not born, do you remember that you were in any way unhappy?—then why be worried when you die? You will be again in the same state. You were not, and you don't remember any unhappiness. One day you will again disappear . . . why be worried? You will be again in the same state: you will not be again—at least not in the way that you are here.

This is what Zen people say: Find out your original face—the face that you had before you were born, and the face that will be there when you are dead. Find out the eternal, and don't pay much attention to the accidental.

If you can drop out of the accidental, you have dropped out of the world. There is no need to go anywhere: it is an inner attitude.

REMEMBER: remain alert that you don't get too much attached to the accidental—*and all is accidental except your consciousness.* Except your awareness, all is accidental. Pain and pleasure, success and failure, fame and defamation—all is accidental. Only your witnessing consciousness is essential. Stick to it! Get more and more rooted in it. And don't spread your attachment to worldly things.

I don't mean leave them. I don't mean leave your house, leave your wife, leave your children—but remember that it is just an accident that you are together. It is not going to be an eternal state. It has a beginning; it will have an end. Remember that you were happy even before it began; and you will be happy when it has ended. If you can carry this touchstone, you can always judge what is accidental and what is essential.

That which is always is truth. That which is momentary is untrue.

In the East and in the West there is a difference in the definition of truth. In the Western philosophy, truth is equivalent to the real. In the East, truth is equivalent to the eternal—

because in the East we say even the momentary is real: real for the moment; but it is not true because it is not eternal. It is just a reflection. The reflection is also real!

You see the moon in the sky and the reflection in the lake — the reflection is also real because it is there! There is a difference between the reflection and no reflection, so it is real. Even a dream is real, because when you dream it is there! It is real as a dream, but it is real. The only difference between the dream and the waking state is that the dream lasts only for a few moments —the waking state lasts longer. But in the East we have come to the ultimate awakening also. Then this waking state also looks momentary, then this too is dreamlike.

The eternal is true. The temporal is untrue. Both are real. The accidental is also real and the essential is also real, but with the accidental you will remain in misery. And with the essential the doors of bliss open, the doors of *satchitanand*—of truth, of consciousness, of bliss.

Remember this story in your day-to-day life. Imbibe its impact. If you can remember it, it can become a transforming influence on your life, it can transfigure you—it can help you to reach to your centre.

CHAPTER 4

How to find out what my
  creativity is?

A white and small aura is
  visible just over your head—
  why is not a coloured one visible?

Aurobindo said India is the
  spiritual centre of the world.

What are the female qualities of God?

How can I know that a woman has fallen in
  love in reality?

How did I get such a wonderful opportunity
  to be at God's feet?

MAN IS ALWAYS AN OPENING

fourteenth august 1976

The first question: *I believed I was uncreative. What else can be creativity besides dancing and painting and how to find out what my creativity is?*

CREATIVITY has nothing to do with any activity in particular —with painting, poetry, dancing, singing. It has nothing to do with anything in particular.

Anything can be creative—you bring that quality to the activity. Activity itself is neither creative nor uncreative. You can paint in an uncreative way. You can sing in an uncreative way. You can clean the floor in a creative way. You can cook in a creative way.

Creativity is the quality that *you* bring to the activity you are doing. It is an attitude, an inner approach—how you look at things.

So the first thing to be remembered: don't confine creativity to anything in particular. A man *is* creative—and if he is creative, whatsoever he does, even if he walks, you can see in his walking there is creativity. Even if he sits silently and does nothing, even non-doing will be a creative act. Buddha sitting under the Bodhi Tree doing nothing is the greatest creator the world has ever known.

Once you understand it—that it is *you,* the *person,* who is creative or uncreative—then this problem disappears.

Not everybody can be a painter—and there is no need also. If everybody is a painter the world will be very ugly; it will be difficult to live. And not everybody can be a dancer, and there is no need. But everybody can be creative.

Whatsoever you do, if you do it joyfully, if you do it lovingly, if your act of doing it is not purely economical, then it is creative. If you have something growing out of it within you, if it gives you growth, it is spiritual, it is creative, it is divine.

You become more divine as you become more creative. All the religions of the world have said: God is the Creator. I don't know whether He is the Creator or not, but one thing I know: the more creative you become, the more godly you become. When your creativity comes to a climax, when your whole life becomes creative, you live *in* God. So He must be the Creator because people who have been creative have been closest to Him.

Love what you do. Be meditative while you are doing it—whatsoever it is! irrelevant of the fact of what it is.

Have you seen Paras cleaning this floor of Chuang Tzu auditorium? Then you will know: cleaning can become creative. With what love! Almost singing and dancing inside. If you clean the floor with such love, you have done an invisible painting. You lived that moment in such delight that it has given you some inner growth. You cannot be the same after a creative act.

Creativity means loving whatsoever you do—enjoying, celebrating it, as a gift of God! Maybe nobody comes to know about it. Who is going to praise Paras for cleaning this floor? History will not take any account of it; newspapers will not publish her name and pictures—but that is irrelevant. She *enjoyed* it. The value is intrinsic.

So if you are looking for fame and then you think you are creative—if you become famous like Picasso, then you are creative—then you will miss. Then you are, in fact, not creative at all: you are a politician, ambitious. If fame happens, good. If it doesn't happen, good. It should not be the consideration. The consideration should be that you are enjoying whatsoever you are doing. It is your love-affair.

If your act is your love-affair, then it becomes creative. Small things become great by the touch of love and delight.

The questioner asks: "I believed I was uncreative." If you believe in that way, you will become uncreative—because belief is not just belief. It opens doors; it closes doors. If you have a wrong belief, then that will hang around you as a closed door. If you believe that you are uncreative, you will become uncreative—because that belief will obstruct, continuously negate, all possibilities of flowing. It will not allow your energy to flow because you will continuously say: "I am uncreative."

This has been taught to everybody. Very few people are accepted as creative: A few painters, a few poets—one in a million. This is foolish! Every human being is a born creator. Watch children and you will see: *all* children are creative. By and by, we destroy their creativity. By and by, we force wrong beliefs on them. By and by, we distract them. By and by, we make them more and more economical and political and ambitious.

When ambition enters, creativity disappears—because an ambitious man cannot be creative, because an ambitious man cannot love any activity for its own sake. While he is painting he is looking ahead; he is thinking, 'When am I going to get a Nobel Prize?' When he is writing a novel, he is looking ahead. He is always in the future—and a creative person is always in the present.

We destroy creativity. *Nobody is born uncreative,* but we make ninety-nine percent of people uncreative.

But just throwing the responsibility on the society is not going to help—you have to take your life in your own hands. You have to drop wrong conditionings. You have to drop wrong, hypnotic auto-suggestions that have been given to you in your childhood. Drop them! Purify yourself of all conditionings . . . and suddenly you will see you *are* creative.

To be and to be creative are synonymous. It is impossible to be and not to be creative. But that impossible thing has happened, that ugly phenomenon has happened, because all your creative sources have been plugged, blocked, destroyed, and your whole energy has been forced into some activity that the society thinks is going to pay.

Our whole attitude about life is money-oriented. And money is one of the most uncreative things one can become interested in. Our whole approach is power-oriented and power is destructive, not creative. A man who is after money will become destructive, because money has to be robbed, exploited; it has to be taken away from many people, only then can you have it. Power simply means you have to make many people impotent, you have to destroy them—only then will you be powerful, can you be powerful.

Remember: these are destructive acts. A creative act enhances the beauty of the world; it gives something to the world, it never takes anything from it. A creative person comes into the world, enhances the beauty of the world—a song here, a painting there. He makes the world dance better, enjoy better, love better, meditate better. When he leaves this world, he leaves a better world behind him. Nobody may know him; somebody may know him—that is not the point. But he leaves the world a better world, tremendously fulfilled because his life has been of some intrinsic value.

Money, power, prestige, are uncreative; not only uncreative, but destructive activities. Beware of them! And if you beware of them you can become creative very easily. I am not saying that your creativity is going to give you power, prestige, money. No, I cannot promise you any rose-gardens. It may give you trouble. It may force you to live a poor man's life. All that I can promise you is that deep inside you will be the richest man possible; deep inside you will be fulfilled; deep inside you will be full of joy and celebration. You will be *continuously* receiving more and more blessings from God. Your life will be a life of benediction.

But it is possible that outwardly you may not be famous, you may not have money, you may not succeed in the so-called world. But to succeed in this so-called world is to fail deeply, is to fail in the inside world. And what are you going to do with the whole world at your feet if you have lost your own self? What will you do if you possess the whole world and you don't possess yourself? A creative person possesses his own being; he is a master.

That's why in the East we have been calling sannyasins 'swamis'. 'Swami' means a master. Beggars have been called swamis—masters. Emperors we have known, but they proved in the final account, in the final conclusion of their lives, that they were beggars. A man who is after money and power and prestige is a beggar, because he continuously begs. He has nothing to give to the world.

Be a giver. Share whatsoever you can! And remember, I am not making any distinction between small things and great things. If you can smile whole-heartedly, hold somebody's hand and smile, then it is a creative act, a *great* creative act. Just embrace somebody to your heart and you *are* creative. Just look with loving eyes at somebody . . . just a loving look can change the whole world of a person.

Be creative. Don't be worried about what you are doing— one has to do *many* things—but do everything creatively, with devotion. Then your work becomes worship. Then whatsoever you do is a prayer. And whatsoever you do is an offering at the altar.

Drop this belief that you are uncreative. I know how this belief is created: you may not have been a gold medalist in the university; you may not have been top in your class; your painting may not have won appreciation; when you play on your flute, neighbours report to the police. Maybe—but just because of these things, don't get the wrong belief that you are uncreative. That may be because you are imitating others.

People have a very limited idea of what being creative is —

87

playing the guitar or the flute or writing poetry—so people go on writing rubbish in the name of poetry. You have to find out what you can do and what you cannot do. Everybody cannot do everything! You have to search and find your destiny. You have to grope in the dark, I know. It is not very clear-cut what your destiny is—but that's how life is. And it is *good* that one has to search for it—in the *very* search, something grows.

If God were to give a chart of your life to you when you were entering into the world—this will be your life: you are going to become a guitarist—then your life would be mechanical. Only a machine can be predicted, not a man. Man is unpredictable. Man is always an opening . . . a potentiality for a thousand and one things. Many doors open and many alternatives are always present at each step—and you have to choose, you have to feel. But if you love your life you will be able to find.

If you *don't* love your life and you love something else, then there is a problem. If you love money and you want to be creative, you cannot become creative. The very ambition for money is going to destroy your creativity. If you want fame, then forget about creativity. Fame comes easier if you are destructive. Fame comes easier to an Adolf Hitler; fame comes easier to a Henry Ford. Fame is easier if you are competitive, violently competitive. If you can kill and destroy people, fame comes easier.

The whole history is the history of murderers. If you become a murderer, fame will be very easy. You can become a prime minister; you can become a president—but these are all masks. Behind them you will find very violent people, terribly violent people hiding, smiling. Those smiles are political, diplomatic. If the mask slips, you will always see Genghis Khan, Timur Leng, Nadir Shah, Napoleon, Alexander, Hitler, hiding behind.

If you want fame, don't talk about creativity. I am not saying that fame never comes to a creative person, but very rarely it comes, *very* rarely. It is more like an accident, and it takes much time. Almost always it happens that by the time fame comes to a creative person, he is gone—it is always posthumous; it is very delayed.

Jesus was not famous in his day. If there were no Bible, there would have been no record of him. The record belongs to his four disciples; nobody else has ever mentioned him, whether he existed or not. He was not famous. He was not successful. Can you think of a greater failure than Jesus? But, by and by, he became more and more significant; by and by, people recognized him. It takes time.

The greater a person is, the more time it takes for people to recognize him—because when a great person is born, there are no criteria to judge him by, there are no maps to find him with. He has to create his own values; by the time he has created the values, he is gone. It takes thousands of years for a creative person to be recognized, and then too it is not certain. There have been many creative people who have never been recognized. It is accidental for a creative person to be successful. For an uncreative, destructive person it is more certain.

So if you are seeking something else in the name of creativity, then drop the idea of being creative. At least consciously, deliberately, do whatsoever you want to do. Never hide behind masks. If you really want to be creative, then there is no question of money, success, prestige, respectability—then you enjoy your activity; then each act has an intrinsic value. You dance because you like dancing; you dance because you delight in it. If somebody appreciates, good, you feel grateful. If nobody appreciates, it is none of your business to be worried about it. You danced, you enjoyed—you are already fulfilled.

But this belief of being uncreative can be dangerous—drop it! Nobody is uncreative—not even trees, not even rocks. People who have known trees and loved trees, know that each tree creates its own space, each rock creates its own space. It is like nobody else's space. If you become sensitive, if you become capable of understanding, through empathy, you will be tremendously benefited. You will see each tree is creative in its own way; no other tree is like that—each tree is unique; each tree has individuality, each rock has individuality. Trees are not just trees—they are people. Rocks are not just rocks—

they are people. Go and sit by the side of a rock—watch it lovingly, touch it lovingly, feel it lovingly.

It is said about a Zen master that he was able to pull *very* big rocks, remove very big rocks—and he was a very fragile man. It was almost impossible looking at his physiology! Stronger men, very much stronger than him, were unable to pull those rocks, and he would simply pull them very easily.

He was asked what his trick was. He said, "There is no trick—I love the rock so the rock helps. First I say to her, 'Now my prestige is in your hands, and these people have come to watch. Now help me, cooperate with me.' Mm?—then I simply hold the rock lovingly . . . and *wait* for the hint. When the rock gives me the hint—it is a shudder, my whole spine starts vibrating—when the rock gives me the hint that she is ready, then I move. You move against the rock; that's why so much energy is needed. I move with the rock, I flow with the rock. In fact, it is wrong to say that I remove it—I am simply there. The rock removes itself."

One great Zen master was a carpenter, and whenever he made tables, chairs, somehow they had some ineffable quality in them, a tremendous magnetism. He was asked, "How do you make them?"

He said, "I don't make them. I simply go to the forest: the *basic* thing is to enquire of the forest, of trees, which tree is ready to become a chair."

Now these things look absurd—because we don't know, we don't know the language. For three days he would remain in the forest. He would sit under one tree, under another tree, and he would talk to trees—and he was a mad man! But a tree is to be judged by its fruit, and this master has also to be judged by his creation. A few of his chairs still survive in China— they still carry a magnetism. You will just be simply attracted; you will not know what is pulling you. After a thousand years! —something tremendously beautiful.

He said, "I go and I say that I am in search of a tree who wants to become a chair. I ask the trees if they are willing; not only willing: cooperating with me, ready to go with me—

only then. Sometimes it happens that no tree is ready to become a chair—I come empty-handed."

It happened: The Emperor of China asked him to make him a stand for his books. And he went and after three days he said, "Wait—no tree is ready to come to the palace."

After three months the Emperor again enquired. The carpenter said, "I have been going continuously. I am persuading. Wait—one tree seems to be leaning a little bit."

Then he persuaded one tree. He said, "The whole art is there!—when the tree comes of its own accord. Then she is simply asking the help of the carpenter."

You can go and ask Asheesh—he has a feel for wood, and wood also has a feel for him.

If you are loving you will see that the whole existence has individuality. Don't pull and push things. Watch, communicate; take their help—and much energy will be preserved.

Even trees are creative, rocks are creative. You are man: the very culmination of this existence. You are at the top—you are conscious. Never think with wrong beliefs, and never be attached to wrong beliefs, that you are uncreative. Maybe your father said to you that you are uncreative, your colleagues said to you that you are uncreative. Maybe you were searching in wrong directions, in directions in which you are not creative, but there *must* be a direction in which you *are* creative. Seek and search and remain available, and go on groping—unless you find it.

Each man comes into this world with a specific destiny—he has something to fulfill, some message has to be delivered, some work has to be completed. You are not here accidentally—you are here meaningfully. There is a purpose behind you. The Whole intends to do something through you.

The second question—it is from Hareesh: *A white and small aura is visible just over your head. Why is not a coloured one visible?*

I T IS a coloured one—but all the colours are there, hence it looks white. White is not colourless. White is the presence of all the colours together. White is the most colourful thing in the world—hence it looks white.

When a white ray passes through a prism it divides into seven colours. That's how a rainbow is created in the rainy season. Small particles of water hanging in the air function as prisms. White rays of sun enter through those hanging particles of water and are divided into seven colours. If you mix all the colours in the right proportions, you will create white. White is all the colours together.

I am not a Buddhist, I am not a Hindu, I am not a Christian, I am not a Jain, I am not a Mohammedan—and I am all. All colours together! Hence white is created. A white aura is the greatest possibility.

People have different auras: somebody has a black aura—black is the lowest possibility. Black is the absence of all colours. Hence, in all the mythologies we paint the Devil as black—that is the aura—we paint the Devil as black. Even negroes paint the Devil as black; they should paint the Devil as white, but they paint the Devil as black.

Black means the absence of all colours—absence of everything. Black is negative. Black is just nihilistic. Black means simply negativity. Black is death. That's why death is also painted black. And when you mourn for a person, you use black dress. White is the opposite polarity of black: black is the absence of all colours; white is the presence of all colours. White is an invisible rainbow.

Go on watching your own face in the mirror. Next time you stand before your mirror, don't be bothered too much with your physiological shape—try to see the aura. In the beginning it will not be visible, but if you go on working, within three months you will be able to see a subtle aura surrounding your face in the mirror. And that will be greatly indicative and helpful for your growth, because it will show the colour where you are. If it is black, then much has to be done. If it is grey, then you are just in the middle of your growth; half the journey is over, half has yet to be travelled.

You ask: "Why is not a coloured one visible?"—because all the colours are there it cannot be a coloured one. A coloured one means simply one colour. And you will be surprised: if you ask the physicists, who know colour well, what it is, you will be surprised. If you are using a red dress, that simply means the red colour is reflected back, is given back to the world. Your dress absorbs all other colours; only the red colour it doesn't absorb but reflects back, shares with the existence, it gives it back. It renounces red—that's why it is red.

This seems paradoxical: red dress is not red! It renounces red; that's why it looks red—people looking at you see it red because the red ray is going back and falls on their eyes and they see it as red. A black dress absorbs all; it doesn't give back anything. It simply absorbs all—the black is miserly, it doesn't share. It is a sort of spiritual constipation. It simply takes in and never gives out.

White simply reflects everything back, gives everything back. Hence, in India white became the colour of renunciation. White means nothing is absorbed; all the rays are returned back to the existence—with thanks, with gratitude. When all the rays fall on your eyes, it looks white. When one ray falls on your eye— red, blue, green—then it is colourful.

A white aura is the best aura. And I would like to tell Hareesh . . . he is a very sensitive man. A new sannyasin in a way, but a very ancient one in another. I have known him before—and he also knows this. May not be very conscious about it, but he feels it somewhere. He is a very sensitive man, an infinitely sensitive man. That's why he has been able to see the aura. If he tries a little, soon he will be able to see his own aura. And if he tries a little more, he can become an aura expert, he can see anybody's aura. And it is going to be helpful in his work. He is a psychotherapist. It will be of tremendous help to him.

In the East, masters have used it as a psychoanalytic device. When a person comes to a master, the first thing to see is his aura—because that will decide everything. He starts analysing his aura because that is very indicative. That shows about the deepest layers of his mind, conscious and unconscious both.

There are people who come to me sometimes who say they don't want to take sannyas, and in their aura I see that they are ready. Just the other day, Prasthan's ex-wife was here. I see she is ready, but she says she has to think about it. Her aura is crystal-clear. She is finished with the world! but is unconscious about it. I told her, "For me you have become a sannyasin—for yourself you can take a little time to think." There are people who want to become sannyasins, and I even initiate them, but I see their aura is still too much involved in the world, too much of the world. I hope for them. Their desire is good, but their preparation is none.

People are not aware of their auras, otherwise they would be able to self-analyse themselves. Hareesh can attain to this capacity very easily.

The third question: *When Sri Aurobindo said that India is the spiritual centre of the world, the thinkers all over the West felt offended. They mocked and laughed at it. Please comment.*

SRI AUROBINDO was never really a very spiritual man. Originally he was a politician, and politics lingered and lingered to the very end. He became religious, he tried hard, but the shadow of politics continued. His assertions should not be given too much value. He was a little chauvinistic about India, as people are about their own country all over the world.

An Indian thinks that he is the very centre of the world spiritually, very highly evolved. All rubbish! No country as such is spiritually evolved, no race as such is spiritually evolved. Spirituality happens only to individuals, not to countries. Yes, Buddha was evolved, so was Jesus; Mahavir was evolved, so was Mohammed; Krishna was evolved, so was Zarathustra—so what! Individuals. Just because Buddha happened to be born in India, India does not become spiritual—because spiritual people have been born all over the world, to every part, to every country, to every century, to every race. But there is a spiritual egoism, and there are reasons also.

India feels very inferior in many ways; it has to compensate. The West is very materially progressive, materially affluent, rich—rich in science, rich in living, rich in every way. India feels inferior: how to compensate for it? This becomes a compensation: that we are spiritually evolved.

No country is spiritually evolved—because spirituality is *basically* individual. It has nothing to do with country and climate; it is not confined to the boundaries of politics. Ask the Indians: "Now what about Pakistan?" Just twenty years ago it was India—then it was spiritually evolved. Now?—now it is the *worst* country in the world—ask an Indian. It was India just twenty years ago! Now it is no more India. Political boundaries. The world is one, the earth is one, for a spiritual man.

So if Aurobindo is talking about the geographical India, he is talking nonsense. But Indians feel good; they have nothing else to claim. Spirituality is good because it is a very invisible thing; you cannot disprove it. If somebody says, "I am very rich," you can prove or disprove it—mm?—you can go and see the bank-balance. And somebody says, "I am spiritual," now what to do? How to prove or how to disprove?

I have heard an anecdote:

A few Christian theologians have concluded that Adam and Eve were Indians. Why? "First," they argue, "they had nothing to wear. Second, they stole apples; and, third, with it all, they thought they were living in the Garden of Eden."

95

They had nothing to wear, were stealing apples, and still thinking that they lived in Paradise! That's what an Indian goes on
thinking. So when somebody like Sri Aurobindo declares that
India is the centre, the spiritual guide, the spiritual guru of the
whole world, Indians feel very good. It enhances their ego. It
helps them to stand a little more erect; it helps them to feel a
little good. It cheers them—that's all. But it is not a truth.

And Sri Aurobindo was definitely talking about the geographical India—because he was very fanatical, chauvinistic. He had
the idea that Indians are very superior, that they have spiritual work to do in the world. No. But in another way, if you take
India not as a geographical thing, not as a political map, but if
you take India as an eternal search for truth, then this country
has been in search long—longer than any other country. It has
sacrificed much for its search. That's how it has become so
poor—because when people start thinking of the inner world,
they start dropping from the outside world, they become
dropouts.

India has been approaching the inner continuously. If you
take India as a symbol of inner search, good—but then you
should remember that it is an inner search and a symbol of inner
search. Then somebody who is born in the West *and* is seeking
God is an Indian; and somebody who is born in India and is seeking money is an American. Then there is no trouble—then
Jesus is Indian, Zarathustra is Indian, Lao Tzu is Indian, Chuang
Tzu is Indian, Bokuju, Rinzai—all are Indians. Then 'India' has
a totally different meaning.

I also say that India *is* significant, but just as a psychological
symbol. Longest India has been searching. And *more* Buddhas
have happened here. The very climate of spirituality, the milieu,
helps. Jesus is rare, Zarathustra is rare. In India, Buddha, Mahavir, Krishna, Ram—it seems almost a normal state of affairs.

But it is just like when somebody says: "The West is symbolic
for science." Yes, the West has been searching scientifically
longest. From the ancient Greeks up to today the Western mind
has been searching in scientific categories. It has been leaning

96

more and more towards logic, mathematics, experimentation. And in the East, India has been leaning more and more illogically, irrationally, towards the inner.

If you can think of the West as a symbol of science, then the East can become a symbol for spirituality. If you think of the Greek mind as logical, then you can think of the Indian mind as religious—but then these are symbols, nothing to brag about.

But every country, every race, goes on bragging about itself. I have heard an anecdote:

The mother superior of a convent was interviewing the three girls graduating from the high school.

"Wee Margaret," she asked the first, "and what will you be doing when you leave us?"

"Oh, Mother," the girl replied, "I'm not going to be leaving you—I'm going to stay here and take the veil!"

"Bless you, Margaret," said the nun, well pleased. Turning to the next one she asked, "And you, Katherine, what are your plans?"

"Oh," replied Katherine, "I'm going to continue to get a good Catholic education and then teach little children in a parochial school."

"Most commendable," said the nun. "And what will you do, Eileen?" she asked of the third student.

Lowering her eyes, the girl replied, "I'm going to become a prostitute."

"A what?" shrieked the mother superior.

"A prostitute," the girl repeated, whereupon the nun fainted to the floor.

They quickly revived her, but even before she rose from the floor, the nun gasped, "Eileen, say that again."

"Mother," the girl replied firmly, "I'm going to be a prostitute!"

"Oh, saints preserve us!" said the nun crossing herself quickly. "I thought you said a Protestant!"

Every religion, every country, every sect, is fanatically mad.

Only they are the right, they are the true ones. They are on the right track and everybody else is wrong, everybody else is condemned.

So, it is natural that the thinkers all over the West felt offended. But to feel offended is to be ill with the same disease. "They mocked and laughed at it." There is no need to mock and laugh.

Sri Aurobindo's statement is absurd—but there is no need to mock and laugh at it, because when you mock and laugh at it then you are carrying the same mind within you. Then an American feels offended—because India, the guru? Then an Englishman feels offended. How can an Englishman ever think of India as the guru?—impossible. But this is the same mind! One extreme is declaring that India is the centre, the supreme-most guru of the world, and then the other is feeling offended.

No need to feel offended—just feel pity for such statements. Just feel sorry that still in this twentieth century there are people who don't belong to this century—very traditional, orthodox; not contemporaries at all. But there is no need to feel offended—because it is ego asserting and it is ego feeling offended. So just see the point; don't feel offended—otherwise you are in the same boat.

The fourth question: *You refer to God always as 'Him', or 'He'. What are some of the female qualities of God?*

Now it is a very delicate problem. . . . In fact, all His qualities are feminine—that's why I call Him 'He' and 'Him'. Otherwise He has no reason to call Himself a male. You can feel sorry for Him! And you can allow this much, can't you? He has all the qualities of a woman, but to call Him 'She' will be too much. Just to compensate I call Him 'He' and 'Him'.

God is more a mother than a father. God is more like a womb

than anything else. Out of God we are born, and back into God we dissolve. He is our birth and He is our death. He is like the ocean: He 'waves' us, we become His waves; He absorbs us — we disappear. He is compassion, love. All His qualities are feminine.

So there is no need to be worried about it, why I call Him 'He'. To call Him 'She' will be too realistic. Mm? This much romance, this much poetry, you can allow me — to call Him 'He'. That balances.

In fact, He is neither — He cannot be, because man is born out of Him, woman is born out of Him. Either He is both or He is neither — because He is all.

But I understand the question. It must be coming from some woman belonging to the Lib movement. They have already started calling Him 'She'. Nothing wrong in it! In fact, it may become by and by more prevalent. The word 'she' is beautiful; in a way, it includes 'he' — s-h-e. 'He' does not include 'she', right; but 'she' includes 'he'. It is a better word, but very confusing.

The whole humanity, in all the ages, has called Him 'He'. Maybe something of the male mind is involved in it, because it is man who has created all the scriptures. It would have been very offensive for men to think that He is a she, God is a woman. It would not have been good for the male ego. Now, there is no need to move to the other extreme. What I am pointing at again and again is that extremes are not good.

Up to now we have called Him 'He' — maybe male chauvinistic attitudes are implied in it. Now we can start calling Him 'She' — then female chauvinistic attitudes will become implied in it. In India, we have a neutral gender: neither masculine nor feminine — neutral. 'Brahma', the word for God in India, is a neuter gender word. We call Him 'It' — that seems to be the best and the most scientific. We call Him 'That' — neither He nor She. *Tatwamasi* Swetketu — That art thou, *That* art thou, Swetketu. This is more scientific.

From He it is very easy for the pendulum to swing to She, but it will be again the same fallacy. God is both or neither.

The fifth question: *How can I know that a woman has fallen in love in reality, not playing games?*

THIS IS DIFFICULT! Nobody has ever been able to know it—because, in fact, love is a game. That is its reality! So if you are waiting and watching and thinking and analysing whether this woman who is in love with you is just playing a game or is in reality in love, you will never be able to love any woman — because love is a game, the suprememost game.

There is no need to ask for it to be real — play the game! that's its reality. And if you are too much of a seeker for reality, then love is not for you. It is a *dream*! It is a fantasy — it is a fiction, it is a romance, it is a poetry. If you are too much of a seeker for reality, obsessed with reality, then love is not for you — then meditate.

And I know the questioner is not that type — the question is from Krishna Gautam. No meditation is possible, at least in this life! He has many karmas to fulfill with women. So he continuously thinks about meditation and continuously goes on moving with this woman or that. Now the women he moves with, they also come to me and they say, "Is he really in love with us?" What to do? And here comes he with a question!

But this problem comes to everybody sometime or other — because there is no way to judge. We are such strangers — we *are* strangers, and our meeting is just accidental. Just on the road suddenly we have come across each other, not knowing who we are, not knowing who the other is. Two strangers meeting on a road, feeling alone, hold each other's hands—and think they are in love. They are in *need* of the other, certainly, but how to be certain that there is love?

I was reading a beautiful joke; listen to it carefully:

A woman arrived at a small midwestern town late at night, only to find there wasn't a single hotel room available. "I'm sorry," said the desk clerk, "but the last room we had was just taken by an Italian."

"What number is it?" said the woman in desperation. "Maybe I can work something out with him."

The clerk told her the room and the woman went up and knocked on the door. The Italian let her in.

"Look, mister," she said, "I don't know you and you don't know me, but I need some place to sleep desperately. I won't be any bother, I promise, if you just let me use that little couch over there."

The Italian thought for a minute and then said, "Okay." The woman curled up on the couch and the Italian went back to bed. But the couch was very uncomfortable and after a few minutes the woman tiptoed over to the bed and tapped the Italian's arm. "Look mister," she said, "I don't know you and you don't know me, but that couch is impossible to sleep on. Could I just sleep here, at the edge of the bed?"

"Okay," said the Italian, "use the edge of the bed."

The woman lay down on the bed, but after a few minutes she felt very cold. Again she tapped the Italian.

"Look mister," she said, "I don't know you and you don't know me, but it's very cold out here. Could I just get under the cover with you."

"Okay," said the Italian, "get under the cover."

The woman snuggled under, but the closeness of a male body stirred her and she started to feel a little horny. Again she tapped the Italian.

"Look mister," she said, "I don't know you and you don't know me, but how about having a little party?"

Exasperated, the Italian bolted up in the bed. "Look lady," he hollered, "I don't know you and you don't know me. In the middle of the night, who we gonna invite to a party?"

But this is how it goes: You don't know me, I don't know you— it is just accidental. Needs are there. People feel lonely; they need somebody to fill their loneliness. They call it love. They show love because that is the only way to hook the other. The other also calls it love because that is the only way to hook you.

101

But who knows whether there is love or not? In fact, love is just a game. Yes, there *is* a possibility of a real love, but that happens only when you don't need anybody—that's the difficulty.

It is on the same lines as banks function. If you go to a bank and you need money, they will not give you any. If you don't need money, you have enough, they will come to you and they will always be ready to give you. When you don't need, they are ready to give you; when you need, they are not ready to give you.

When you don't need a person at all, when you are totally sufficient unto yourself, when you can be alone and tremendously happy and ecstatic, then love is possible. But then too you cannot be certain whether the *other's* love is real or not—you can be certain about only one thing: whether your love is real. How can you be certain about the other? But then there is no need.

This continuous anxiety—whether the other's love is real or not—simply shows one thing: that your love is not real. Otherwise, who bothers? Why be worried about it? Enjoy it while it lasts! Be together while you can be together! It is a fiction, but you need fiction.

Nietzsche used to say that man is such that he cannot live without lies, he cannot live with truth. Truth will be too much to tolerate, to bear. You need lies. Lies, in a subtle way, lubricate your system; they are lubricants. Mm? You see a woman, you say, "How beautiful! I have never come across such a beautiful person." These are just lubricating lies—you know it!

You have said the same thing to other women before, and you know you will say the same thing again to other women in the future. And the woman also says that you are the only person that has ever attracted her. These are lies. Behind these lies there is nothing but need. You want the woman to be with you to fill your inner hole; you want to stuff that inner emptiness with her presence. She also wants. You both are trying to use each other as a means.

That's why lovers, so-called lovers, are always in conflict—because nobody wants to be used, because when you use a person the person becomes a thing, you have reduced him to a commodity. And every woman feels, after making love to a man, a little sad, deceived, cheated, because the man turns over and goes to sleep—finished is finished!

Many women have told me that they cry and weep after the man, their man, has made love to them—because after love he is no longer interested. His interest was only for a particular need; then he turns over and goes to sleep. And he is not even bothered about what has happened to the woman. And men also feel cheated. They, by and by, start suspecting that the woman loves them for something else—for money, power, security. The interest may be economical—but it is not love.

But it is true. This is how it can be; only this is how it can be! The way you are, living almost asleep, moving in a stupor, somnambulistic, this is the only way it is possible. But don't be worried about it, whether the woman loves you really or not. While you are asleep you will need somebody's love—even if it is false, you will need it. Enjoy it! Don't create anxiety. And try to become more and more awake.

One day when you are really awake you will be able to love—but then you will be certain about your love only. But that's enough! Who bothers? Because right now you want to use others. When you are really blissful on your own, you don't want to use anybody. You simply want to share. You have so much, so much is overflowing, you would like somebody to share it. And you will feel thankful that somebody was ready to receive. Finished! That is the full point.

Right now, you are worried too much whether the other loves you really—because you are not certain about your own love. One thing. You are not certain about your worth. You cannot believe that somebody can really love you. You don't see anything in yourself. *You cannot love yourself*—how can somebody else love you? It seems unreal, it seems impossible.

Do you love yourself? You have not even asked the question. People *hate* themselves. People condemn themselves—they go on condemning; they go on thinking that they are rotten. How can the other love you? such a rotten person. No, nobody can love you really. The other must be befooling, cheating;

there must be some other reason. She must be after something else; he must be after something else.

I have heard:

A dirty, smelly, filthy-looking old Jewish bum, sat down on a park bench next to a sweet young girl. The girl took one look at the bum and looked away in revulsion. Pretty soon she heard a noise and turned her head to see what was happening. She watched in horror as the Jewish bum took a sandwich from a brown bag and took a big bite of it. The meat was rancid, the lettuce was brown, and the bread mouldy.

Sensing the girl's eyes on him, the Jewish bum turned towards her and said, "Pardon me, miss, would you like a bite of my sandwich? I suppose to make love would be out of the question."

This is what goes on happening. You know about yourself—love seems to be out of the question. You know your rottenness, worthlessness—love seems to be out of the question. And when some woman comes and says she adores you, you cannot trust. When you go to a woman and you say you adore her, and she hates herself, how can she believe you? It is self-hatred that is creating the anxiety.

There is no way to be certain about the other—first be certain about yourself. And a person who is certain about himself is certain about the whole world. A certainty achieved at your innermost core becomes a certainty about everything that you do and everything that happens to you. Settled, centred, grounded, in yourself, you never worry about such things. You accept.

If somebody loves you, you accept it because you love yourself. You are happy with yourself; somebody else is happy—good! It does not get in your head; it does not make you madly egoistic. You simply enjoy yourself; somebody else also finds you enjoyable—good! While it lasts, live the fiction as beautifully as possible—it will not last forever. That too creates a problem.

When a love is finished, you start thinking it was false—that's why it has come to an end. No, not necessarily—*not* necessarily. It may have had some glimmer of truth in it, but you were both unable to keep and hold that truth. You killed it. It was there—you murdered it. You were not capable of love. You *needed* love, but you were not capable of it. So you meet a woman or a man; things go very well, very smoothly, fantastically beautifully—in the beginning. The moment you have settled, things start getting sour, bitter. The more you have settled, the more conflict arises. That kills love.

As I see it, every love has in the beginning a ray of light in it, but the lovers destroy that. They jump on that ray of light with all their darknesses within—dark continents, great Africas within. They jump on it and they destroy it. When it is destroyed they think it was false. *They have killed it!* It was not false—they are false. The ray was real, true.

So don't be worried about the other; don't be worried whether the love is real or not. While it is there, enjoy it. Even if it is a dream, good to dream about it. And become more and more alert and aware so sleep is dropped.

When you are aware, a totally different kind of love will arise in your heart—which is absolutely true, which is part of eternity. But that is not a need—it is a luxury. And you have so much of it that you hanker for somebody to share it with.

Just like clouds when they are so full of rainwater: they would like to shower anywhere, upon anybody. And they don't bother whether it is a hilly track they are showering on, whether it is rocky ground they are showering on, or whether it is fertile soil thirsty for them—they don't bother. They go on raining on rocks, on fertile soil, on everybody—good and bad, thirsty, non-thirsty; needed, not needed. Because it is not a question now of whether *you* need; it is a question now that they are so full they have to share.

I love you—not because I need. I love you simply because what else can I do now? It is there and I would like to shower it on you, and I *go* on showering—unconditionally. It is *not* that you deserve it—never think that. You know and I know that you don't deserve it, but that is not the point. What else can I do?

I have heard a very old Tibetan story:

There was a great sage who would not initiate anybody, who would not make anybody a disciple. And his fame spread far and wide, and thousands of people would come every year to his hilltop and they would touch his feet and they would cry and weep and they would say, "Accept us! Initiate us into the truth you have achieved! Open the door of your temple to us also—we are thirsty."

But he would say, "You are not worthy, you don't deserve. First become worthy of me!" And his conditions were such that nobody was ever able to fulfill them: Be truthful for three years, not a single lie; for three years be celibate, not even a thought of a woman or a man—and so on and so forth. Those conditions were impossible! And those conditions are such that the more you try to fulfill them, the more you will feel it is impossible. You can be a celibate if you don't bother too much about it; but if you think too much about celibacy then you will be surrounded by many, many women in your mind.

Many people had tried and nobody was successful, so nobody was initiated. Then the man was dying. Just three days before he died, many people had gathered and he told his closest people, "Now you go, and whosoever wants to be initiated I will initiate—only three days are left!"

The people knew him well and they said, "What about your conditions?"

He said, "Forget all about those conditions! In fact, I was not ready to initiate anybody; hence, I was insisting too much on the conditions. *Now I am ready!* and I am full and I want to share. Now forget all about the conditions—whosoever wants to come, fetch them! And be in a hurry because only three days are left."

He initiated any and everybody, whosoever came. People could not believe it! They asked, "What are you doing? We are sinners!"

He said, "Forget about it. I was not a saint up to now—that was the only trouble. I had nothing to initiate you into. There was no door—I was standing outside the door myself. But now the door has opened—now I *have* to share. Now there is no question of any conditions."

When you are aware, you are not in need of love. When you are not in need of love, you become capable of love. This is the paradox. When you are in need you are not capable.

And in this sleepy state, full of needs and desires, you go on stumbling. Why bother? Let me tell you one anecdote:

> Two very proper English gentlemen were drunk in the pubs looking for women. They finally got lucky and were about to bed with their respective finds. As they were lurching their way through the crowded London streets, one turned to the other and said, "Look here, old man, do you mind switching bitches?"
>
> "No, I don't mind old thing, but can you tell a fellow why?"
>
> "Well," slobbered the first, "don't you know, between the grog and the fog and the smog, I seem to have picked up my old auntie!"

In the darkness of desire, in the madness of passion, between the grog and the fog and the smog, don't be too worried whether the other's love is real or not. Right now, as you are, the real cannot happen to you. The real happens only to real persons. Gurdjieff used to say: "Don't seek reality—become real!" because the real happens to real persons only. To unreal persons only the unreal happens.

The last question: *How is it that I got such a wonderful opportunity to be at God's feet, and not just God, but such a beautiful God?*

IT IS Sheela's question. You are also beautiful, Sheela—and everybody is beautiful. It is just a question of realization. It is not only that God is beautiful; in fact, because God is beauti-

107

ful, everything is beautiful—because everything is out of God, everything is in God.

You may not know your own beauty, you may not have looked into your own being, but let me remind you again and again: You are beautiful, Sheela—everybody is beautiful. In fact, there is no way of being otherwise: only beauty exists and only beauty can exist. Truth is beauty: beauty is truth.

CHAPTER 5

A WRESTLER named O-nami, Great Waves, was immensely strong and highly skilled in the art of wrestling. In private he defeated even his very teacher, but in public his own young pupils could throw him.

In his trouble he went to a Zen master who was stopping at a nearby temple by the sea, and asked for counsel.

"Great Waves is your name," said the master, "so stay in this temple tonight and listen to the waves of the sea. Imagine you are those waves. Forget you are a wrestler, and become those huge waves sweeping everything before them."

O-nami remained. He tried to think only of the waves, but he thought of many things. Then gradually he did think only of the waves. They rolled larger and larger as the night wore on. They swept away the flowers in the vases before the Buddha; they swept away the vases. Even the bronze Buddha was swept away. By dawn the temple was only surging water, and O-nami sat there with a faint smile on his face.

That day he entered the public wrestling and won every bout, and from that day no one in Japan could ever throw him.

LISTEN TO THE WAVES

fifteenth august 1976

SELF-CONSCIOUSNESS IS A DISEASE. Consciousness is health, self-consciousness is disease—something has gone wrong. Some tie has arisen, some complex. The river of consciousness is not flowing naturally—something foreign has entered into the river of consciousness, something alien; something that cannot be absorbed by the river; something that cannot become part of the river; something that resists becoming part of the river.

Self-consciousness is morbidity. Self-consciousness is a frozen state, blocked. It is like a dirty pool—going nowhere; just drying, evaporating and dying. Of course, it stinks.

So the first thing to be understood is the difference between self-consciousness and consciousness.

Consciousness has no idea of 'I', of ego. It has no idea of one's separation from existence. It does not know any barrier, it knows no boundaries. It is one with existence; it is in a deep

at-onement. There is no conflict between the individual and the Whole. One is simply flowing into the Whole, and the Whole is flowing into one. It is like breathing: you breathe in, you breathe out—when you breathe in the Whole enters you, when you breathe out you enter the Whole. It is a constant flow, a constant sharing. The Whole goes on giving to you, and you go on giving to the Whole. The balance is never lost.

But in a self-conscious man something has gone wrong. He takes in but he never gives out. He goes on accumulating and he has become incapable of sharing. He goes on making boundaries around himself so nobody can trespass. He goes on putting boards around his being: No Trespassing Allowed. By and by, he becomes a grave, a dead being—because life is in sharing.

A self is a dead thing, alive only for the name's sake. Consciousness is infinite life, life abundant. It knows no boundaries. But ordinarily everybody is self-conscious.

To be self-conscious is to be unconscious. This paradox has to be understood: to be self-conscious is to be unconscious; and to be unself-conscious, or to be self-unconscious, is to become conscious. And when there is no self, when this small, tiny self disappears, you attain to the real Self with a capital 'S'—call it the supreme Self, the Self of all.

So it is both: no-self in the sense that it is not only yours, and the ultimate Self also because it is the self of all. You lose your tiny centre and you attain to the centre of existence itself. Suddenly you become infinite; suddenly you are no longer bound, you have no cage around your being. And infinite power starts flowing through you. You become a vehicle—clear, with no obstructions. You become a flute and Krishna can sing through you. You become just a passage—empty, nothing of your own. This is what I call surrender.

Self-consciousness is a non-surrendering attitude—it is the attitude of conflict, fight, struggle. If you are fighting with existence you will be self-conscious and, of course, you will be defeated again and again and again. Each step is going to be a step in more and more defeat—your frustration is certain. You are doomed from the very beginning because you cannot hold this self *against* the universe. It is impossible. You cannot exist separately. You cannot be a monk.

This word 'monk' is good. You must be aware of similar words like 'monopoly'—that comes from the same root; or 'monastery'—that comes from the same root; or 'monologue'—that comes from the same root. A monk is one who is trying to be himself, who is trying to define his boundaries, and who is trying to exist separate from this total existence. His whole effort is egoistic—it is bound to fail. No monk can ever succeed.

You can succeed only with God, never against Him. You can succeed only with the Whole, never against It. So if you *are* frustrated, in deep misery, remember: you are creating that misery. And you are creating it by a subtle trick: you are fighting against the Whole.

It happened—it must have been a rainy season like this—and the village river was flooded. And people came running to Mulla Nasrudin and said, "Your wife has fallen in the flooded river. Run fast! Save her!"

Nasrudin ran. He jumped into the river and started swimming upstream. The people who had gathered to see, they shouted, "What are you doing, Nasrudin? Your wife cannot go upstream—the stream has taken her downwards."

Nasrudin said, "What are you talking about? I know my wife: *she can only go upstream!*"

The ego is always an effort to go upstream. People don't like to do easy things. Before they want to do them, they want to make them hard, difficult. People enjoy doing hard things. Why? Because when you face a hard thing, your ego becomes subtle, sharp; there is a challenge.

When the first group reached to the top of Everest, somebody asked Edmund Hillary, "Why did you take such a risk? It was dangerous—many others have died before you and have not been able to reach." And the person who was asking was unable to understand why people go on trying to reach Everest and losing their lives. What is the point of it? What is *there* to achieve?

Edmund Hillary is reported to have said, "We cannot rest as

115

long as this Everest remains unconquered. We *have* to conquer it!" There is nothing to get in it, but the very presence of Everest unconquered is a challenge. To whom is it a challenge?—to the ego.

You watch your own life: many things you are doing only because of the ego. You want to make a big house. You may be perfectly comfortable in your house as it is, but you want to make a big palace. That big palace is not for *you;* that big palace is for the ego. You may be perfectly comfortable as you are, but you go on accumulating money. That money is not for you; that money is for the ego. How can you rest unless you have become the richest man in the world?—but what are you going to do by becoming the richest man in the world? You will become more and more miserable—because misery comes out of conflict. Misery is an indication that you are in conflict. So don't throw your responsibility on something else.

People are very rationalizing: if they are miserable they will say, "What can we do?—the past lives' karmas are making us miserable." All rubbish! Past life karmas must have made you miserable, but in past lives! Why should they wait up to now? There is no point in waiting. Your present karmas are making you miserable. Throwing it on past lives makes it easy—what can you do? You have to be the way you are. Now nothing can be done; the past cannot be undone—you cannot erase it just by waving your hand. There is no magic trick that can help you to erase your past. It has happened and it has happened forever; now it is going to remain absolute; there is no possibility of changing it. That relieves you of the burden, and you think: "So okay, I have to be miserable because of the past karmas."

You can throw the responsibility on the Devil as Christians go on doing. Hindus go on throwing the responsibility on past karmas; Christians go on throwing the responsibility on the Devil—he must be creating traps for you. It is not *you*—it is the Devil who goes on trapping you into miseries, and who goes on pulling you down towards hell. Who is bothered with you? Why should this Devil be bothered with you?

Then there are Marxists, Communists, Socialists—they say it

116

is the social structure, the economic system, that makes people miserable. Then there are Freudians, psychoanalysts; they say it is the child and mother relationship. But it is always something else—it is never you. It is never *you* in the present.

And I would like to tell you: It is you. If you are miserable, you and only you are responsible. Neither the past nor the social structure nor the economic system—nothing is going to help.

If you remain you, in any sort of a society, you will remain miserable; in any economic system you will remain miserable; in any world you will remain miserable—if you remain you.

And the first, basic change happens when you start dropping this conflict with existence. That is the only meaning of all the great religions when they emphasize: Drop the ego! They are saying: Drop the conflict. I would like you to remember it more, because 'drop the ego' seems too metaphysical. 'Ego'?—where is the ego? what is the ego? The word seems to be known, you seem to be well acquainted with it, but it seems to be very vague, cannot be grasped. I would like to make it more practical: drop the conflict—because ego is a by-product of your conflicting attitude.

People talk of conquering nature, people talk of conquering this and that—how can you conquer nature? You are part of it. How can the part conquer the Whole? See the foolishness of it, the stupidity. You can be with the Whole in harmony, or you can be in conflict with the Whole in disharmony. Disharmony results in misery; harmony results in bliss.

Harmony naturally results in a deep silence, joy, delight. Conflict results in anxiety, anguish, stress, tension.

THE EGO IS NOTHING but all the tensions that you have created around yourself. And in the first place there is no need to create it—but why does man go on creating it? There must be some reason. Why does everybody go on creating the self? The real Self is unknown—that's why. And it is very difficult to live without a self, so we create a pseudo-self, a substitute self. The real Self is unknown.

In fact, the real Self never becomes absolutely known; it remains mysterious, it remains ineffable, indefinable. The real Self is so vast that you cannot define it, and the real Self is so mysterious that you cannot penetrate it to the very core. The real Self is the self of the Whole. It is not possible for human intellect to penetrate, to ponder, to contemplate it.

I have heard, there is a famous story of a wise man who was called by Alexander the Great. And Alexander asked him, "I have heard that you have come to know what God is, so please tell me. I have been in search, and people say you have attained, so enlighten me about God, what God is."

It is said the wise man said, "You give me at least twenty-four hours to think over it."

Twenty-four hours passed, and Alexander was waiting very eagerly. The wise man came and he said, "Seven days, will be needed."

And then seven days passed, and Alexander was very impatient. The wise man came and he said, "One year will be needed."

Alexander said, "What do you mean, one year will be needed? You know or you don't? If you know, you know—tell me. Why waste time?"

The wise man laughed and he said, "The more I ponder, the more it becomes unknowable. The more I know, the more difficult it becomes to say that I know. Twenty-four hours I tried and tried, and it started slipping from my hands. It is very elusive—it is like mercury. Then I asked for seven days—that didn't help. Now, at least one year—and I am not certain that I will be able to bring a definition."

The wise man did well. He must have been really wise, because there is no way to define the *real* Self. But man cannot live without a self—then one feels so empty! Then one feels like a wheel without a hub; then one feels like a circumference without a centre. No, it is hard to live without a self.

To know the real Self is arduous; one has to travel long to arrive home. One has to knock on many doors before one comes to the right door. The easy trick is: you can create a false self. To grow real roses is difficult; you can purchase plastic roses. They will not deceive you, but they will deceive the neighbours. Mm?—

that is the point of the self, the ego. It cannot deceive you; you know well that you yourself don't know who you are—but at least it can deceive the neighbours. In the outside world at least you have a certain label, who you are.

Have you ever thought about it? If somebody asks, "Who are you?" what do you answer? You say your name. Name is not yours, because you came in the world without a name; you came nameless. It is not your property—it has been given to you. And any name—A-B-C-D—would have been useful; it is arbitrary. It is not essential in any way.

If you are called 'Ram', good; if you are called 'Hari', good—it makes no difference. Any name would have been as applicable to you as any other. It is just a label. A name is needed to call you by, but it has nothing to do with your being. Or you say, "I am a doctor"; or you say, "I am an engineer"— or a businessman, or a painter, or this and that—but nothing says anything about you.

When you say, "I am a doctor," you say something about your profession, not about you; you say how you earn your living. You *don't* say anything about life; you say something about your living. You may be earning your living as an engineer, or as a doctor, or as a businessman—it is irrelevant. It does not say anything about you.

Or you say your father's name, your mother's name, your family tree—that too is irrelevant because that doesn't define you. Your being born in a particular family is accidental; you could as well have been born in another family, and you would not even have noticed the difference.

These are just utilitarian tricks—and man becomes a self. This self is a pseudo-self, a created, manufactured self, home-made. And your own real Self remains deep down hidden in mist and mystery.

I was reading:

A Frenchman was crossing the desert with an Arab guide. Day after day, the Arab never failed to kneel on the burning sand and call upon his God. At last, one evening the unbeliever said to the Arab, "How do you know there is a God?"

The guide fixed his eye upon the scoffer for a moment and then replied: "How do I know there is a God? How did I know that a camel and not a man passed last night? Was is not by the print of his hoof in the sand?" And pointing to the sun whose last rays were fading over the horizon, he added, "That footprint is not of man."

Your Self cannot be created by you; it cannot be man-made. Your Self you have brought with you; it *is* you. How can you create it? To create it you will have to be there in the first place. That is the meaning when Christians, Mohammedans, Hindus, say that man is a creature. That means that man has not created himself, that's all. The creator is somewhere hidden in the unknown. We have come out of some mysterious life-source. Your Self is not yours!

This false self is not yours because you have created it; and your real Self is not yours because it is still in God, you are still rooted in God.

THIS FALSE SELF that we go on carrying in our lives like a flag is always in danger of being damaged; it is very fragile, it is very weak—it has to be: it is man-made. How can man make something deathless? He himself has to pass through many deaths, so whatsoever he produces is always mortal.

Hence the fear, continuous fear that: "I may be lost. My self may be destroyed." A continuous fear goes on trembling into your being; you can never be certain about this false self of yours—you know it is false. You may avoid the fact, but you know it is false. It is gathered together, manufactured, it is mechanical; it is not organic.

Have you observed the difference between an organic unity and a mechanical unity? You make a car engine; you can purchase parts from the market and you can fix those parts, and the engine starts functioning like a unity. Or you can purchase parts of a radio from the market and you can fix them, and the radio starts functioning like a unity. Somehow it comes to have a self. No part in itself can function as a radio; all parts together start functioning like a radio—but still the unity is mechanical, forced from the outside. Then you throw seeds into the ground, and those seeds die into the soil and a plant arises. This unity is organic; it is not forced from outside—it was in the seed itself. The seed goes on spreading, goes on gathering a thousand and one things from the earth, from the air, from the sun, from the sky—but the unity is coming from within. The centre comes first and then the circumference. In a mechanical unity the circumference comes first and then the centre.

Man is an organic unity. You were a seed one day, like any tree; in the soil of your mother's womb you started gathering your circumference. Centre came first, centre preceded circumference. And now you have forgotten the centre completely. You live on the circumference and you think this is your whole life. This circumference, and continuously living on it, creates a sort of self, a pseudo-self, which gives you a feeling that yes, you are somebody. But it is always trembling because it has no organic unity in it.

Hence, the fear of death. If you know your real Self you will never be afraid of death—there is no question, because the organic unity never dies. Organic unity is immortal. Only mechanical unities are put together and die. That which is put together, one day will fall apart. Mechanical unity has a beginning and an end. The organic unity has no beginning and no end—it is an eternal process.

Do you know your centre? If you don't know it then you will be continuously afraid. Hence, self-consciousness is always afraid, always trembling. And you always need support from others— somebody to appreciate you; somebody to clap; somebody to say how beautiful you are or how intelligent. You need somebody to say these things to you, like suggestions, so that you can believe that yes, you are intelligent, you are beautiful, you are strong. But see the point: you depend on others.

A foolish man comes to you and says you are very intelligent. And in fact, you can look intelligent only to a foolish man. If he is more intelligent than you, of course, you will not look intelligent to him. So a foolish man comes and certifies your intelligence, and

121

you are very happy. You can look beautiful only to an ugly man. If he is more beautiful than you, you will look ugly—because it is all relative. And you are certified by ugly people that you are beautiful, and you are tremendously happy.

What type of intelligence is this which has to be certified by foolish people? What type of beauty is this which has to be certified by ugly people? It is completely false. It is idiotic. But we go on searching. We go on searching in the outside world to find some support for our ego, somebody to give a little support, to become a prop. Otherwise there is always the danger that our ego will collapse. So we have to support it from this side and from that and continuous worry arises.

That's why you are more graceful when you are alone—because you are not worried. Nobody is there to see you. You are more innocent when you are alone—in your bathroom you are more innocent, you are more like a child. Again you stand before the mirror and make faces, and you enjoy it. But if you become aware that your small child is looking through the keyhole, immediately you are totally different. Now the ego is at stake. That's why people are so much afraid of others. Alone, there is no anxiety.

There is a famous Zen story:

A Zen master was making a painting, and he had his chief disciple sit by his side to tell him when the painting was perfect. The disciple was worried and the master was also worried, because the disciple had never seen the master do anything imperfect. But that day things started going wrong. The master tried, and the more he tried, the more it was a mess.

In Japan or in China, the whole art of calligraphy is done on rice-paper, on a certain paper, a very sensitive paper, very fragile. If you hesitate a little, for centuries it can be known where the calligrapher hesitated—because more ink spreads into the rice-paper and makes it a mess. It is very difficult to deceive on rice-paper. You have to go *on* flowing; you are not to hesitate. Even for a single moment, split moment, if you hesitate—what to do?— missed, already missed. And one who has a keen eye will immediately say, "It is not a Zen painting at all"—because a Zen painting has to be a spontaneous painting, flowing.

The master tried and tried and the more he tried—he started perspiring. And the disciple was sitting there and shaking his head again and again negatively: 'No, this is not perfect.' And more and more mistakes were being made by the master.

Then the ink was running out so the master said, "You go out and prepare more ink." While the disciple was outside preparing the ink, the master did his masterpiece. When he came in he said, "Master, but this is perfect! What happened?"

The master laughed; he said, "I became aware of one thing: your presence. The very idea that somebody is there to appreciate or to condemn, to say no or yes, disturbed my inner tranquillity. Now I will never be disturbed. I have come to know that I was *trying* to make it perfect and that was the only reason for its not being perfect."

Try to make something perfect and it will remain imperfect. Do it naturally and it is always perfect. Nature is perfect; effort is imperfect. So whenever you are doing something too much, you are destroying.

That's why it happens: everybody talks so beautifully; everybody is a talker; people talk their whole life—but just put them on a platform and tell them to talk to a crowd, and suddenly they become dumb; suddenly they forget everything, suddenly they cannot utter a single word. Or, even if they do utter, it is not graceful, it is not natural, it is not flowing. What has happened? And you have known this man talking so beautifully to his friends, to his wife, to his children. These are also people, the same people—why are you afraid? You have become self-conscious. Now the ego is at stake: you are trying to perform something.

Listen carefully: whenever you try to perform something, you are searching food for the ego. Whenever you are natural and let things happen, they are perfect, and then there is no problem. When you are natural and let things happen, God is at the back with you. When you are afraid, trembling, trying to

123

prove something, you have lost God. In your fear, you have forgotten Him. You are looking more at the people and you have forgotten your source. Self-consciousness becomes a weakness. A person who is unself-conscious is strong, but his strength has nothing to do with himself — it comes from the beyond.

WHEN YOU ARE SELF-CONSCIOUS, you are in trouble. When you are self-conscious, you are really showing symptoms that you don't know who you are. Your very self-consciousness indicates that you have not come home yet.

It happened:

As a pretty girl passed by, Mulla Nasrudin turned to look. His wife said with a pout, "Every time you see a pretty girl you forget you are married."

"That's where you are wrong," said the Mulla. "Nothing makes me more aware of the fact!"

Whenever you are self-conscious you are simply showing that you are not conscious of the Self at all. You don't know who you are. If you had known, then there would have been no problem — then you are not seeking opinions; then you are not worried what others say about you. It is irrelevant! In fact, nobody ever says anything about you — whenever people say something about you, they are saying it about themselves.

One day it happened: I was in Jaipur and a man came in the morning to see me, and he said, "You are divine."

I said, "You are right!"

He was sitting there and another man came and he was very much against me, and then he said, "You are almost devilish."

I said, "You are right!"

The first man became a little worried. He said, "What do you mean? You told me also, 'You are right,' and you say to this man also, 'You are right' — we can't be both right."

I told him, "Not only two — millions of people can be right about me, because whatsoever they say about me they say about themselves. How can they know me? It is impossible — they have

124

not even known themselves yet. Whatsoever they say is their interpretation."

So the man said, "Then who are you? If this is my interpretation that you are divine, and this is his interpretation that you are evil, then who are you?"

I said, "I am just myself. And I have no interpretation about myself, and there is no need. I am simply delighted in being myself! — whatsoever that means. I am happy in being myself."

Nobody can say anything about you. Whatsoever people say is about themselves. But you become very shaky, because you are still clinging to a false centre. That false centre depends on others, so you are always looking to what people are saying about you. And you are always following other people, you are always trying to satisfy them. You are always trying to be respectable. You are always trying to decorate your ego. This is suicidal.

Rather than being disturbed by what others say, you should start looking inside yourself. To know the real Self is not so cheap. But people are always hankering for cheap things.

It happened:

When the pain in Mulla Nasrudin's back became unbearable, he reluctantly went to a specialist to diagnose his problem.

"Well," said the doctor, "your problem can be cured by an operation, two weeks in the hospital and six months totally horizontal."

"Doctor, I can't afford the cost of all that!" shouted Nasrudin.

"Well then, for twenty-five rupees I can retouch the X-ray," suggested the doctor.

This is cheap! — retouch the X-ray — but that is not going to make you healthy. That's what we are doing: continuously retouching the X-ray, and thinking that somehow the miracle will happen. When you are decorating your ego you are retouching the X-ray. That is not going to help in any way; it is not going to help you become healthy. But it is cheaper: no operation is needed; at no cost. But what is the point? Your misery remains.

You become respectable and your misery remains. You become

highly praised by the society—your misery remains. You are decorated by medals, gold medals—Padma Bhushan, Victoria Cross—but your misery remains. These gold medals are not going to destroy your misery: they are like retouching the X-ray. All decoration on the ego, for the ego, is nothing but deceiving yourself.

And continuously you go on becoming weaker and weaker and weaker—because the ego goes on becoming weaker every day. Your body will become weaker, your mind will become weaker, and by and by the ego that you have created out of the body and mind combination will become weaker. Fear will become greater and greater; you will be continuously sitting on a volcano that can any day explode. It will not allow you rest. It will not allow you relaxation. It will not allow you any moments of peace.

Once you understand it then the whole energy is put into another direction. One has to know oneself. One has not to be worried about what others say about you.

Madhuri has sent me a very beautiful joke:

So there was this guy, and nobody ever noticed him. He did not have any friends. He was at a salesman's convention in Miami, see, and he saw that everybody else was happy and laughing and paying attention to each other, but not to him.

One evening he was sitting really bummed out when he got to talking with another salesman. He told him his problem. "Oh, I know how to fix that up," cried the other. "You just get a camel and ride it around in the streets, and in no time everybody will notice you and you will have all the friends you want."

So, whaddya know? There was a circus going out of business and they wanted to sell a camel. The man bought it and rode up and down the streets on it, and, sure enough, everybody paid attention to him and noticed him. He felt on top of the world.

But then a week later, the camel disappeared. The man was heartbroken and immediately phoned the local newspaper to place an ad for his lost camel.

"Is it a boy or a girl camel?" enquired the guy on the phone.

"A boy or a girl? How should I know?" raged the man. Then

he thought, "Oh, yeah, of course, it was a boy, that's right."

"How do you know?" enquired the adman.

"Because," said the man, "every time I rode up and down the streets people yelled, 'Look at that schmuck on the camel!'"

'Schmuck' is a Yiddish word, a very beautiful word. It has two meanings, and very relevant meanings. One meaning is 'the idiot'; another meaning, in the beginning looks very far-fetched, means the male genital organ. But in a way both meanings are very deeply related. Idiots live only as sexual beings—they don't know any other life. So 'schmuck' is beautiful. If a person has known only sex as life, he is stupid, he is an idiot.

Now, people were saying, "Look at that idiot on the camel!" but the man thinks they were talking about the male genital organ of the camel, not about him.

The ego is very deceptive. It goes on hearing what it wants to hear. It goes on interpreting what it wants to interpret. It never sees the fact. It never allows the fact to reveal itself to you. People who live in the ego live behind curtains. And those curtains are not inactive—they are active curtains. Whatsoever passes through the curtain, the curtain changes it.

People go on living in a mental world of their own creation. Ego is the centre of their world, of the false world—call it 'illusion', 'maya'—and around the ego they go on creating a world. . .which is nobody else's world. Only they live in that world.

When you drop the ego, you drop a whole world that you have created around it. For the first time you are able to see things *as they are*—not as you would like them to be. And when you are capable of knowing the facts of life, you become capable of knowing the truth.

The facticity of life is the first step towards truth. And ego is the most falsifying agent.

Now this story

*A wrestler named O-nami, Great Waves, was
immensely strong and highly skilled in the art
of wrestling. In private he defeated even his
very teacher, but in public his own young pupils
could throw him.*

*In his trouble he went to a Zen master who
was stopping at a nearby temple by the sea, and
asked for counsel.*

*"Great Waves is your name," said the master,
"so stay in this temple tonight and listen to the
waves of the sea. Imagine you are those waves;
forget you are a wrestler and become those huge
waves sweeping everything before them."*

*O-nami remained. He tried to think only of
the waves, but he thought of many things. Then
gradually he did think only of the waves. They
rolled larger and larger as the night wore on.
They swept away the flowers in the vases before
the Buddha; they swept away the vases. Even the
bronze Buddha was swept away. By dawn the
temple was only surging water, and O-nami sat
there with a faint smile on his face.*

*That day he entered the public wrestling and
won every bout, and from that day no one in
Japan could ever throw him.*

This is a story of self-consciousness and how to lose it, and how
to drop it, and how to get rid of it. We will try to enter into it
step by step.

*A wrestler named O-nami, Great Waves, was
immensely strong. . .*

Everybody is immensely strong. You don't know your strength;
that is another matter. Everybody is immensely strong — has to be,
because everybody is rooted in God, everybody is rooted in this

universe. However small you may look, you are not small — you cannot be by the very nature of things.

Now physicists say that in a small atom so much energy is confined — Hiroshima and Nagasaki were destroyed by atomic energy. And the atom is so small — nobody has yet seen it! It is just an inference, a deduction. Nobody has seen the atom. With all the sophisticated instruments science has today, nobody has seen the atom — so small and such vast energy.

If the atom can have so much energy, what to say about man? What to say about this small flame of consciousness in man? If some day this small flame bursts forth, it is bound to become an infinite source of energy and light. That's how it has happened to a Buddha, or to a Jesus.

Everybody is immensely strong because everybody is immensely divine. Everybody is strong because everybody is rooted in God, in the very origin of existence. Remember it.

The human mind tends to forget it. When you forget it, you become weak. When you become weak, you start trying some artificial ways to become strong. That's what millions of people are doing.

Searching for money, what are you really searching? You are searching power, you are searching strength. Searching for prestige, political authority, what are you searching? You are searching power, strength — and strength is all the time available just by the corner. You are searching in wrong places.

A wrestler named O-nami, Great Waves. . .

We are all great waves of the ocean. We may have forgotten it, but the ocean has not forgotten us. We may have so much forgotten it that we have no idea of what an ocean is — still we are in the ocean. Even if a wave forgets and becomes oblivious of the ocean, it is still in the ocean — because the wave cannot exist without the ocean. The ocean can exist without the wave — maybe it can exist without the wave — but the wave cannot exist without the ocean. The wave is nothing but waving of the ocean; it is a process, it is not an entity. It is just the ocean delighting in its being.

129

God in His delight peoples the earth; God in His delight peoples existence. It is ocean searching ocean—just playful. It has tremendous energy—what to do with it?

> *A wrestler named O-nami, Great Waves, was immensely strong...*

But this strength is possible only when the wave knows that it is a wave of a great, infinite ocean. If the wave forgets this, then the wave is very weak. And our 'forgetory' is tremendous; our memory is very small, very tiny—forgetory tremendous. We go on forgetting. And that which is very obvious, we forget very easily. That which is very close, we forget very easily. That which is always available we forget very easily.

Do you remember your breathing? You remember only when there is some trouble: you have a cold, breathing trouble or something; otherwise, who remembers breathing? That's why people remember God only when they are in trouble. Otherwise, who remembers? And God is closer than your breathing, closer than you are to yourself; He is more close than yourself. One tends to forget.

Have you watched it? If you don't have something, you remember. When you have it, you forget—you take it for granted. Because God cannot be lost, it is very difficult to remember. Only very rare people become capable of remembering God. To remember that which we have *never* been away from is very difficult.

A fish in the ocean forgets the ocean. Throw the fish on the shore, in the sands, hot sands, and then the fish knows, then the fish remembers. But there is no way to throw you out of God; there is no shore to Him—God is a shoreless ocean. And you are not like a fish, you are like a wave. You are exactly like God; your nature and God's nature are the same.

That's the symbolic meaning of choosing this name for this story.

> *He was highly skilled in the art of wrestling. In private he defeated even his own teacher...*

but in private, because in private he must have been capable of forgetting his self.

Remember this sutra: When you remember your self, you forget God; when you forget your self, you remember God — and you cannot remember both together. When the wave thinks of herself as a wave she forgets that she is an ocean. When the wave knows herself as the ocean, how can she remember herself now as a wave? Only one is possible. Either the wave can think about herself as a wave, or as the ocean. It is a gestalt. You cannot remember both together — that is impossible.

> *In private he defeated even his own master, but*
> *in public his own young pupils could throw him.*

In privacy he must have been completely forgetful of his own self, the ego. Then he was tremendously powerful. In public he must have been becoming too self-conscious. Then he was weak. Self-consciousness is weakness. Self-forgetfulness is strength.

> *In his trouble he went to a Zen master who was*
> *stopping at a nearby temple by the sea, and asked*
> *for counsel.*
> *"Great Waves is your name," said the master,*
> *"so stay in this temple tonight and listen to the*
> *waves of the sea."*

A MASTER IS ONE who can create devices for *everybody*. A master is one who has no fixed device. He looks at the man, this man O-nami, Great Waves — just his name and he creates a device around his name.

That's what I go on doing: I give you a name and create a device around it. I give you a name so that you can remember your device, you can remember your technique, so that it becomes a constant mindfulness for you, a reminder, an arrow pointing out your path continuously.

Just coming to know that his name is O-nami, Great Waves, the master said:

131

"Great Waves is your name, so stay in this temple tonight and listen to the waves of the ocean."

Listening is one of the basic secrets of entering into the temple of God. Listening means passivity. Listening means forgetting yourself completely—only then can you listen. When you listen attentively to somebody, you forget yourself. If you cannot forget yourself, you never listen. If you are too self-conscious about yourself, you simply pretend that you are listening—you don't listen. You may nod your head; you may sometimes say yes and no—but you are not listening.

When you listen, you become just a passage, a passivity, a receptivity, a womb: you become feminine. And to arrive one has to become feminine. You cannot reach God as aggressive invaders, conquerors. You can reach God only. . .or it will be better: God can reach you only when you are receptive, a feminine receptivity. When you become *yin,* a receptivity, the door is open. And you wait.

Listening is the art for becoming passive. Buddha has emphasized listening so much, Mahavir has emphasized listening so much, Krishnamurti goes on emphasizing right listening so much. The ears are symbolic. Have you watched?

Your ears are nothing but passages, just holes—nothing else. Your ears are more feminine than your eyes; your eyes are more male. Your ears are a *yin* part; your eyes are a *yang* part. When you look at somebody, you are aggressive. When you listen to somebody, you are receptive.

That's why looking at somebody for too long a time becomes vulgar, impolite, unmannerly. There is a certain limit; psychologists say three seconds. If you look at a person for three seconds it's okay; it can be tolerated. More than that, then you are not looking—you are staring; you are offending the person; you are trespassing.

But listening to a person has no limit, because ears cannot trespass. They simply remain wherever they are. Eyes need rest. Have you seen in the night—eyes need rest, ears need no rest.

132

They are open twenty-four hours—year in, year out. Eyes cannot remain open even for minutes—continuous blinking, continuously tiring. Aggression tires, because aggression takes your energy out; so the eyes have to blink continuously to rest. It is a continuous rest. Ears are rested always.

That's why music has been used by many religions as an approach towards prayer—because music will make your ears more vibrant, more sensitive. One has to become more of the ears and less of the eyes.

> *"Great Waves is your name, so stay in this*
> *temple tonight and listen to the waves of the sea."*

"You just become ears," said the master. "You just listen. There is nothing else to do—just go on listening with no idea why, with no idea of what is happening. Just go on listening with no interpretation, with no activity on your part." And then:

> *"Imagine you are those waves."*

"First listen, get in tune with the waves, and when you feel that now you are completely silent and receptive, then imagine that you are those waves. That is the second step. First: don't be aggressive; become receptive. And when you have become receptive, then just melt into those waves, start imagining that you are those waves."

The master is giving him a device so that he can forget his self, the ego. First step is receptivity, because in receptivity ego cannot exist—it can exist only in conflict. And when you are receptive, suddenly your faculty of imagination becomes tremendously powerful.

Receptive people, sensitive people, are imaginative people. Those who can see the greenery of the trees, just without any aggression on their part, not even a subtle aggression on their part, who can just drink the greenery of the trees, who can simply absorb it as if they are sponges—they become very creative, they become very imaginative. These are the poets, the painters, the dancers, the musicians—they absorb the universe in deep recep-

133

tivity, and then they pour whatsoever they have absorbed into their imagination.

Imagination is the one faculty you have which comes closest to God. God must have a great imagination — mm? — just look at His world! Just to think! — such an imaginative world, with so many flowers and so many butterflies and so many trees and so many rivers, and so many people. Just think about His imagination! With so many stars, and so many worlds — worlds beyond worlds, non-ending. . . . He must be a great dreamer.

In the East, Hindus say the world is God's dream, His imagination. The world is His magic, His imagination. He is dreaming it. We are part of His dream.

When the master said to O-nami, "Then you imagine yourself as those waves," he was saying, "Then you become creative. First you become receptive and then you become creative. And once you have dropped your ego, you become so flexible that whatsoever you imagine will happen. Then your imagination will become your reality."

> *"Forget you are a wrestler and become those*
> *huge waves sweeping everything before them."*
> *O-nami remained. He tried to think only of*
> *the waves . . .*

Of course, it was difficult in the beginning: *He thought of many things.* It is natural — but he remained. He must have been very patient. *Then gradually he did think only of the waves.* Then a moment came. . . . If you pursue, if you persist, one moment is bound to come when the thing that you have been desiring for many lives happens — but patience is needed.

> *Then gradually he did think only of the waves.*
> *They rolled larger and larger as the night wore*
> *on.*

Now these are not the real waves of the ocean that are rolling larger and larger. Now there is no distinction between his waves of imagination and the real waves. That distinction is lost. Now he does not know what is what; what is dream and what is real

134

he does not know. He has become a small child again. Only children have that capacity.

In the morning you can find a child weeping for a toy he had seen in the dream, and he wants it back, and he says, "Where is my toy?" And you go on insisting that it was just a dream, but he says, "Still, where is it now?" He makes no distinction between the dream and the waking. He knows no distinctions. He knows reality as one.

When you become very receptive, you become childlike.

Now these waves:

> *They rolled larger and larger as the night wore on. They swept away the flowers in the vases before the Buddha; they swept away the vases.* Not only that — *even the bronze Buddha was swept away.*

This is beautiful! It is very difficult for a Buddhist to imagine that the Buddha is being swept away. If he had been too much attached to his religion, that would have been the point where he would have been completely cut off from his imagination. He would have said, "Enough is enough! Buddha being swept away! — what am I doing? No, I am no more a wave." He would have stopped at the feet of the Buddha, he would have touched the feet of the Buddha, but not more than that.

But remember: one day, even those feet that have helped you tremendously on the path, they have to go; Buddhas also have to be swept away. Because the door can become a hindrance if you cling to it.

> *Larger and larger — they swept away the flowers in the vases before the Buddha; they swept away the vases. Even the bronze Buddha was swept away. By dawn the temple was only surging water. . .*

Not that it really happened: it happened to O-nami. Remember it: if you had been in that temple that time, you would not have seen the surging water in the temple — it was happening only to

135

O-nami. It was happening in a totally different dimension of his being. It is the dimension of poetry, imagination, dream; the intuitive, the feminine, the childlike; innocence.

He had opened the doors of his imaginative faculty. By listening to the waves, by becoming receptive, he became imaginative. His imagination flowered as a thousand-and-one-petalled lotus.

> *By dawn the temple was only surging water, and*
> *O-nami sat there with a faint smile on his face.*

HE BECAME A BUDDHA! The same faint smile as one day came to Buddha under the Bodhi Tree must have come to O-nami, Suddenly he was no more there! — and that was the smile, the smile of coming back home. The smile that one has arrived. The smile that now there is no longer anywhere to go. The smile that one has reached the source. The smile that one has died and is resurrected.

> *O-nami sat there with a faint smile on his face.*
> *That day he entered the public wrestling and*
> *won every bout, and from that day no one in*
> *Japan could ever throw him.*

Because now it is not *his* energy. He is no more O-nami — he is no more the waves, he is the ocean now. How can you defeat the ocean? You can only defeat the waves.

Once you have dropped the ego you have dropped all defeat, all failure, all frustration. Carry the ego and you are doomed to failure. Carry the ego and you will remain weak. Drop the ego and infinite strength starts flowing through you. By dropping the ego you become a river, you start flowing, you start melting, you start streaming — you become alive.

All life is of the Whole. If you are trying to live on your own, you are simply being stupid. It is as if a leaf on a tree is trying to live on its own — not only that, but fighting the tree; fighting other leaves, fighting the roots, thinking that those are all inimical to him. We are just leaves on a tree, a great tree — call it 'God', or 'the Whole', or you name it, but we are small leaves on an infinite tree of life. There is no need to fight. The only way to come home is to surrender.

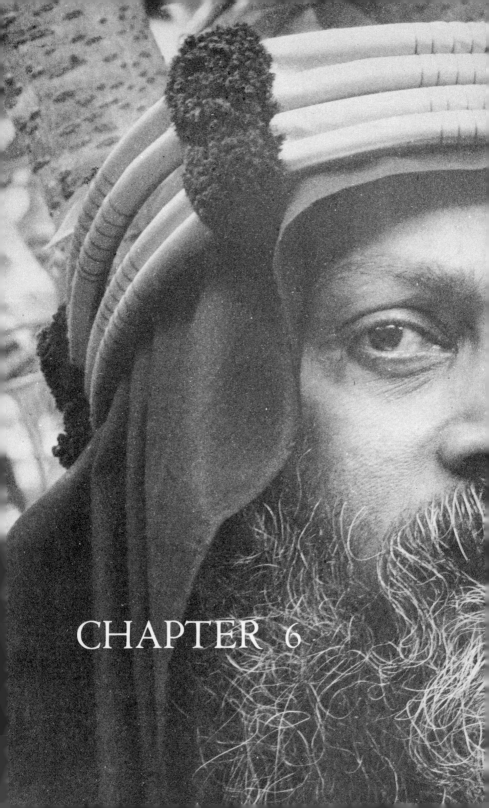

CHAPTER 6

Have I missed you?

"This would be a nice time to die!"

Compassion is so foreign and new to me.

LIFE UNDEFINED IS WHAT GOD IS

sixteenth august 1976

The first question: *Leaving soon for the West*
I look back on the five months with you and
think:
I have been with Bhagwan and I have not
been with Bhagwan.
I have seen him and yet something
remains unseen.
I have heard him yet still I am deaf
to his teaching.
I leave with no feeling of security,
no sense of certainty,
nothing to rely on.
Have I missed you?

T HE QUESTION is from Swami Anand Subhuti. No—you have
not missed me at all. People who leave me with certainty,
security, they are the ones who have missed me.

I am not here to give you a dogma. A dogma makes one certain. I am not here to give you any promise for the future—any promise for the future makes one secure.

I am here simply to make you alert and aware. That is: to be herenow—with all the insecurity that life is; with all the uncertainty that life is; with all the danger that life is.

I know you come here seeking some certainty, some creed, some 'ism', somewhere to belong to, someone to rely upon. You come here out of your fear. You are searching a sort of beautiful imprisonment—so that you can live without any awareness.

I would make you more insecure, more uncertain, because that's how life is, that's how God is. When there is more insecurity and more danger, the only way to respond to it is by awareness.

There are two possibilities. Either you close your eyes and become dogmatic—become a Christian or a Hindu or a Mohammedan . . . then you become like an ostrich. It doesn't change life: it simply closes your eyes; it simply makes you stupid; it simply makes you unintelligent. In your unintelligence you feel secure—all idiots feel secure. In fact, only idiots feel secure. A really alive man will always feel insecure. What security can there be?

Life is not a mechanical process. It cannot be certain. It is an unpredictable mystery. Nobody knows what is going to happen the next moment. Not even God that you think resides somewhere in the Seventh Heaven, not even He—if He is there—not even He knows what is going to happen, because if *He* knows what is going to happen then life is just bogus, then everything is written beforehand, then everything is destined beforehand. How can He know what is going to happen next if the future is open? If God knows what is going to happen the next moment, then life is just a dead mechanical process, then there is no freedom. And how can life exist without freedom? Then there is no possibility to grow, or not to grow. If everything is predestined then there is no glory, no grandeur. Then you are just robots.

No—nothing is secure. That is my message. Nothing can be secure, because a secure life will be worse than death. Nothing is certain. Life is full of uncertainties, full of surprises—that is its beauty! You can never come to a moment when you can say,

"Now I am certain." When you say you are certain, you simply declare your death, you have committed suicide.

Life goes on moving with a thousand and one uncertainties. That's its freedom. Don't call it insecurity. I can understand why mind calls freedom insecurity.

Have you lived in a jail for a few months or a few years? If you have lived in a jail for a few years, when the day of release comes the prisoner starts feeling uncertain about the future. Everything was certain in the jail; everything was dead routine. Food was supplied to him, protection was given to him; there was no fear that he would be hungry next day and there would be no food—nothing! Everything was certain. Now, suddenly, after many years the jailer comes and says to him, "Now you are going to be released." He starts trembling. Outside the wall of the prison, again uncertainties; again he will have to seek, search; again he will have to live in freedom. . .

Freedom creates fear. People talk about freedom but they are afraid. And a man is not yet a man if he is afraid of freedom. I give you freedom—I don't give you security. I give you understanding—I don't give you knowledge. Knowledge will make you certain. If I can give you a formula, a set formula, that there is a God and there is a Holy Ghost and there is an only begotten son, Jesus; there is Hell and Heaven; and these are the good acts and these are the bad acts; do the sin and you will be in Hell; do what I call the virtuous acts and you will be in Heaven—finished!—then you are certain.

That's why so many people have chosen to be Christians, to be Hindus, to be Mohammedans, to be Jains—they don't want freedom. They want fixed formulas.

A Jew was dying—suddenly, in an accident on a road. Nobody knew that he was a Jew. A priest was called, a Catholic priest. He leaned close to the Jew—and the man was dying, in the last throes of death—and the priest said, "Do you believe in the Trinity of God the Father, the Holy Ghost and the son Jesus?"

The Jew opened his eyes and he said, "Look, here I am dying—

143

and he is talking riddles? Here I am dying and he is talking in riddles!"

When death knocks at your door, all your certainties will be simply riddles and foolish. Don't cling to any certainty. Life *is* uncertain—its very nature is uncertain. And an intelligent man always remains uncertain.

This very readiness to remain in uncertainty is courage. This very readiness to be in uncertainty is trust. An intelligent person is one who remains alert whatsoever the situation—and responds to it with his whole heart. Not that he knows what is going to happen; not that he knows that 'do this' and 'that will happen'. Life is not a science; it is not a cause and effect chain. Heat the water to a hundred degrees and it evaporates—it is a certainty. But like that, in real life, nothing is certain.

Each individual is a freedom, an unknown freedom. It is impossible to predict, impossible to expect. One has to live in awareness *and* in understanding.

You come to me seeking knowledge; you want set formulas so that you can cling to them. I don't give you any. In fact, if you have any I take them away. By and by, I destroy your certainty; by and by, I make you more and more hesitant; by and by, I make you more and more insecure. That is the only thing that has to be done. That's the only thing a master needs to do!—to leave you in total freedom. In total freedom, with all the possibilities opening, nothing fixed . . . you will have to be aware. Nothing else is possible.

This is what I call understanding. If you understand, insecurity is an intrinsic part of life—and *good* that it is so, because it makes life a freedom, it makes life a continuous surprise. One never knows what is going to happen. It keeps you continuously in wonder. Don't call it uncertainty—call it wonder. Don't call it insecurity—call it freedom.

"I leave you with no feeling of security, no sense of certainty, nothing to rely on." Precisely that's what I have been always hoping. "Have I missed you?" No, not at all. You have understood me well. Go with this uncertainty into the world; go with this insecurity into the world. And never be a coward, and don't regress back into some dogma.

"I have been with Bhagwan and I have not been with Bhagwan."

YES, IT IS SO. This is the paradox of love. You possess your beloved and yet you don't possess. You *are* with your beloved and yet you are not with. This is the paradox of love.

You cannot possess your beloved like a thing; you cannot become a possessor—yet in a certain sense you possess your beloved, and in a certain sense you don't possess. In fact, the more you love, the more you make your beloved free. In fact, the more freedom you give to your beloved, the more you possess. The more you possess, the less you possess. This is the paradox of love.

Here being with me is an act of love. I have nothing else to give to you—except my love. I have nothing else to share with you except my love. While you are here with me you will be in this paradox continuously: you will feel you have been with me, and you will feel that you have not been with me. Both are true— *and both are true together!* That's the paradox of love.

The more you have been with me, the more you will feel that you have not been with me. The less you have been with me, the more you will feel that you have been with me.

There are foolish people, unloving people, who come and listen once or twice and think they have known me. And they go with certainty, with decisions, conclusions. They don't know what love is. They don't know what truth is. They come with certain prejudices, and if they feel that I am agreeing with their prejudices, they think they have understood me and they say I am right. If I am not agreeing with their prejudices, they think they have understood me and 'this man is wrong'.

If you are here for a longer period . . . and the period is not as important as the depth of the relationship. That is the meaning of sannyas: it is a plunge into a deeper intimacy, into a deeper commitment.

Just the other night a woman was asking: "If I don't take

sannyas, won't you accept me?" I told her: "Yes, I accept you—whether you take sannyas or not is irrelevant—but you will not be able to accept me if you don't take sannyas."

If you are able to accept me, then sannyas is just a gesture of your acceptance, nothing else. It is just a gesture that 'I am coming with you', that 'I am ready to be with you', that 'even if you are going to hell I would rather be with you in hell than be in heaven alone'—that's all. I am not promising you that I will take you to heaven—nothing of the sort. Nobody should be hoping that. I am not promising you anything of that sort. Maybe I am going to hell.

A sannyasin is one who has trusted me, who says, "Okay, so I am also coming—but I am coming with you." Then something starts transpiring between me and you. It is not only changing your clothes, it is not only changing your name. It is simply dropping your *whole* past and starting from A-B-C. That's why I change your name—mm?—just to give you a new start, as if you are born again.

The day of your initiation into sannyas becomes your real birthday. You disown the past and you tell me: "I am ready for a new future—I will not continue my past; I am ready to discontinue it. And I will not insist on my past—I disclaim, I disown it. And I am absolutely open: wherever you lead, I am ready. I have no prejudices."

If you have been here with me in a deep intimate relationship, if you have loved me, and if you have tasted my love, this is bound to happen: "I have been with Bhagwan and I have not been with Bhagwan." Yes, you will feel that paradox. "I have seen him and yet something remains unknown, unseen." That will always remain—unless you also become Bhagwan. Unless you also reclaim your divinity, unless you also become a God, something will remain unknown—because we can know only that of which we have become capable.

Another woman last night came to me and she said, "I love you, but I cannot love you as a divine being—I love you as a human being." That's okay! In fact, how can you see divineness if some-

146

thing of the divine has not already stirred in your heart? How can you see beyond yourself?

And the woman who said it is a dogmatic Christian. In fact she thinks—maybe not very consciously, but unconsciously—that Jesus is the only God there ever has been. But you must know that Jesus was crucified, and the people who crucified him, they were not crucifying a God—they were crucifying a vagabond, they were crucifying a criminal; they were crucifying a man who was creating mischief.

The people who crucified Jesus were not able to see his godliness at all; they could only see the mischief in him. So whether Jesus was a God or not is not the question—whether you can see or not is the question. And you can see only that which you are; you cannot see beyond yourself.

The moment you start seeing God in me, something of the God has been born in you. And then it is not going to remain confined to me. The moment you start seeing God in me, by and by you will see God in Jesus, in Buddha, in Krishna. And, by and by, you will see God in other people. By and by, you will be able to see God in birds, in trees, in rocks—and one day you will see that only God exists and nothing else. In fact, only God exists and nothing else.

The more you hear me, the more you will feel something has been left unheard. The more you see me, the more you will feel something is missing, you have not seen me totally. The more close you are to me, the more intense your thirst will become. The more you love me, the more passionate you will become in your love; a burning desire will arise in you to become a God yourself.

Now there is a problem with Christians, Mohammedans, Jews, who think of God as a person—there is a problem. They think God is the one who created the world. In the East we have a deeper understanding of God than that. Creation is not something separate from God: it is His play; it is He Himself hiding in many forms. Here He has become a rock, there He has become a flower. Here He is a sinner and there He is a saint. The whole play is His.

147

And He is the only actor, and He goes on dividing His roles. He is in Jesus and He is in Judas.

In the East, God is not a person—God is the very stuff the universe is made of. God is not a creator—God is creativity. And the creator and the creation are just two aspects of the same creative energy.

In the West, the idea is something like a painter making a picture, a painting. By the time the painting is complete, the painting is separate from the painter. Then the painter can die, but the painting will remain. In the East, we don't think of God and the world as a painter and a painting—we think of God as a dancer, *natraj.* You cannot separate the dancer from the dance; if the dancer goes, the dance goes. If the dance stops, then the person is no more a dancer. Dancer and dancing exist together; they cannot exist separately; you cannot separate them.

God is more like a dancer. I am one of His movements; you are also one of His movements—you may recognize it, you may not recognize it. The only difference in the world is that a few people recognize that they are Gods and a few people don't recognize that they are Gods. The difference is not of your being, it is only of recognition.

The more and more you love, the more and more you become understanding and aware, the more and more you will feel something is missing.

"I have heard him and yet still I am deaf to his teaching"— you have really heard me. Only then can this feeling arise. If hearing me you think you have understood me, you are really deaf—not only deaf, you are stupid also.

I am saying something about the ineffable. I am saying something about the ultimate mystery. You can understand it, yet you can never understand it totally. It is elusive, it escapes. It is within reach, but it is not within grasp. You are always coming closer and closer to it, but you never arrive. And the day you arrive, then you are no more there; the distinction between the seeker and the sought disappears. *Then you are it.* That art thou—then you *are* it! That is the moment of culmination.

I would like to tell Anand Subhuti: Go happily, go in insecurity, go in freedom; go independent—there is no need to lean on anything or anybody. Don't use me as a crutch. Allow me to help you to become independent, to be free of me and to be free of everything. You have not missed me. I have fallen like a seed into your heart. Just watch prayerfully, wait with deep gratitude, and in the right time the seed will sprout.

The second question: *While in a peaceful state of being, I watched a bird flying by. I thought, "This would be a nice time to die!" Yet during the "stop" exercise when I was feeling some discomfort, I experienced maybe as much separation as ever.*

Do the conditions of the particular moment of death determine something about the nature of an Enlightened being? or vice versa?

FIRST: this is a sort of calamity that has befallen human beings. Somehow, when things are going beautifully, and you feel calm and quiet and collected, why do you start thinking of death?

The questioner says: "While in a peaceful state of being, I watched a bird flying by. I thought, 'This would be a nice time to die!'" Why not think: This would be a nice time to live! Why think: This would be a nice time to die! Something is implied in it.

All over the world, and in the West more so, people have been taught not to be happy, not to enjoy life, not to be ecstatic. People have been taught that to be happy is somehow to be guilty. People have become deep down very much conditioned: when they feel happy, they almost always feel guilt arising. When they feel sad, everything is good. When they are depressed, nothing is wrong. When they are serious, there is no guilt.

Have you watched it? Dancing with a woman, suddenly you

149

feel guilty. Making love to a woman, suddenly you feel guilty. Enjoying your food, suddenly you start looking guilty. Have you watched? Whenever there is happiness something of guilt arises in you. This never happens when you are sad; when you are depressed, when you are carrying a long face, then this never happens. But if you are smiling . . . people even feel afraid to laugh; they laugh reluctantly, as if they are going to do something wrong. The whole humanity has been conditioned to be unhappy. *All* happiness has been condemned as sin.

That's why saints are painted as if they never laugh. Christians, in fact, say that Jesus never laughed. This is absurd! If Jesus was an Enlightened man, only he is entitled to laugh. But Christians say he never laughed. Have you ever seen a picture of Jesus laughing? So dead, dull, serious, deathlike.

All Jesus' pictures are falsifications; they cannot be about the real Jesus. This real man must have been totally different, because we *know* he enjoyed drinking—it is impossible to think of a person who enjoys drinking and not laughing. He enjoyed women—it is difficult to think of a man who enjoys women and not laughing. He was friendly, almost in love, with a prostitute, Mary Magdalene. It is difficult to move with a prostitute—he was not moving with a Catholic monk, not with a priest, not with the Pope . . . with a prostitute! These were the condemnations against him.

And he was moving with simple people, simple folk—carpenters, farmers—very uneducated people. You cannot expect them to be serious. He was not moving with scholars, with professors, with vice-chancellors—no. He was moving with very simple people, ordinary people, down-to-earth people. It is impossible to think that he was not laughing. Late in the nights they would enjoy food and drink. He must have been gossiping, he must have been telling jokes.

But Jesus has been depicted as a serious man. And Christians say he never laughed. Then what is the function of an Enlightened man? If Jesus cannot laugh, then who is going to laugh in this world?

Somehow man has been conditioned to be unhappy. Happiness

150

seems to be hedonistic, epicurean, pagan. A religious man has to be serious, has to carry a long face, a mask; he cannot smile. He cannot enjoy the small things of life—his ego won't allow it. His ego keeps aloof, away, distant. He will not meet and mingle with ordinary people, and he will not enjoy ordinary gossiping. He will always remain aloof, far away.

This is an egoistic attitude, this is pious ego—and a pious ego is more poisoned than ordinary egos because it is purer: it is pure poison. And *these* people have conditioned the human mind. They are neurotic people. Something is missing—they are not normal, they are not healthy; they are morbid, ill. These ill people have conditioned humanity's mind. They have destroyed laughter from the earth, they have destroyed festivity. They have destroyed celebration—and destroying celebration they have destroyed the very foundation of God. Life is a celebration!

Because of this conditioning, whenever you are feeling happy you think, "This is the right moment to die." Why not to live?! When you are miserable, that is the right moment to live; and when you are feeling happy, this is the right moment to die. Drop this nonsense! When a bird flies by and you are feeling peaceful, this is the moment to live and love and dance. Why be in a hurry for death? Death is coming on its own. It need not have any support from you. It is already coming.

While you are alive, be so alive that even death when it comes cannot kill you. A really alive person transcends death. Death happens only to dead people. Let me repeat it: Death happens only to dead people; who are already dead, only to those people does death happen. A really alive person transcends death, goes beyond death. Death comes, but misses the target.

How can you kill a person like Buddha? How can you kill a person like Jesus? How can you kill Krishna with his flute on his lips?—impossible. Death itself will start dancing around him! His life is so abundant that death itself will fall in love with him.

Always remember that to be happy is to be religious, to be happy is to be virtuous. To be celebrating is to be prayerful. To be festive, and to remain in a festive dimension continuously, is to be a sannyasin. Then you enjoy whatsoever happens. You enjoy health when it happens; you enjoy illness also when it happens. Then both become beautiful. In health you enjoy activity; when you are ill you enjoy relaxation.

It is beautiful sometimes to be ill and just lying on the bed, resting, not worrying about the world; allowing yourself a good holiday; singing, praying, meditating on the bed; reading a little bit, listening to music; or just doing nothing, just being lazy. It is beautiful! If you know how to enjoy health, you will be able to know how to enjoy illness also. Then you become a master, you become skillful.

This is the whole art of life!

You enjoy your youth, and when you become old you enjoy your old age. Old age has its own beauties; no young man can have those beauties. Youth is shallow; full of energy but shallow. Old age is not so full of energy, but things are settling and depth is arising.

If you miss your youth, you will miss your old age also — remember. So I am not saying become old while you are young. I am saying be whatsoever you are; let that moment be your totality. When a child, be a child; never enforce your wisdom on any child because that is a crippling thing. Don't try to make a child old before he is old, don't crush him.

That's what has happened in the world: old people are dominating children, and they want to pull them out of their childhood faster than nature allows. They kill and they crush — the child loses something forever. And when a child was not a child when he was a child, he will not be young when he is young. Something will always go on missing. He will always be late in life — he will miss the train.

That's why so many people dream of missing the train. This is one of the commonest dreams in the world: people rushing towards the railway station, doing everything in a hurry; somehow they reach on the platform and the train is moving, or has moved, and they just see the last bogie leaving the platform.

This is the commonest dream; it is very significant. It simply shows that somehow you have been missing the train that life is. You always reach late; you are never in time. And the wonder of wonders is that everybody is studying the timetable so much. People go on studying the timetable, but when they reach they are always late. They waste their time with the timetable.

This is what is happening when you read the Bible or you read the Koran or you read the Gita — these are timetables. And reading the timetables you miss the train of life. Good sometimes to read them, when you have nothing else to do — but don't make them a substitute for life. They are nothing compared to life.

While you can read the book of life, don't substitute it by any other book. When you can read a tree, read the tree! When you can read the rosebush, read the rosebush! When you can read a man, read the man! When you can read a woman, read the woman! These are *alive* books, the *real* Bibles. But you are too much concerned with dead books, and by the time you raise your eyes, the train has left.

A child has to be a child when he is a child. A young man has to be a young man when he is a young man. An old man has to be an old man when he is old. If you miss your youth then you will be in difficulty: you will never be really old; your body will start deteriorating and your mind will hanker around your youth. The unfulfilled desires, the sensuality, the sexuality, the greed, the ambition — all that you always wanted to do and could not because at that time you were reading the Bible or the Gita — now will haunt you. Now your mind will go after those things.

I was reading one beautiful story about a missionary:

He went to Africa to teach Christianity to a cannibal tribe. He was talking to the chief of the cannibal tribe — a very old man, near about eighty-five, ninety. The cannibal listened very attentively, then he asked a few questions. One he said: "So do you mean to say to me that I should not fall in love with my neighbour's wife?"

The missionary said, "Yes, you have understood rightly."

And then the chief said, "And do you mean to say to me that I should not kill anybody in a fight?"

153

The missionary was very happy. He said, "Perfectly right! You have understood me."

The cannibal said, "Do you mean to say that robbing somebody of his property or killing him in the fight or taking his wife as your own wife is wrong, immoral, a sin?"

The missionary said, "Absolutely, absolutely!"

The chief said, "But I can't understand—because I am too old to do all these things. So do you mean to say that to be an old man and to be a Christian are the same?"

Your so-called religions are just religions created by dead people. They don't allow you life. They don't allow you love. They go on condemning all that is beautiful and all that is right at the time.

My whole emphasis is to live the moment whatsoever it is, and live it with tremendous energy.

If you are a young man while young, you will be an old man while old—very wise. You will have known all that is good and bad in life: the day and night, the summer and winter—all you will have have known. By your own experience a wisdom will arise. And when you are dying, you will have enjoyed your life so tremendously that you will be able to enjoy your death also.

Only a person who has enjoyed his life becomes capable of enjoying his death. And if you are capable of enjoying your death, you have defeated death. Then there is no more birth for you and no more death for you—you have learnt the lesson.

This is what we call Enlightenment: learning the lesson that life can teach you.

The questioner says: "While in a peaceful state of being, I watched a bird flying by. I thought, 'This would be a nice time to die.'"

This thought must have come out of your Christian background, the so-called, the pseudo-religious background, life-negating background—otherwise you would have thought: "Nice time to live!" And you *are* alive so think in terms of life. Why do you think in terms of death? There must be some suicidal tendency in you. This I have watched in many people.

Once I took one of my professors—he was my teacher—I took

him to a very beautiful place. Nothing like it exists. anywhere in the world. I used to live in Jabalpur, and just thirteen miles away from there flows the beautiful River Narmada. Two miles amidst hills of marble, two miles' stretch of marble hills: it is something not of this world. On a full-moon night it is unbelievable; you cannot believe that it is there. It is *so* unreal! It has such a hypnotic energy in it.

I took my old professor on a full-moon night, just in the middle of the night when the moon is just on the head. He could not believe that such a beautiful thing is possible on this earth. He said, "What a beautiful place to die!"

But why does this idea arise? "What a beautiful place to live!" would have been absolutely relevant. "What a beautiful place to love! What a beautiful place to dance! and sing!" would have been relevant. But the idea arises: "What a beautiful place to die!" Why this death-obsession? Can't you enjoy anything? Can't you delight in anything?

Become aware of such tendencies. And next time when a beautiful moment passes by—dance! sing! paint! love! Death will take care of itself. It will come one day. Be *ripe* when it comes—and the only ripeness that is possible is through living.

Live deeply, live totally, live wholly, so when death comes and knocks at your door you are ready—ready like a ripe fruit to drop. Just a small breeze comes and the fruit drops; sometimes even without the breeze the fruit drops from its own weight and ripeness. Death should be like that. And the readiness has to come through living.

THE QUESTIONER asks: "Yet during the 'stop' exercise when I was feeling some discomfort I experienced maybe as much separation as ever."

You think about death and you become disturbed by small things: a headache, an ant crawling on your body. You become distracted by such small things, small discomforts—and you talk about death. Maybe you don't know what death is; maybe you have only heard the name. And you have seen people dying, but you yourself have never seen death.

In fact, when a person dies you see him lying in repose—silent, relaxed, with no discomfort. You think death is not a discomfort? You are seeing only a dead person; you have not seen his inner misery, you have not seen his inner conflict. You have not seen his inner struggle with death. You have not seen his inner anguish and turmoil. You just see the dead body—painted, dressed well, washed, cleaned.

One man died. Mulla Nasrudin went to see with his wife. And the wife said, "Looks so beautiful and so silent!"

Nasrudin said, "Has to look beautiful and silent—is coming from Kashmir, three months' holiday!"

Watch a dead person—every person looks beautiful, silent. Not that he died in silence, not that he died beautifully—rarely does a person die beautifully. Ninety-nine percent of people struggle very badly—fight, great stress arises.

Just think!—a small ant crawling on your body, a small thorn in your foot, and how uncomfortable you become. A small headache, stomach a little disturbed, and how much you become concerned. Just think!—the body and soul are being taken apart. With the body you have become so involved; you have completely forgotten that you are a soul—and you are being taken apart. You *cling!* You leave your claim with great difficulty, very reluctantly—fighting, struggling, crying. But nobody can see it; it is something inside you—only you can see it. You cannot even say anything.

You die in misery. Only a few people die blissfully. And when death becomes a bliss, it is a *samadhi*. When death is a relaxation . . . *real* relaxation. Deep inside you surrender, you welcome. You have *known* life, now you want to know death also. You have *lived* life, you have enjoyed it. A great trust has arisen in you about life—and you know death is the culmination of life, the crescendo. It must be beautiful! When the whole journey has been beautiful, why not the goal? There is no reason to be afraid. When the *whole* journey has been such a tremendous joy, why not the end? It is the culmination. You have come home. You welcome, you are ready to embrace death. You relax, you simply slip into death.

And that's the moment! If you can die without any fight, you don't die—and you are never born again. You have simply slipped out of the body confinements—of the world. You live!—you live eternally. But then you live as an unembodied existence, with no limitations, with no boundaries.

Body gives you a boundary. Death takes away all boundaries from you. Body gives you a definition, makes you a man or a woman, makes you ugly or beautiful, makes you intelligent or unintelligent, makes you this and that—body gives you definition. Death takes all definitions away. It simply leaves life undefined.

Life undefined is what God is. But to know this death you will have to know life well.

So if you can accept my suggestion: next time when a beautiful moment passes by, think in terms of life—"What a beautiful moment to live and dance and be alive!" Then one day when death comes, you will say the same to death: "What a beautiful moment to die!"

All moments are beautiful, only you have to be receptive and surrendering. All moments are blessings, only you have to be capable of seeing. All moments are benedictions. If you accept with a deep gratitude, nothing ever goes wrong.

"Do the conditions of the particular moment of death determine something about the nature of an Enlightened being? or vice versa?"

Vice versa. Death does not determine, neither does the time of death determine anything. It is *you,* conscious or unconscious, who determine the meaning of death. It is an Enlightened consciousness that makes death so beautiful, so tremendously beautiful. You are making even life ugly, and an Enlightened man makes even death beautiful.

It is you in the final analysis, always you, the decisive factor, who decide whatsoever happens to you. Remember it. This is the very key. If you are unhappy, it is you. If you are not living rightly, it is you. If you are missing, it is you. The responsibility is totally yours. Don't be afraid of this responsibility.

Many people become too much afraid of the responsibility because they don't see the other side of the coin. On one side is written 'responsibility'; on another side is written 'freedom'. Responsibility means freedom. If somebody else is forcing you to be in misery, then you cannot get out of it—how can you get out of it if somebody else is forcing you into misery? Unless the other decides not to make you miserable you can never get out of it. If it is *you* who are responsible for your misery, then it is for you to decide. If you are enjoying being miserable, be miserable thousandfold—there is no problem. Enjoy! If you are not enjoying it, then drop it. Be clear-cut.

What I see is: people go on thinking that they want to be happy, but what can they do?—they are being forced to be miserable. This is absolutely absurd. Nobody is forcing anybody—nobody can force anybody—to be miserable. A man who knows how to be happy becomes happy in *any* sort of situation. You cannot give him any situation in which he will not find something to be happy about.

And there are persons who have learnt the trick of being unhappy. You cannot give them any situation in which they will not find something to be unhappy about.

Whatsoever you want to find, you will find. Life goes on supplying all sorts of things to you. You choose!

I have heard:

Two men were imprisoned. It was a full-moon night; both were standing near the window of their dark cell. The full moon was there. One was looking at the moon, and it was the rainy season—must have been like these days—and there was much water and mud just in front of the window. Dirty, and it was smelling and stinking.

One man continued to look at the moon, the other continued to look at the mud. And the man who was looking at the mud, of course, was feeling very miserable. And the man who was looking at the moon was aflame, aglow; his face was reflecting the moon; his eyes were full of beauty. He had completely forgotten that he was imprisoned.

Both are standing at the same window, but they are choosing different things. There are people: if you take them to a rosebush they will count the thorns; they are great calculators—their mathematics is always right. And when they have counted thousands of thorns, it is simply logical that they will not be able to see the one roseflower. In fact, their inner world will say, "How is it possible?—amidst so many thorns, how is a roseflower possible? It must be a deception, it must be illusory. Or even if it is possible, it is worthless."

Then there are people who have never known the thorns of a rosebush—they look at the rose. And looking at the rose, feeling the rose, the beauty of it, celebrating the moment, they come to feel that even thorns are not so thornlike. "How can they be when they are growing on the same rosebush as the roseflower?" When their mind is focused on the roseflower, they start looking at thorns also in a different way: they start thinking that thorns are there to protect the roseflower. They are no longer ugly, they are no longer irrelevant; they are no longer anti—a positive attitude arises.

It is up to you to make whatsoever you want out of your life. An enlightened consciousness makes even death beautiful. An unenlightened consciousness makes even life ugly. For an enlightened consciousness, only beauty exists—only beauty; only bliss exists—only bliss.

So the question is not how to change ugliness into beauty, how to change pain into pleasure, how to change misery into happiness. No. The question is how to change the unconscious into conscious, the unenlightened attitude into the enlightened attitude—how to change your inner world of being, how to attain to life-affirmative values and drop life-negative values.

159

The third question: *I am a so-called psychologist. Usually I enjoy it. Recently I have begun to appreciate witnessing. I wonder now if I am "qualified" to be a psychologist. Carl Rogers used the phrase "unconditional positive regard" as the core of psychotherapy. Compassion is so foreign and new to me.*
Kindly advise.

ALL PSYCHOLOGISTS are so-called psychologists—because the real psychology does not exist yet, because man is still not known. Psychology is just a groping. It is still not a science; it is just in a very primary stage.

So every psychologist is a so-called psychologist because psychology is a so-called psychology. The real psychology is yet to be born. But the so-called psychology is paving the way for it, so it *is* valuable. When I say it is so-called psychology, I am not condemning it.

It is just like alchemy preceded chemistry and astrology preceded astronomy. This so-called psychology is preceding, is a requirement, for the real psychology to be born. Just as alchemists are no longer remembered, forgotten, you cannot even mention their names, sooner or later Freud and Jung and Adler will be forgotten the same way—they are alchemists of the inner world.

Sooner or later, you will be surprised, a few other names will become more important which are already there but known only to a few people. For example, Gurdjieff will become more important than Freud in the coming century—because he has tried to give a few keys for a real, objective psychology. Ouspensky's name will become more important than Jung's. And a few completely unknown names will bubble up into prominence.

But Freud, Jung and Adler have done a great service. They have paved the way. Without alchemy chemistry would not have been born. *It is a must*—but it is so-called. We call it psychology because nothing else exists, but it is not yet real. It simply watches human beings from the lowest rung of the ladder.

You go to a pond; you see a lotus—the lotus comes out of dirty

160

mud. The modern psychology reduces the lotus to the dirty mud: it says the lotus is nothing but the dirty mud. It is *right* in a way, and yet absolutely wrong. Right in a way because the lotus needs the dirty mud; it comes out of the dirty mud. But to reduce it back to the dirty mud is not right.

The real psychology, if you ask a Buddha, or you ask a Patanjali, who are the pioneers of a real psychology — which has not yet settled, which has not yet found its place in the human consciousness, which is still hovering around, seeking, searching for a nest — they will say that rather than reduce the lotus to the dirty mud, why not raise the value of dirty mud to the lotus itself? Why say that the lotus comes out of the dirty mud? Why not say that the dirty mud carries a lotus within itself? that the dirty mud is an abode of the lotus, a temple? Why not raise the value of the dirty mud? And that seems to be better, more objective.

The higher should never be explained by the lower. The lower cannot explain the higher, but the higher can explain the lower.

Watch . . . Darwin says man comes from the monkeys, so he is nothing but a monkey. Freud says art comes out of sexuality, so it is nothing but sexuality; meditation, religion, God, are nothing but frustrations, repressions, complexes. Then religion looks like a mass neurosis.

Darwin or Freud, they reduce the higher to the lower — mm? But then go on the whole way. From where do the monkeys come? Then reduce them back, further back, go on, go on . . . finally you will come to matter. Then everything is reduced to matter. Then even Darwin is reduced to matter. You reduce religion to repressed sexuality, then how will you treat Freud himself? Then what is psychology? Then that too is reduced.

I have heard an anecdote: Adler was talking to a few friends and a few visitors. A group of Americans had come to see him, and he was talking about his famous theory about the inferiority complex. And he said, "If a man is inferior in one way, he tries to compensate for it in another.

"For example: Lenin was very small, his legs were very short, out of proportion. When he sat on a chair, his legs would not reach to the ground. That was the reason he rose so high: to prove that he was very powerful and he was not a weakling." Adler talked on and on, and he gave many examples as to why people who lack something always become ambitious for power.

Then somebody stood and said, "And what about psychologists? Do they lack something in their minds so that they become psychologists? Do they have a smaller mind than other people so that they try to compensate for it by thinking and talking and creating theories about mind?"

I don't know what Adler said to it, but in fact there is no answer to it. If religion is repressed sexuality, art is repressed sexuality, science is repressed sexuality, then what is psychology? What are Freud, Jung and Adler? Then you go on reducing backwards, and finally nothing is left—only matter.

But everything comes out of this matter!—that means everything is implied in matter; then matter is no more material; then matter carries gods hidden behind it . . . because a Buddha is born, a lotus flowers.

In the East we have a totally different attitude about psychology, and the attitude is: Always explain the lower by the higher. We say that sex is nothing but the lowest rung of *samadhi;* sex is nothing but the lowest rung of your superconsciousness. Then the whole view changes. Then there is a possibility to grow.

The modern psychology leaves no possibility for growth. It reduces everything to dirt—and there is no possibility to grow. In fact, there is no point in growing because all is going to be just repressed sexuality. If you listen to the modern psychologists, their definition of the normal man makes life worthless.

Einstein is abnormal, because a normal man never bothers about the mathematics of the world—why should he bother? Michelangelo is abnormal; he must have some psychological problem—that's why he becomes so imaginative. Van Gogh is abnormal. Buddha, Jesus, Krishna—all are in some way neurotic. They are not normal: abnormal. They are all condemned. Then who is normal?

The man who only lives in unconsciousness is normal: he gets up early in the morning, goes to the marketplace, earns his living, gives birth to children, makes a house—goes on moving in a routine for seventy years, then dies. This is the normal man. Not creative, not innovative, not original in any way; has nothing to contribute—no art, no science, no religion.

Just think about a really normal world according to Freud: it will be the most boring world possible. There will be no music because it is repressed sexuality. There will be no poetry because it is just fantasy. There will be no science, because to be a scientist is just nothing but a deep instinct of voyeurism.

If you remain clean, you like a shower, you use beautiful clothes, then it is exhibitionism. Then everything is condemned. Then everything is suspected and doubted. Then only animals are normal—and if man is to be normal he has to just live an animal life. Then you cannot soar high. Then the whole sky is taken away from you, and you live caged in your small cages of normal routine life.

A world of normal people according to Freud is going to be worse than hell. Hell at least must be interesting! The world is beautiful because people soar high—because there are Buddhas and Michelangelo's and Van Goghs and Picasso's; musicians and dancers and philosophers, and psychologists and poets and painters. The world is beautiful *because not all are normal*— a few people try to be abnormal, a few people try to go beyond the norm, beyond the ordinary. And they try to raise themselves a little higher, to see more, to perceive more, to live more.

People who are *not* satisfied with a dead, routine life, people who are adventurous, people who take risks, people who dare, and people who go into the unknown and the unfamiliar . . . you are all abnormal according to Freud! Otherwise, what are you doing here with me? Meditating? Meditation is not a good term with Freud. Then something has gone wrong; otherwise, an ordinary, normal person never thinks of meditation.

According to Freud, a normal person never thinks about himself. To think about the self is to become morbid. A normal person only thinks about others, never thinks about himself. Self-knowledge is a disease. The very idea of knowing oneself is ill. You are all abnormal. In fact, all great people, all rare people, are abnormal.

This psychology cannot be a real psychology. It cannot help us to explain Buddha, Jesus Christ, Mahavir, Patanjali; it cannot help us to understand the lotus — it can only help us to understand the dirty mud. What type of psychology is this? It does not help us to see above the boundaries, beyond the boundaries. It confines us to the boundaries. I call it a so-called psychology. Necessary, a preparation for the real psychology to come and take over. That's why I call all psychologists 'so-called'.

And the person who has asked the question says: "I am a so-called psychologist." Good that you are aware of the so-calledness of your science, that you are aware that it is not enough, that you are humble. It is very difficult to find a psychologist who is humble, because he thinks he has known man, he has known all that is possible to know. He becomes very, very egoistic. Good! It is a religious quality to be humble.

"Usually I enjoy it." It is good to help people; it is good to help them grow. Just one thing remember always: Don't help them just to be normal — help them to grow; help them to become unique. *Don't help them to become normal!* Normal, they will be just part of a collectivity. Help them to become individuals. Help them to become rare, unique. Enjoy it!

"Recently I have begun to appreciate witnessing. I wonder now if I am 'qualified' to be a psychologist."

If you ask me, and if my certificate can mean anything: To whomsoever it concerns, I certify you. By becoming a witness, the first rays are entering in you. You are really becoming qualified to be a psychologist. How can you be a psychologist if you have not witnessed even your own self? Then all your observations are from the outside. You see people's behaviour — you can be a behaviourist but not a psychologist.

When you have watched your innermost core. . .and that is the only way to watch it. You cannot watch it in somebody else — because watching somebody else, you are always outside. You can watch the real human soul only from the inside. You have to become an introvert — witnessing. That's why the questioner has

164

become suspicious whether he can call himself qualified, because if he goes and asks Freudians they will say, "You are dropping out of the profession. An introvert is morbid. Witnessing? There is nothing to witness. You are losing your track." But I will say to you: For the first time you are really becoming a psychologist.

"Carl Rogers used the phrase 'unconditional positive regard' as the core of psychotherapy."

Yes, it is—compassion. An unconditional acceptance of the other's being as he is. Ordinarily psychology has a condemnatory attitude—it goes on labelling. You say something and they will say you are a schizophrenic. You say something and you are a split personality. You say something, you are a neurotic or a psychotic. And they go on labelling—as if man is just a thing to be labelled. Man is not a thing to be labelled: man is something to be revered, with deep regard.

"Compassion is so foreign and new to me."

Yes, it is foreign to psychologists because they take people as patients not as persons. They have to treat you. Something has gone wrong; they have accepted it. It is new. If you start witnessing your being, you will feel more and more compassion. Allow it to happen more and more.

In deep compassion you will be able to help many more people—because, in fact, compassion is the only thing that helps. Compassion is therapeutic. Compassion is the only therapy there is.

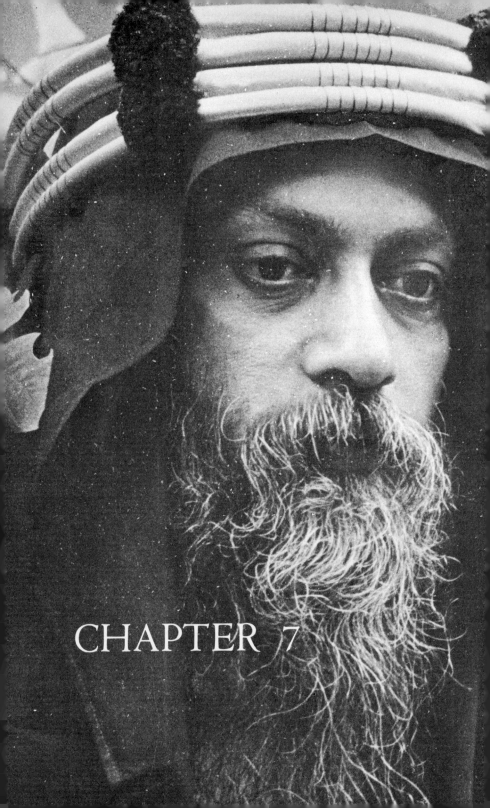

CHAPTER 7

ONCE there was a man of Ch'i who wanted gold. At dawn he put on his coat and cap and set out for the market.

He went to the stall of a dealer in gold, snatched his gold, and made off.

The police caught him and questioned him. "Why did you snatch somebody else's gold, and in front of so many people?"

The man replied:

"At the time when I took it I did not see the people—I only saw the gold."

ONLY THE GOLD

seventeenth august 1976

LET ME tell you first one small anecdote:

"My doctor insisted that I came to see you," the patient told the psychiatrist. "Goodness knows why—I am happily married, secure in my job, lots of friends, no worries . . ."

"Hmmm," said the psychiatrist, reaching for his notebook, "and how long have you been like this?"

HAPPINESS IS UNBELIEVABLE. It seems that man cannot be happy. If you talk about your depression, sadness, misery, everybody believes it. It seems natural. If you talk about your happiness nobody believes you—it seems unnatural.

Sigmund Freud, after forty years of research into the human mind, working with thousands of people, observing thousands of disturbed minds, came to the conclusion that happiness is a fiction: man cannot be happy. At the most, we can make things a little more comfortable, that's all. At the most we can make unhappiness a little less, that's all. But happy man cannot be.

Looks very pessimistic—but looking at the modern man it seems to be exactly the case, it seems to be a fact.

Buddha says that man can be happy, tremendously happy. Krishna sings songs of that ultimate bliss—*satchitanand.* Jesus talks about the Kingdom of God. But how can you believe so few people, who can be counted on the fingers, against the whole mass, millions and millions of people down the centuries, remaining unhappy, growing more and more into unhappiness, their whole life a story of misery and nothing else? And then comes death! How to believe these few people?

Either they are lying or they are deceived themselves. Either they are lying for some other purpose, or they are a little mad, deceived by their own illusions. They are living in a wish-fulfillment. They wanted to be happy and they started believing that they were happy. It seems more like a belief, a desperate belief, rather than a fact. But how did it come to happen that very few people ever become happy?

If you forget man, if you don't pay much attention to man, then Buddha, Krishna, Christ, they will look more true. If you look at the trees, if you look at the birds, if you look at the stars, then everything is shimmering in tremendous happiness. Then bliss seems to be the very stuff the existence is made of. Only man is unhappy.

Something deep down has gone wrong.

Buddha is not deceived and he is not lying. And I say this to you, not on the authority of the tradition—I say this to you on my own authority. Man can be happy, more happy than the birds, more happy than the trees, more happy than the stars—because man has something which no tree, no bird, no star, has. Man has consciousness!

But when you have consciousness then two alternatives are possible: either you can become unhappy or you can become happy. Then it is your own choice! Trees are simply happy because they cannot be unhappy. Their happiness is not their

170

freedom—they *have* to be happy. They don't know how to be unhappy; there is no alternative.

These birds chirping in the trees, they are happy! not because they have chosen to be happy—they are simply happy because they don't know any other way to be. *Their* happiness is unconscious. It is simply natural.

Man can be tremendously happy, *and* tremendously unhappy— and he is free to choose. This freedom is hazardous. This freedom is very dangerous—because *you* become responsible. And something has happened with this freedom, something has gone wrong. Man is somehow standing on his head.

You have come to me seeking meditation. Meditation is needed only because you have not chosen to be happy. If you have chosen to be happy there is no need for any meditation. Meditation is medicinal: if you are ill then the medicine is needed. Buddhas don't need meditation. Once you have started choosing happiness, once you have decided that you have to be happy, then no meditation is needed. Then meditation starts happening of its own accord.

Meditation is a function of being happy. Meditation follows a happy man like a shadow: wherever he goes, whatsoever he is doing, he is meditative. He is intensely concentrated.

The word 'meditation' and the word 'medicine' come from the same root—that is very significant. Meditation is also medicinal. You don't carry bottles of medicines and prescriptions with you if you are healthy. Of course, when you are not healthy you have to go the doctor. Going to the doctor is not a very great thing to brag about. One should be happy so the doctor is not needed.

So many religions are there because so many people are unhappy. A happy person needs no religion; a happy person needs no temple, no church—because for a happy person the whole universe is a temple, the whole existence is a church. The happy person has nothing like religious activity because his whole life is religious.

Whatsoever you do with happiness is a prayer: your work

becomes worship; your very breathing has an intense splendour
to it, a grace. Not that you constantly repeat the name of God—
only foolish people do that—because God has no name, and by
repeating some assumed name you simply dull your own mind.
By repeating His name you are not going to go anywhere. A
happy man simply comes to see God is everywhere. You need
happy eyes to see Him.

What has gone wrong?

I have heard about a man who became very famous in
Germany—even today his statues are there and some squares
and some streets are still named after him. His name was
Dr. Daniel Gottlieb Schreber. He was the real founder of
Fascism. He died in 1861, but he created the situation for
Adolf Hitler to come—of course, unknowingly.

This man ". . . had very pronounced views on how to bring
up children. He wrote many books. Those books were translat-
ed into many languages. Some of them ran into fifty editions."
His books were loved tremendously, respected tremendously,
because his views were not exceptional—his views were very
common. He was saying things which everybody has believed
down the centuries. He was the spokesman for the ordinary
mind, the mediocre mind.

"Hundreds of clubs and societies were set up to perpetuate
his thoughts, his ideas, and when he died many statues were
installed, many streets were named after him.

"He believed in disciplining children from the time they
were six months old"—because he said if you don't discipline a
child when he is six months old you will miss the real opportunity of disciplining him. When a child is very tender and soft,
unaware of the ways of the world, make a deep imprint—then
he will always follow that imprint. And he will not even be
aware that he is being manipulated. He will think he is doing all
this of his own will—because when a child is six months old he
has no will yet; the will will come later on, and the discipline
will come earlier than the will. So the will will always think:
'This is my own idea.'

This is corrupting a child. But all the religions of the world

172

and all the demagogues and all the dictatorial people of the world, and all the so-called gurus and the priests, they all have believed in doing this.

This seems to be the basic cause why man is unhappy, because no man is moving freely, no man is sensing, groping his path with his own consciousness. He has been corrupted at the very root.

But Schreber called it discipline, as all parents call it. "He believed in disciplining children from the time they were six months old in such a way that they would never after question their parents and *yet believe* that they were acting of their own free will. He wrote that on the first appearance of self-will one has to . . ." stop it immediately, kill it immediately. When you see the child becoming a person, an individual, you have to destroy the first ray of his individuality, immediately, not a single moment should be lost.

When the first appearance of self-will is noticed ". . . one has to step forward in a positive manner . . . stern words, threatening gestures, rapping against the bed . . . bodily admonishments, consistently repeated until the child calms down or falls asleep.

"This treatment was needed only once or twice or at the most thrice," the doctor told people.

Make the child so afraid, shake him to his very roots! And those roots are very tender yet — a six-month-old child. Threaten him with gestures, with a deep hatred, enmity in your eyes, as if you are going to destroy the child himself. Make it clear to the child that either he can live or his self-will — both cannot be allowed to live. If he wants his self-will then he will have to die. Once the child comes to know that he can live only at the cost of self-will, he will drop his self-will and he will choose survival. That's natural! Survival one has to choose first; everything else comes secondary.

"And then one is master of the child forever. From now on, a glance, a word or a single threatening gesture is sufficient to rule the child."

What happened to his own children? Nobody bothered. Everybody liked the idea. Parents all over the world became very enthusiastic and everybody started trying to discipline their children. And that's how, according to Schreber, the whole of Germany was disciplined. That paved the way for Adolf Hitler.

Such a beautiful country, intelligent, became the victim of a fool who was almost mad. And he ruled the whole country. How was it possible? It is still a question which has not been answered. How could he rule so many intelligent people so easily, with such foolish ideas?

These people were trained to believe; these people were trained not to be individuals. These people were trained always to remain in discipline. These people were trained that obedience is the greatest virtue. It is not! Sometimes it is disobedience which is the greatest virtue. Sometimes, of course, it is obedience. But the choice has to be yours: you have consciously to choose whether to obey or not to obey. That means you have consciously to remain the master in every situation, whether you obey or you disobey.

What happened to his own children? Just now the whole history of his children has come to light.

"One of his daughters was melancholic and her doctor suggested putting her in a mad asylum. One of his sons suffered a nervous breakdown and was institutionalized. He recovered, but eight years later had a relapse and died in a madhouse. His other son went mad and committed suicide." And the autopsies of both the sons proved that there was nothing wrong physically with their brains — still both went mad: one died in a madhouse, another committed suicide.

What happened? Physically their brains were perfect, but psychologically they were damaged. This mad father damaged all of his children. And that is what has happened to the whole of humanity.

Down the centuries, parents have been destroying people. They were destroyed by their parents, and so on and so forth. It seems to be a chronic state. Your parents were not happy; whatsoever they knew made them only more unhappy and more unhappy — and they trained you for it, and they have made a replica of themselves in you.

Arthur Koestler has coined a beautiful word for this whole nonsense. He calls it 'bapucracy'. 'Bapu' means father — it is an Indian term. Indians used to call Mahatma Gandhi, 'bapu'. This word 'bapucracy' is perfect. India suffers more than any other country from bapucracy. The Indian leadership is still suffering from its bapu, Mahatma Gandhi.

Each child is destroyed by the bapus. Of course, they were destroyed by their bapus. So I am not saying that it is their responsibility; it is an unconscious, chronic state that perpetuates itself. So there is no need of complaining against your parents — that is not going to help. The day you understand it, you have to consciously drop it and come out of it.

Be an individual if you want to be happy. If you want to be happy, then start choosing on your own. There are many times when you will have to be disobedient — be! There are many times when you will have to be rebellious — be! There is no disrespect implied in it. Be respectful to your parents. But remember that your deepest responsibility is towards your own being.

Everybody is dragged and manipulated, so nobody knows what his destiny is. What you really always wanted to do you have forgotten. And how can you be happy? Somebody who could have been a poet is just a moneylender. Somebody who could have been a painter is a doctor. Somebody who could have been a doctor, a beautiful doctor, is a businessman. Everybody is displaced. Everybody is doing something that he never wanted to do — hence unhappiness.

Happiness happens when you fit with your life, when you fit so harmoniously that whatsoever you are doing is your joy. Then suddenly you will come to know: meditation follows you. If you love the work that you are doing, if you love the way you are living, then you are meditative. Then nothing distracts you. When things distract you, that simply shows that you are not really interested in those things.

The teacher goes on telling the small children: "Pay attention to me! Be attentive!" They *are* attentive, but they are attentive somewhere else. A cuckoo is crying with all its heart outside the

175

school building, and the child *is* attentive — nobody can say he is not attentive, nobody can say he is not meditative, nobody can say he is not in deep concentration — he *is*. In fact, he has completely forgotten the teacher and the arithmetic that he is doing on the board. He is completely oblivious. He is completely possessed by the cuckoo. And the teacher says: "Be attentive! What are you doing? Don't be distracted!" In fact, the teacher is distracting.

The child is attentive — it is happening naturally. Listening to the cuckoo, he is happy. The teacher is distracting and the teacher says: "You are not attentive." He is simply stating a lie. The child *was* attentive. The cuckoo was more attractive to him, so what can he do? The teacher was not so attractive. The arithmetic has no appeal. But we are *not* born here to be mathematicians. There are a few children who will not be interested in the cuckoo. The cuckoo may go on getting madder and madder, and they will be attentive to the blackboard. Then arithmetic is for them. Then they have a meditation, a natural meditative state.

We have been distracted into unnatural motivations: money, prestige, power. Listening to the cuckoo is not going to give you money. Listening to the cuckoo is not going to give you power, prestige. Watching the butterfly is not going to help you economically, politically, socially. These things are not paying, but these things make you happy.

A real person takes the courage to move with things that make him happy. If he remains poor, he remains poor; he has no complaint about it, he has no grudge. He says: "I have chosen my way — I have chosen the cuckoos and the butterflies and the flowers. I cannot be rich, that's okay! But *I am rich* because I am happy."

This type of man will never need any method to concentrate, because there is no need — he *is* in concentration. His concentration is spread all over his life. Twenty-four hours he is in concentration.

Man has gone topsy-turvy. I was reading:

176

Old Ted had been sitting on the edge of the river for some hours without getting a bite. The combination of several bottles of beer and a hot sun caused him to nod off, and he was completely unprepared when a lively fish got himself hooked, tugged at his line and woke him up. He was caught completely off balance and, before he could recover, found himself in the river.

A small boy had been watching the proceedings with interest. As the man struggled to get out of the water, he turned to his father and asked, "Dad, is that man catching a fish or is that fish catching a man?"

Man has gone completely topsy-turvy. The fish is catching you and dragging you; you are not catching the fish. Wherever you see money, you are no more yourself. Wherever you see power, prestige, you are no more yourself. Wherever you see respectability, you are no more youself. Immediately you forget everything — you forget the intrinsic values of your life, your happiness, your joy, your delight.

You always choose something of the outside, and you bargain with something of the inside. You lose the within and you gain the without. But what are you going to do? Even if you get the whole world at your feet and you have lost yourself, even if you have conquered all the riches of the world and you have lost your own inner treasure, what are you going to do with it? This is the misery.

I F YOU CAN learn one thing with me, then that one thing is: Be alert, aware, about your own inner motives, about your own inner destiny. Never lose sight of it, otherwise you will be unhappy. And when you are unhappy, then people say: "Meditate and you will become happy!" They say: "Concentrate and you will become happy; pray and you will become happy; go to the temple, be religious, be a Christian or a Hindu and you will be happy!" This is all nonsense.

Be happy! and meditation will follow. Be happy, and religion will follow. Happiness is a basic condition. People become religious only when they are unhappy—then their religion is pseudo. Try to understand why you are unhappy.

Many people come to me and they say they are unhappy, and they want me to give them some meditation. I say: First, the basic thing is to understand why you are unhappy. And if you don't remove those basic causes of your unhappiness, I can give you a meditation, but that is not going to help very much— because the basic causes remain there.

The man may have been a good, beautiful dancer, and he is sitting in an office, piling up files. There is no possibility for dance. The man may have enjoyed dancing under the stars, but he is simply going on accumulating a bank-balance. And he says he is unhappy: "Give me some meditation." I can give him!— but what is that meditation going to do? what is it supposed to do? He will remain the same man: accumulating money, competitive in the market. The meditation may help in this way: it may make him a little more relaxed to *do* this nonsense even better.

That's what TM is doing to many people in the West—and that is the appeal of transcendental meditation, because Maharishi Mahesh Yogi goes on saying, "It will make you more efficient in your work, it will make you more successful. If you are a salesman, you will become a more successful salesman. It will give you efficiency." And American people are almost crazy about efficiency. You can lose everything just for being efficient. Hence, the appeal.

Yes, it can help you. It can relax you a little—it is a tranquillizer. By constantly repeating a mantra, by continuously repeating a certain word, it changes your brain chemistry. It is a tranquillizer! a sound-tranquillizer. It helps you to lessen your stress so tomorrow in the marketplace you can be more efficient, more capable to compete—but it doesn't change you, it is not a transformation.

Just the other day, a small sannyasin asked me—whenever he comes he asks beautiful questions—very small, maybe seven years old. When he took sannyas . . . he must be courageous— he took sannyas before his mother decided to take sannyas; he took sannyas before his father decided to take sannyas. Has an individuality of his own. He took sannyas and I asked him, "Have you something to say?"

He said, "Yes, what group should I do?"

And the other night he came and I asked, "Now, what do you have to say?"

He said, "What do you think about Maharishi?" A seven-year-old child!

I told him, "Maharishi is a good man, a very nice guy—but doing very ordinary work."

You can repeat a mantra, you can do a certain meditation; it can help you a little bit here and there—but it can help you to remain whatsoever you are. It is not a transformation.

Hence, my appeal is only for those who are really daring, dare-devils who are ready to change their very pattern of life, who are ready to stake everything—because in fact you don't have anything to put at the stake: only your unhappiness, your misery. But people cling even to that.

I have heard:

In a certain remote training camp, a squad of rookies had just returned to their billet after a day's route-march under the boiling sun.

"What a life!" said one new soldier. "Miles from anywhere, a sergeant who thinks he's Attila the Hun, no women, no booze, no leave—and on top of all that, my boots are two sizes too small."

"You don't want to put up with that, chum," said his neighbour. "Why don't you put in for another pair?"

"Not likely," came the reply. "Taking 'em off is the only pleasure I've got!"

What else do you have to put at the stake? Just the misery. The only pleasure that you have got is talking about it. Look at people talking about their misery: how happy they become! They pay for it: they go to psychoanalysts to talk about their misery— they pay for it! Somebody listens attentively, they are very happy.

People go on talking about their misery again and again and

again. They even exaggerate, they decorate, they make it look bigger. They make it look bigger than life-size. Why? Nothing do you have to put at the stake. But people cling to the known, to the familiar. The misery is all that they have known — that is their life. Nothing to lose, but so afraid to lose.

With me, happiness comes first, joy comes first. A celebrating attitude comes first. A life-affirming philosophy comes first. Enjoy! If you cannot enjoy your work, change. Don't wait! because all the time that you are waiting you are waiting for Godot. Godot is never to come. One simply waits — and wastes one's life. For whom, for what are you waiting?

If you see the point, that you are miserable in a certain pattern of life, then all the old traditions say: *You* are wrong. I would like to say: The pattern is wrong. Try to understand the difference of emphasis. *You are not wrong!* Just your pattern, the way you have learnt to live is wrong. The motivations that you have learnt and accepted as yours are not yours — they don't fulfill your destiny. They go against your grain, they go against your element.

The village policeman stopped his son in the road as he saw him going home after a day's fishing.

"Any luck, son?" he asked.

"Yes, Dad," said the lad, opening his basket to show half a dozen lovely trout.

"That's marvellous! Where did you catch all those?"

"Just down there, Dad. There's a narrow lane marked 'Private' and you go down there until you come to a notice saying 'Trespassers Will Be Prosecuted'. A few yards further on there's a pool with a big sign 'No Fishing Allowed' — and that's the place."

Remember it: nobody else can decide for you. All their commandments, all their orders, all their moralities, are just to kill you. You have to decide for yourself. You have to take your life in your own hands. Otherwise, life goes on knocking at your door and you are never there — you are always somewhere else.

If you were going to be a dancer, life comes from that door

180

because life thinks you must be a dancer by now. It knocks there but you are not there—you are a banker. And how is life expected to know that you would become a banker? God comes to you the way He wanted you to be; He knows only that address— but you are never found there, you are somewhere else, hiding behind somebody else's mask, in somebody else's garb, under somebody else's name.

How do you expect God to find you? He goes on searching for you. He knows your name, but you have forgotten that name. He knows your address, but you never lived at that address. You allowed the world to distract you.

It happened:

"I dreamt I was a kid last night," Joe was telling Al, "and I had a free pass to all the rides at Disneyland. Boy, what a time I had! I didn't have to choose which rides to go on—I rode them all."

"That's interesting," remarked his friend. "I had a vivid dream last night too. I dreamt a beautiful dreamgirl blonde knocked on my door and knocked me out with her desire. Then just as we were getting started, another visitor, a gorgeous well-stacked brunette came in and wanted me too!"

"Wow," interrupted Joe. "Boy, would I have loved to be there! Why didn't you call me?"

"I did," responded Al. "And your mother told me you were at Disneyland."

God can find you only in one way, only in one way can He find you, and that is your inner flowering: as He wanted you to be. Unless you find your spontaneity, unless you find your element, you cannot be happy. And if you cannot be happy, you cannot be meditative.

WHY DID this idea arise in people's minds? that meditation brings happiness. In fact, wherever they found a happy person they always found a meditative mind—both things got associated. Whenever they found the beautiful meditative milieu surrounding a man, they always found he was tremendously happy — vibrant with bliss, radiant. They became associated. They thought: Happiness comes when you are meditative. It was just the other way round: meditation comes when you are happy.

But to be happy is difficult and to learn meditation is easy. To be happy means a drastic change in your way of life, an abrupt change — because there is no time to lose. A sudden change — a sudden clash of thunder — a discontinuity.

That's what I mean by sannyas: a discontinuity with the past. A sudden clash of thunder, and you die to the old and you start afresh, from ABC. You are born again. You again start your life as you would have done if there had been no enforced pattern by your parents, by your society, by the state; as you would have done, must have done, if there had been nobody to distract you. But you were distracted.

You have to drop all those patterns that have been forced on you, and you have to find your own inner flame.

Don't be too much concerned about money, because that is the greatest distraction against happiness. And the irony of ironies is that people think they will be happy when they have money. Money has nothing to do with happiness. If *you* are happy and you have money, you can use it for happiness. If you are unhappy and you have money, you will use that money for more unhappiness. Because money is simply a neutral force.

I am not against money, remember. Don't misinterpret me: I am not against money — I am not against anything. Money is a means. If you are happy and you have money, you will become more happy. If you are unhappy and you have money, you will become more unhappy because what will you do with your money? Your money will enhance your pattern, whatsoever it is. If you are miserable and you have power, what will you do with your power? You will poison yourself more with your power, you will become more miserable.

But people go on looking for money as if money is going to bring happiness. People go on looking for respectability as if respectability is going to give you happiness. People are ready, at any moment, to change their pattern, to change their ways, if more money is available somewhere else.

I have heard:

The treasurer of a black civil rights organization picked up the phone and heard a Southern voice drawling on the other end of the line, "Hey there, boy, I want to talk to the head nigger."

Shocked and outraged, the treasurer said, "My dear sir....."

"I want to contribute $50,000 to your cause, so let me talk to the head nigger," the redneck said.

"Hold the line there, brother," the treasurer said. "I think I see that ugly jigaboo coming in the door right now."

Once money is there immediately everything changes.

I have heard:

Mulla Nasrudin's daughter came home and she said she was pregnant and the richest man of the town was the father of the unborn child. Mulla Nasrudin was, of course, mad. He rushed with his gun towards the rich man's house; he forced the rich man into a corner and said, "Now you can breathe your last, or if you have any prayer to say to God, say it!"

The rich man smiled and he said, "Listen, before you do anything neurotic. Yes, I know your daughter is pregnant by me — but if a boy is born I have kept one lakh rupees in the bank for the boy. If a daughter is born I have kept fifty thousand rupees in the bank for the daughter."

Mulla took his gun away and said, "Sir, if something goes wrong, if there is a miscarriage or something, are you ready to give her another chance?"

Once the money is there, then suddenly you are no more yourself; you are ready to change.

This is the way of the worldly man. I don't call those people worldly who have money — I call those people worldly who change their motives for money. I don't call those people unworldly who have no money — they may be simply poor. I call those people unworldly who don't change their motives for money. Just being poor is not equivalent to being spiritual; and just being rich is not equivalent to being a materialist. The materialistic pattern of life is that where money predominates over everything. The non-materialistic life is that where money is just a means—happiness predominates, joy predominates; your own individuality predominates. You know who you are and where you are going, and you are not distracted. Then suddenly you will see your life has a meditative quality to it.

But somewhere on the way, everybody has missed. You were brought up by people who have not arrived. You were brought up by people who were unhealthy themselves. Feel sorry for them! I am not saying be against them; I am not condemning them—remember. Just feel compassion for them. The parents, the school-teachers, the university professors, the so-called leaders of the society—they were unhappy people. They have created an unhappy pattern in you.

And: you have not yet taken charge of your life. They were living under a misinterpretation—that was their misery. And you are also living under a misinterpretation.

It happened:

In the days of the British Raj in India, a young subaltern travelled to a distant part of the Punjab to join his first regiment. He reported to the Colonel who welcomed him and then said, "You must understand, Skiffington-Smythe, that we need a very special type of officer out here. Someone who can handle the natives, someone who can think for himself and keep cool in a tight spot. So we have devised a little test which all new officers are requested to undergo. Are you willing to have a try?"

"Certainly, sir," said the keen young officer, "anything you say, sir."

"Very good," said the Colonel. "Now, the test is quite simple. It's in two parts: first of all you must go down to the village marketplace, where you will take hold of the first woman you see, rip off her veil and kiss her full on the lips. This is quite a dangerous procedure, since the men here are very jealous of their womenfolk and carry wicked-looking knives with them at all times. So you must kiss this woman and make good your escape. Then you must go into the jungle and shoot the first tiger you see right between the eyes. You must kill it with one shot—right between the eyes. All clear?"

"Yes, sir," replied the subaltern.

And with that the Colonel handed the young officer a rifle with one round, and one round only, up to the spout. The brave young man saluted, turned on his heel, and was gone.

A week later the Colonel heard a scratching at his door. He shouted for whoever it was to come in: the door slowly opened and a figure collapsed across the mat. It was Skiffington-Smythe!

Bruised, battered and bleeding from a dozen wounds, he crawled across the floor, hauled himself painfully to his feet at the Colonel's desk, saluted weakly and gasped, "Right, sir . . . . . . where's this woman I've got to shoot between the eyes?!"

Get it?! He kissed a tiger!—got mixed up. And when I look at you, I see the same problem. Something has gone very deeply wrong. You have misunderstood the instructions.

MEDITATION comes naturally to a happy person. Meditation comes automatically to a joyous person. Meditation is very simple to a person who can celebrate, who can delight in life. You are trying it from the other way—which is not possible.

This is the whole meaning of this small Zen anecdote— simple and yet very significant.

> Once there was a man of Ch'i who wanted gold. At dawn he put on his coat and cap and set out for the market.
>
> He went to the stall of a dealer in gold, snatched his gold, and made off.

The police caught him and questioned
him. "Why did you snatch somebody else's
gold, and in front of so many people?"
The man replied:
"At the time when I took it I didn't see
the people—I only saw the gold."

It is a parable. It says: If you know exactly what you want, you
only see that. Concentration comes easy. If you know exactly
what you want, then the whole life and the whole world goes
on its own way—you don't see it even. You go like an arrow
You are not distracted.

But if you don't know what you are meant to be here, if you
don't know what your destiny is, if you don't know what you
really want, then everything is a distraction, then you are pulled
in this direction and that. Then continuously you go on being
pulled in many directions—and that creates a mess out of you.

You are pulled in so many directions together that your personality becomes broken, split. Only fragments: one fragment
going to the north, another fragment going to the south. You
are continuously in conflict. You don't know where you are
going, because you are not one any more. You become one when
you know what you want.

Many people come to me and I ask them: "What do you want
really?" They shrug their shoulders. They say, "We don't
know." Then it is obvious that your life cannot have any organic
unity in it. You don't have any sense of direction. You have
been misguided. But—it is never too late. You can take posses-
sion of your life any moment. If you decide, then the first thing
is: don't listen to the parental voice within you, don't listen to
the school-teacher's voice within you.

You can do a small technique to get rid of all this. You can
just sit on your bed every night before you go to sleep, close your
eyes, and just try to feel: whatsoever you want, is it your own?
that wanting, that desiring. And try to find out, try to check it
out, to whom that voice belongs.

If you listen silently you will be surprised: your mother is saying, "Become a doctor!" And you will be able to know exactly who is saying this. Your father is saying, "Become rich!" Your brother is saying something else, your teachers are saying something else, your neighbours are saying something else.

And not only that: your father is saying something with his lips and another thing with his eyes; saying one thing, meaning another thing. He says, "Be honest, be true!" and you know he himself is not honest and is not true. And you can see it in his eyes—children are very perceptive. They look deep; their eyes go very deep, they can penetrate—they can see the father is lying. He himself is not honest, he himself is not true.

It happens: he is inside the house and somebody knocks at the door, and he sends the child to tell him that the father has gone out. He lies! The father is saying, "Don't beat your small brother—you are stronger, you are bigger," and the father goes on beating him himself—and he is very strong and very big, and takes every advantage that he can. One thing he is saying, another thing the child is reading. He goes on reading the indirect message.

In the school something is taught, and life needs something else. Confusion arises, conflict arises, contradictions go on getting together, and then they pull you in different directions— then you are no longer together, your unity is lost. A child is born as an organic unity. By the time you have become young, you are no more an individual, you are no more a unity. You are a crowd, a mad crowd.

This you have to understand: it is something that you have *learnt* from others. And remember—one of the basic truths of life—that which you have learnt can be unlearnt. That which you have learnt from others is nothing natural to you: you can erase it. Just a conscious awareness is needed; it can be erased and the slate can become clean again.

So the first thing is to erase all that has been forced on you, and only then will you be able to listen to your own heart's voice.

Many people come to me and they say, "How to distinguish what is what—what is mind's voice and what is heart's voice?" It is difficult to distinguish right now: first you have to clean the mind. The heart's voice is very still and very small. The mind's is very noisy: it goes on shouting things. The heart whispers. The mind shouts.

Your father used to shout at you. Your mother used to shout at you. The teachers in the school used to shout at you. The mind shouts. God speaks in whispers. First this shouting has to be dropped, otherwise it is very difficult. And many people have followed Dr. Daniel Gottlieb Schreber's methods. They have put their voice in you at such an early stage that it seems as if it is your own heart's voice.

One thing is certain: you can never become anything other than yourself, and unless you become yourself you cannot be happy. Happiness happens only when a rosebush grows rose-flowers; when it flowers, when it has its own individuality. You may be a rosebush and trying to flower as lotus flower—that is creating insanity.

Erase the mind. And the way to erase it is not by fight: the way to erase it is just to become aware.

Every night for at least one hour, sit in your bed and just watch from where you hear something—just go to the very roots of it. Trace it out, go backwards, find out from where it comes. You will always find the source, and the moment you have found the source you will feel an unburdening. Suddenly it is no more yours—now you are not deceived by it.

It is slow work, but if you work, after a few months you will be feeling so clean—your book clean, nobody else writing in it. Then, only then will you be able to hear that still small voice. And once you hear it, the very hearing is like a sudden clash of thunder. Suddenly you are together, suddenly you have a direc-tion—suddenly you know where your gold is. And then you don't see anybody; you simply go like an arrow towards your destiny.

I T IS very easy to follow your parents, it is very easy to follow your teachers, it is very easy to follow the society, it is very easy to be obedient—to be rebellious, to be on your own, is very difficult. But growth comes the hard way.

188

Let me tell you one small anecdote to end with:

There was once a farmer who, after a poor crop, complained: "If God would only let me control the weather, everything would be better, because He apparently does not know very much about farming."

That's true! Nobody has ever heard about God being a farmer — how can He know?

The Lord said to him: "For one year I will give you control of the weather; ask for whatever you wish and you will get it."

In the old days God used to do that. Then He got fed up.

The poor man became very happy and immediately said, "Now I want sun," and the sun came out. Later he said, "Let the rain fall," and it rained. For a whole year first the sun shone and then it rained. The seed grew and grew, it was a pleasure to watch it. "Now God can understand how to control the weather," he said proudly. The crop had never been so big, so green, such a luscious green.

Then it was time to harvest. The farmer took his sickle to cut the wheat, but his heart sank. The stalks were practically empty. The Lord came and asked him, "How is your crop?"

The man complained, "Poor, my Lord, very poor!"

"But didn't you control the weather? Didn't everything you wanted turn out all right?"

"Of course! and that is the reason I am perplexed—I got the rain and the sunshine I asked for, but there is no crop."

Then the Lord said, "But have you never asked for wind, storms, ice and snow, and everything that purifies the air and makes the roots hard and resistant? You asked for rain and sunshine, but not for bad weather. That's the reason there is no crop."

Life is possible only through challenges. Life is possible only when you have both good weather and bad weather, when you have both pleasure and pain, when you have both winter and

189

summer, day and night. When you have both sadness and happiness, discomfort and comfort. Life moves between these two polarities.

Moving between these two polarities you learn how to balance. Between these two wings you learn how to fly to the farthest star.

If you choose comfort, convenience, you choose death. That's how you have missed real happiness: you have chosen convenience instead. It is very convenient to follow the parental voice, convenient to follow the priest, convenient to follow the church, convenient to follow the society and the state. It is very easy to say yes to all these authorities—but then you never grow. You are trying to get life's treasure too cheap. It requires that you have to pay for it.

Be an individual and pay for it. In fact, if you get something without paying for it, don't accept it—that is insulting to you. *Don't* accept it; that is below you. Say: "I will pay for it—only then will I accept it." In fact, if something is given to you without your being ready for it, without your being capable for it, without your being receptive for it, you will not be able to possess it for long. You will lose it somewhere or other. You will not be able to appreciate its value.

God never gives you anything cheap—because given without any effort on your part, you will never be able to rejoice in it.

Choose the hard way. And to be an individual is the hardest thing in the world, because nobody likes you to be an individual. Everybody wants to kill your individuality and to make a sheep out of you. Nobody wants you to be on your own. Hence, you go on missing happiness, you go on missing direction, and, naturally, meditation has become impossible, concentration seems to be almost non-existent. You cannot concentrate, you cannot meditate, you cannot be with anything for more than a split second. How can you be blissful?

Choose your own destiny. I cannot show it to you, what your destiny is—nobody else knows it, not even you. You have to sense it, and you have to move slowly.

190

First, drop all that is borrowed on your being and then you will be able to feel. It always leads you to the right place, to the right goal. The thing that you call conscience right now, it is not your conscience. It is a substitute—pseudo-conscience, fake, counterfeit. Drop it! and by its very dropping, you will be able to see hidden behind it your real conscience which has been waiting for you. Once that conscience comes into your consciousness your life has a direction, meditation follows you like a shadow.

Yes, that man was right. He said:

> *"At the time when I took it I did not see*
> *the people—I only saw the gold."*

When you have felt and sensed your destiny, you see only your destiny, you see only the gold.

CHAPTER 8

Only compassion is therapeutic.

The dilemma: which centre to choose?

*What is the difference between
non-doing and being lazy?*

Comparative studies. . .?

CHOICELESSNESS IS BLISS

eighteenth august 1976

The first question: *"Only compassion is therapeutic" you said. Could you comment on the word 'compassion', compassion for oneself and compassion for the other?*

Yes, only compassion is therapeutic—because all that is ill in man is because of lack of love. All that is wrong with man is somewhere associated with love. He has not been able to love, or he has not been able to receive love. He has not been able to share his being. That's the misery. That creates all sorts of complexes inside.

Those wounds inside can surface in many ways: they can become physical illness, they can become mental illness—but deep down man suffers from lack of love. Just as food is needed for the body, love is needed for the soul. The body cannot survive without food, and the soul cannot survive without love.

In fact, without love the soul is never born—there is no question of its survival.

You simply think that you have a soul; you believe that you have a soul because of your fear of death. But you have not known unless you have loved. Only in love does one come to feel that one is more than the body, more than the mind.

That's why I say compassion is therapeutic. What is compassion? Compassion is the purest form of love. Sex is the lowest form of love, compassion the highest form of love. In sex the contact is basically physical; in compassion the contact is basically spiritual. In love, compassion and sex are both mixed, the physical and the spiritual are both mixed. Love is midway between sex and compassion.

You can call compassion prayer also. You can call compassion meditation also. The highest form of energy is compassion. The word 'compassion' is beautiful: half of it is 'passion' —somehow passion has become so refined that it is no more like passion. It has become compassion.

In sex, you use the other, you reduce the other to a means, you reduce the other to a thing. That's why in a sexual relationship you feel guilty. That guilt has nothing to do with religious teachings; that guilt is deeper than religious teachings. In a sexual relationship *as such* you feel guilty. You feel guilty because you are reducing a human being to a thing, to a commodity to be used and thrown away.

That's why in sex you also feel a sort of bondage—*you* are also being reduced to a thing. And when you are a thing your freedom disappears, because your freedom exists only when you are a person. The more you are a person, the more free; the more you are a thing, the less free.

The furniture in your room is not free. If you leave the room locked and you come after many years, the furniture will be in the same place, in the same way; it will not arrange itself in a new way. It has no freedom. But if you leave a man in the room, you will not find him the same—not even the next day—not even the next moment. You cannot find the same man again.

Says old Heraclitus: *You cannot step in the same river twice.*

196

You cannot come across the same man again. It is impossible to meet the same man twice—because man is a river, continuously flowing. You never know what is going to happen. The future remains open.

For a thing, future is closed. A rock will remain a rock, will remain a rock. It has no potentiality for growth. It cannot change, it cannot evolve. A man never remains the same. May fall back, may go ahead; may go into hell or into heaven—but never remains the same. Goes on moving, this way or that.

When you have a sexual relationship with somebody, you have reduced that somebody to a thing. And in reducing him you have reduced yourself also to a thing, because it is a mutual compromise that 'I allow you to reduce me to a thing, you allow me to reduce you to a thing. I allow you to use me, you allow me to use you. We use each other. We both have become things.'

That's why . . . watch two lovers: when they have not yet settled, the romance is still alive, the honeymoon has not ended, and you will see two persons throbbing with life, ready to explode—ready to explode the unknown. And then watch a married couple, the husband and the wife, and you will see two dead things, two graveyards, side by side—helping each other to remain dead, forcing each other to remain dead. That is the constant conflict of the marriage. Nobody wants to be reduced to a thing!

Sex is the lowest form of that energy 'X'. If you are religious, call it 'God'; if you are scientific, call it 'X'. This energy, X, can become love. When it becomes love, then you start respecting the other person. Yes, sometimes you use the other person, but you feel thankful for it. You never say thankyou to a thing. When you are in love with a woman and you make love to her, you say thankyou. When you make love to your wife, have you ever said thankyou? No, you take it for granted. Has your wife said thankyou to you ever? Maybe, many years before, you can remember some time when you were just undecided, were just trying, courting, seducing each other—maybe. But once you were settled, has she said thankyou to you for anything? You have been doing so many things for her, she has been doing so

197

many things for you, you are both living for each other—but gratitude has disappeared.

In love, there is gratitude, there is a *deep* gratefulness. You know that the other is not a thing. You know that the other has a grandeur, a personality, a soul, an individuality. In love you give total freedom to the other. Of course, you give and you take; it is a give-and-take relationship—but with respect.

In sex, it is a give-and-take relationship with no respect. In compassion, you simply give. There is no idea anywhere in your mind to get anything back—you simply share. Not that nothing comes! millionfold it is returned, but that is just by the way, just a natural consequence. There is no hankering for it.

In love, if you give something, deep down you go on expecting that it should be returned. If it is not returned, you feel complaining. You may not say so, but in a thousand and one ways it can be inferred that you are grumbling, that you are feeling that you have been cheated. Love seems to be a subtle bargain.

In compassion, you simply give. In love, you are thankful because the other has given something to you. In compassion, you are thankful because the other has taken something from you; you are thankful because the other has not rejected you. You had come with energy to give, you had come with many flowers to share, and the other allowed you, the other was receptive. You are thankful because the other was receptive.

Compassion is the highest form of love. Much comes back—millionfold, I say—but that is not the point, you don't hanker for it. If it is not coming there is no complaint about it. If it is coming you are simply surprised! If it is coming, it is unbelievable. If it is not coming there is no problem—you had never given your heart to somebody for any bargain. You simply shower because you *have*. You have so much that if you don't shower you will become burdened. Just like a cloud full of rainwater *has* to shower. And next time when a cloud is showering *watch* silently, and you will always hear, when the cloud has showered and the earth has absorbed, you will always hear the cloud saying to the earth "Thankyou." The earth helped the cloud to unburden.

When a flower has bloomed, it has to share its fragrance to the winds. It is natural! It is not a bargain, it is not a business — it is simply natural! The flower is full of fragrance — what to do? If the flower keeps the fragrance to itself then the flower will feel very, very tense, in deep anguish. The greatest anguish in life is when you cannot express, when you cannot communicate, when you cannot share. The poorest man is he who has nothing to share, or who has something to share but has lost the capacity, the art, of how to share it — then a man is poor.

The sexual man is very poor. The loving man is richer comparatively. The man of compassion is the richest — he is at the top of the world. He has no confinement, no limitation. He simply gives and goes on his way. He does not even wait for you to say a thankyou. With tremendous love he shares his energy.

This is what I call therapeutic.

Christians believe that Jesus did many miracles. I cannot see him doing any miracle. The miracle was his compassion. If anything happened, it happened without his doing it. If anything ever happens in the highest plane of being, it always happens without any effort. He moved; many sorts of people came to him. He was there like a tremendous pool of energy — anybody who was ready to share, shared.

Miracles happened! He *was* therapeutic. He was one of the greatest healers the world has ever known. Buddha, or Mahavir, or Krishna — they are all great healers, on different levels. Yes, you cannot find in Buddha's life any miracle of healing an ill person, or healing a blind man, or bringing a dead person to life. You will be surprised: Was Jesus' compassion more than Buddha's? What happened? Why were many people not healed through Buddha's energy? No. It is not a question of more or less. Buddha's compassion functioned on a different level. He had a different type of audience and a different type of people around him from Jesus.

It always happens — almost always — I go on watching: continuously a stream of people comes to me from the West — they never ask anything about their bodies. They don't come to me and say, "I have a constant headache. Bhagwan, help me, do something!" Or, "My eyes are weak," or, "My concentration is not good," or, "My memory is being lost"—no, never. But Indians come and always something of the physical they bring. Mm? They have had an upset stomach for many years— "Bhagwan, do something!"

Almost always I feel: Why? What has happened to India? Why do these people come only for some bodily, physical problems? They have only those problems. A poor country, a very poor country, has no spiritual problems. A rich country has spiritual problems; a poor country has physical problems.

Buddha's time in India was the golden age. That was the time for India at its peak. The country was rich, tremendously rich, affluent. The whole world was poor, and India was very rich. The people coming to Buddha were bringing spiritual problems. Yes, they were also bringing wounds, but they were spiritual wounds.

Jesus moved in a very poor country, lived in a very poor country. The people who were coming to him had no spiritual problems, in fact, because to have a spiritual problem you have to attain to a certain standard of living. Otherwise, your problems go on being of the lower levels. A poor man has a problem.

Just a few days before, one of my relatives was here. For one month he was here, meditating, doing things. And then on the last day I was hoping he would ask something meaningful. What did he ask? He asked that his son is not doing well. Living one month here, listening to me for one month, this was the only question that came to his mind: his son is not doing well. He drives a taxi, and they have purchased such a car that every day there is some problem or other—"Bhagwan, do something!" I am not a car mechanic! So I told him, "Sell that car!" He said, "Nobody will purchase it, so do something!"

When people are poor, their problems are of the world. When people are rich, their problems are of a higher quality. Only an affluent country can be really spiritual; a poor country cannot be. I am not saying that a poor man cannot be—yes, a poor man can be, exceptions are there—but a poor country cannot be. A poor country, on the whole, thinks in terms of money, medicine, house, car, this and that. And it is natural, it is logical! Jesus moved in a very poor world. People were seeking their own solutions. Many were helped — not that Jesus was helping — they were helped. And Jesus says again and again: "It is your faith that has healed you." When you have faith, compassion can pour into you. When you have faith, you are open to compassion. Buddha did miracles, but those miracles are of the invisible. Mahavir did miracles, but those miracles are of the invisible. You cannot see them — they can only be seen by the person to whom they have happened.

But compassion is always therapeutic; whatsoever your level, it helps you. Compassion is love purified — so much so that you simply give and don't ask anything in return.

Buddha used to say to his disciples, "After each meditation, be compassionate — immediately — because when you meditate, love grows, the heart becomes full. After each meditation, feel compassion for the whole world so that you share your love and you release the energy into the atmosphere and that energy can be used by others."

I would also like to say that to you: After *each* meditation, when you are celebrating, have compassion. Just feel that your energy should go and help people in whatsoever ways they need it. Just release it! You will be unburdened, you will feel very relaxed, you will feel very calm and quiet, and the vibrations that you have released will help many. End your meditations always with compassion.

And compassion is unconditional. You cannot have compassion only for those who are friendly towards you, only for those who are related to you.

It happened in China: When Bodhidharma went to China, a man came to him. He said, "I have followed your teachings: I meditate and then I feel compassion for the whole universe — not only for men, but for animals, for rocks and rivers also. But there is one problem: I cannot feel compassion for my neighbour. No — it is impossible! So you please tell me: can I exclude my neighbour from my compassion? I include the whole existence, known, unknown, but can I exclude my neighbour? — because it is very difficult, impossible. I cannot feel compassion for him."

Bodhidharma said, "Then forget about meditation, because if compassion excludes anybody then it is no more there."

Compassion is all-inclusive — intrinsically all-inclusive. So if you cannot feel compassion for your neighbour, then forget all about meditation — because it has nothing to do with somebody in particular. It has something to do with your inner state. Be compassion! unconditionally, undirected, unaddressed. Then you become a healing force into this world of misery.

Jesus says: "Love thy neighbour as thyself" — again and again. And he also says: "Love thy enemy as thyself." And if you analyse both the sentences together, you will come to find that the neighbour and the enemy are almost always the same person. "Love thy neighbour as thyself" and "Love thy enemy as thyself." What does he mean?

He simply means: don't have any barriers for your compassion, for your love. As you love yourself, love the whole existence — because in the ultimate analysis the whole existence is yourself. It is *you* — reflected in many mirrors. It is *you* — it is not separate from you. Your neighbour is just a form of you; your enemy is also a form of you. Whatsoever you come across, you come across yourself. You may not recognize because you are not very alert; you may not be able to see yourself in the other, but then something is wrong with your vision, something is wrong with your eyes.

COMPASSION is therapeutic. "Could you comment on the word 'compassion', compassion for oneself and compassion for the other?"

Yes, you have to understand that to be compassionate one has to have compassion for oneself in the first place. If you don't love yourself you will never be able to love anybody else. If you are not kind to yourself you cannot be kind to anybody else. Your so-called saints who are so very hard on themselves are just pretenders that they are kind to others. It is not possible. Psychologically it is impossible. If you cannot be kind to yourself, how can you be kind to others?

Whatsoever you are with yourself you are with others. Let that be a basic dictum. If you hate yourself you will hate others — and you have been taught to hate yourself. Nobody has ever said to you, "Love yourself!" The very idea seems absurd — loving oneself? The very idea makes no sense — loving oneself? We always think that to love one needs somebody else. But if you don't learn it with yourself you will not be able to practise it with others.

You have been told, constantly conditioned, that you are not of any worth. From every direction you have been shown, you have been told, that you are unworthy, that you are not what you should be, that you are not accepted as you are. There are many shoulds hanging over your head — and those shoulds are almost impossible to fulfill. And when you cannot fulfill them, when you fall short, you feel condemned. A deep hatred arises in you about yourself.

How can you love others? So full of hatred, where are you going to find love? So you only pretend, you only show that you are in love. Deep down you are not in love with anybody — you cannot be. Those pretensions are good for a few days, then the colour disappears, then reality asserts itself.

Every love-affair is on the rocks. Sooner or later, every love-affair becomes very poisoned. And how does it become so poisoned? Both pretend that they are loving, both go on saying that they love. The father says he loves the child; the child says he loves the father. The mother says she loves her daughter, and the daughter goes on saying the same thing. Brothers say they love each other. The *whole* world talks about love, sings about love — and can you find any other place so loveless? Not an iota of love exists — and mountains of talk! Himalayas of poetry about love.

It seems all these poetries are just compensations. Because we cannot love, we have somehow to believe through poetry, singing, that we love. What we miss in life we put in poetry. What we go on missing in life, we put in the film, in the novel. Love is absolutely absent, because the first step has not been taken yet.

The first step is : accept yourself as you are; drop all shoulds. Don't carry any ought on your heart! You are *not* to be somebody else; you are not expected to do something which doesn't belong to you — you are just to be yourself. Relax! and just be yourself. Be respectful to your individuality, and have the courage to sign your own signature. Don't go on copying others' signatures.

You are not expected to become a Jesus or a Buddha or a Ramakrishna—you are simply expected to become yourself. It was good that Ramakrishna never tried to become somebody else, so he became Ramakrishna. It was good that Jesus never tried to become like Abraham or Moses, so he became Jesus. It is good that Buddha never tried to become a Patanjali or Krishna—that's why he became a Buddha.

When you are not trying to become anybody else, then you simply relax—then a grace arises. Then you are full of grandeur, splendour, harmony—because then there is no conflict! nowhere to go, nothing to fight for; nothing to force, enforce upon yourself violently. You become innocent.

In that innocence you will feel compassion and love for yourself. You will feel so happy with yourself that even if God comes and knocks at your door and says, "Would you like to become somebody else?" you will say, "Have you gone mad?! I am perfect! Thankyou, but never try anything like that—I am perfect as I am."

The moment you can say to God, "I am perfect as I am, I am happy as I am," this is what in the East we call *shraddha* — trust; then you have accepted yourself and in accepting yourself you have accepted your creator. Denying yourself you deny your creator.

If you go and see a painting of Picasso's and you say, "This is wrong and that is wrong, and this colour should have been this way," you are denying Picasso. The moment you say, "I should be like this," you are trying to improve upon God. You are saying, "You committed blunders—I should have been like this, and you have made me like this?" You are trying to improve upon God. It is not possible. Your struggle is in vain—you are doomed to failure.

And the more you fail, the more you hate. The more you fail, the more you feel condemned. The more you fail, the more you feel yourself impotent. And out of this hatred, impotency, how can compassion arise? Compassion arises when you are perfectly grounded in your being. You say, "Yes, this is the way I am." You have no ideals to fulfill. *And immediately fulfillment starts happening!*

The roses bloom so beautifully because they are not trying to become lotuses. And the lotuses bloom so beautifully because they have not heard the legends about other flowers. Everything in nature goes so beautifully in accord, because nobody is trying to compete with anybody, nobody is trying to become anybody else. Everything is the way it is.

Just see the point! Just be yourself and remember you cannot be anything else, whatsoever you do. All effort is futile. You have to be just yourself.

There are only two ways. One is: rejecting, you can remain the same; condemning, you can remain the same; or: accepting, surrendering, enjoying, delighting, you can be the same. Your attitude can be different, but you are going to remain the way you are, the person you are. Once you accept, compassion arises. And then you start accepting others!

Have you watched it?—it is very difficult to live with a saint, very difficult. You can live with a sinner; you cannot live with a saint—because a saint will be condemning you continuously: by his gesture, by his eyes, the way he will look at you, the way he will talk at you. A saint never talks with you—he talks at you. He never just looks at you; he has always some ideals in his eyes, clouding. He never sees *you.* He has something far away and he goes on comparing you with it—and, of course, you always fall short. His very look makes you a sinner. It is very difficult to live with a saint—because he does not accept himself, how can he accept you? He has many things in him, jarring notes he feels, he has to go beyond. Of course, he sees the same things in you in a magnified way.

But to me only that person is a saint who has accepted himself, and in his acceptance has accepted the whole world. To me, that state of mind is what sainthood is: the state of total acceptance. And that is healing, therapeutic. Mm?—just being with somebody who accepts you totally is therapeutic. You will be healed.

As life is. . . . I divide it in three parts : breakfast, lunch, supper. The childhood is the breakfast-time. And as it happens if you have not been given your breakfast today, you will feel very, very hungry, out of all proportion, at lunchtime. And if you have missed lunch also, then of course at supper you will be almost mad. Love is food—that's why I divide life in three: breakfast, lunch, supper.

Love is food: food for the soul. When a child sucks at his mother's breast for the first time, he is sucking two things, not only milk—milk is going into his body and love is going into his soul. Love is invisible, just as soul is invisible; milk is visible just as body is visible. If you have eyes to see, you can see two things together dripping into the child's being from the mother's breast. Milk is just the visible part of love; love is the invisible part of milk—the warmth, the love, the compassion, the blessing.

If the child has missed at his breakfast, then when he is young he will be too needy for love—and that creates trouble. Then he will be too impatient for love—that creates trouble. Then he will be in such a hurry for love—that creates trouble. Because love grows very slowly, it needs patience. And the more you are in a hurry, the more is the possibility that you will miss.

Have you watched it in yourself and in others? The people who are too much in need of love always suffer, because they always feel that nobody is going to fulfill them. In fact, nobody is going to be their mother again. In a mother-child relationship, nothing was expected from the child. What can a child do?—helpless. He cannot return anything. At the most he can smile—that's all—or follow with his eyes where the mother is going—that's all. Small, beautiful gestures—but nothing else can he do. The mother has to give, the child has to receive.

If at breakfast-time you have missed this, then you will be looking for a woman who can be your mother. Now, a woman is looking for a lover, not for a son—trouble is bound to be there. Unless by chance, by accident, you can find some woman who is looking for a son—then things will settle; then two illnesses will fit together.

It always happens: a pessimist always finds an optimist to fit; a sadist always finds a masochist to fit; a dominating person always finds one who is in need of being dominated, then they fit. You cannot find two masochists living together, never. I have watched thousands of couples: up to now I have not been able to come to a single couple in which both the partners are sadists or both the partners are masochists. It is impossible to live together—they have to fit. Only opposites fit, and people always fall in love with the opposite.

If you can meet a woman who is in search of a son . . . that too is ugly, that too is ill, because a woman naturally should be seeking a lover, not a child. And this is the problem, and the problem becomes more complicated: even if she is looking for a son, she is unaware of it; and even if you are looking for a mother, you are unaware of it. In fact, if a woman tries to mother you, you will feel hurt. You will say, "What are you doing? Am I a child?" And you *are* looking for a mother. Thousands, millions of people are looking for a mother.

That's why man seems so much interested in women's breasts— otherwise there is no need to be so much interested in women's breasts. The interest simply shows that in your childhood, at your breakfast-time, you have missed something. It continues, it hovers on your mind, it haunts you. Breasts are for breakfast-time. Now why do you go on thinking and painting—mm? . . .

Just a few days before, a painter was here and he brought a few of his paintings; just breasts and breasts. He became a sannyasin so I said to him, "Now at least you start to grow a little. This is childish!" And he has won many prizes; he is a world-famous painter. His paintings have been exhibited all over the world: in New York, in London, in Paris, in Berlin, and everywhere. And he has been appreciated very much. Of course, must have been appreciated by other children! There is no point in it.

So I told him, "Do something else—breakfast-time is over! You are old enough to do something else."

He said, "I will try."

Now he sends a painting in which I am sitting in the middle—and breasts and breasts all around. So now I am also part! He has tried his best, but difficult to get out of it.

Watch deep down, because it is nothing of your responsibility, it is nothing to do with you—you cannot change your mother now. It happened as it happened—but you can become conscious. You can become conscious of all these things inside. And by becoming conscious a miracle happens. If you become conscious of these things, they start dropping. They can cling to you only in deep unconsciousness. A profound consciousness begins to be a transforming force.

So just become conscious! If you have some childish attitudes towards love, become conscious, find out, search deep. And just by becoming conscious, they drop. So nothing else is needed. Not that first you have to become conscious and then you have to ask "What to do now?" The moment you become conscious they disappear—because by becoming conscious you are becoming adult.

A child is not conscious. A child lives in a deep unconsciousness. By becoming conscious you are becoming adult, mature, so all that was clinging to your unconsciousness will disappear. Just as you bring light in a room and the darkness disappears: bring consciousness deep in your heart.

Then there are people who miss their lunch also. Then in their old age they become what you call 'dirty old people'. Then in their old age they continuously think of sex and nothing else. They may not talk about sex in a direct way—they may start talking *against* sex—but they will talk about sex. Their being against makes no difference.

You go and listen to the so-called saints in India, and you will always find them continuously talking against sex and praising *brahmacharya*. These people have even missed their lunch. Now suppertime has come—and they are mad. Now they know that death is coming any moment. And when death is approaching

208

near, and time is disappearing from their hands, if they become neurotic it seems natural.

These neurotic people have stories in the old scriptures that when they meditate, *apsaras*—beautiful women from heaven—descend. Naked they dance around them. Why should they do such a thing? Who is bothered about an old man sitting in the Himalayas meditating—who is bothered? dead almost—who is bothered? Those *apsaras* from heaven, they can find better people.

In fact, so many people are chasing *apsaras,* how can they find time to chase rishis, these so-called saints? No, it has nothing to do with *apsaras* or with heaven or anything. It is just that these people have missed breakfast and lunch both. And by suppertime their imagination is playing tremendous games with them. It is *their* imagination, starved imagination.

You do one thing: you just go on a fast for three weeks, and then everywhere you will start seeing food—everywhere! Even you may see a full moon rushing into the sky and you will say it looks like bread, a chapati. That's how it will happen. You will start projecting, your imagination will be playing games with you.

If this happens, then compassion never arises. Move slowly, alert, watching, be loving. If you are sexual I don't say drop sex: I say make it more alert, make it more prayerful, make it more profound, so that it can become love. If you are loving, then make it even more grateful; bring deeper gratitude, joy, celebration, prayer to it, meditation to it, so that it can become compassion.

Unless compassion has happened to you, don't think that you have lived rightly or that you have lived at all. Compassion is the flowering. And when compassion happens to one person, millions are healed. Whosoever comes around him is healed. Compassion is therapeutic.

The second question: *Each centre opening brings a different jewel: kundalini, balance, love, expression, a diamond mind. This is the dilemma: which to choose? You say choicelessness is bliss, but society rewards specialists. Also, on the cellular level, the evolution of complex organisms arises out of the increasing specialization of its cells.*

Y ES, my emphasis is not to choose—be choiceless. Because if you choose, you become narrow. Every choice narrows you down. Every choice says, "Now I will have a window to the sky, not the whole sky." Why? Why have a frame to the sky? The sky is frameless. When you stand at a window and look into the sky, you have falsified the sky—because your window-frame looks as if it is framed on the sky. Then you have only a limited vision, narrow.

Why be poor? Why not come out of the house and see the sky as it is—infinite? To me, life is an infinite expanding energy. Don't make any choice!

That's why I don't put sannyas against the world. I say be a sannyasin and be in the world, because a sannyasin, if he chooses the life of the monk and escapes from the world, will be poorer for that—because the world has many things to give to you. It is a tremendously beautiful device of God's—to help you grow, to give you challenges, to give you new adventures; to give you opportunities to test yourself, your awareness, your being.

If you escape from the world you will be escaping from all these opportunities. Sitting in a cave in the Himalayas you will be very poor—poor in the sense that you will not have richness of experience. And by and by you will become stupid. You *will* become silent—that's true—because there will be nothing to distract you. But that silence also *is* of the Himalayas, it is not yours. Come back to the world and in the marketplace you will see your silence has disappeared. It was not yours—it was part of the Himalayan silence. You were deceived by yourself.

When silence happens in the marketplace then it is true, then

210

it is *yours*—now nobody can take it away. Now *no* distraction can be a distraction to you. You can remain anywhere; whatsoever the situation, your silence will remain there as a deep substratum to your being. It is inner.

So I don't say leave the world. I say be in the world and yet be beyond it—so that you can have both the experiences of the sansari, the worldly, and the sannyasi, the other-worldly. When both are possible, why choose? Make life as big as possible. Don't narrow it down.

"Each centre opening brings a different jewel . . . the dilemma is which to choose."

No, no need to choose any centre. All the centres, all the seven chakras of the body, have to function well. All the centres of the body have to function in a unity, in an organic unity. From sex to sahasrar, from the first to the seventh, they should vibrate like an orchestra.

You can choose one centre. That's what people have done: some people have chosen the sex centre—they remain, around and around they go. They move in a circle. Their whole life remains just a process of sexuality—very poor. I don't call them sinners; I simply call them very poor people. And poor by their own choice—when more was possible.

It is as if you have an aeroplane and you yoke bullocks to it and use it as a bullock-cart. You are poor—not a sinner. You are simply foolish, stupid! Or you can use the aeroplane like a truck, like a bus—a little better than the bullock-cart, but still you are foolish. Such a costly vehicle, and you are using it as a bus! A vehicle that can fly into the skies, you are using it as a truck on the road.

That's what is happening. You have a beautiful orchestra within you, the full range, all the colours, all the notes—all that is possible is possible within you, but you cling to one centre: the sex. Somebody clings to some other centre, somebody to some other. And then there are people who think: "Leave all this, and we should just remain in the *ajna* chakra—in the third-eye centre." That too is narrowing down your being. Better than being a bullock-cart but still you are a truck on the road.

Then there are a few who think that they have to use only the sahasrar against all the six—then again you are confining your being. Then you have an aeroplane, but you never get down on the earth. You are going to have a big accident sooner or later because sooner or later the gas will be finished, the petrol will not be there. Flying continuously is dangerous. Sometimes come back to the earth, down to earth; refill the petrol, rest, relax; get ready to fly again. That's the way.

And the earth is beautiful—as much as the sky. The stars are beautiful, but have you watched, sitting in an aeroplane?—you cannot look very long in the sky, it is boring. It is beautiful, but it is monotonous. People start falling asleep sooner or later. They look outside the window for a little while and then they feel bored—it is monotonous. Earth is tremendously beautiful, never monotonous. So many flowers, so many trees, so many birds, so many people.

My emphasis is to live in all the seven centres together. Never lose contact with the lowest, and never avoid flying with the highest. Use all the centres! Then your wings will be in the sky and your roots will be in the earth. And a perfect man is a meeting of heaven and earth—that's what Taoists say: a meeting of heaven and earth. That's what a perfect man is: meeting of the physical and the spiritual, meeting of the body and the soul, meeting of the world and renunciation, meeting of prose and poetry.

AND THE questioner asks: "You say choicelessness is bliss, but society rewards specialists." That's true—society is not interested in your bliss: society is interested in its own efficiency. Society is not bothered whether you are ecstatic or not—that is none of its business. Society wants you to be just efficient mechanisms, robots. Do the work that society wants you to do, and then the society is finished with you. What you do with your own being is none of its business.

In fact, the society wants you not to do anything on your own, because that can become a distraction from efficiency. A man who is very happy cannot be so efficient—because he is so bubbling with happiness that efficiency seems trivial. What does it matter whether you earn one thousand rupees a month or ten thousand rupees a month? If his needs are fulfilled, a happy man doesn't bother. He stops at a point; he is not obsessed with money.

If a happy man sees that five days working is enough, then two days he rests—goes fishing or to the mountains. If he sees that only two days working is enough, then he works two days—in five days there are many more important things to do. He has to compose poetry, and he has to play his guitar, and he has to dance; and he has to just sit with friends and gossip; he has to meditate, pray, dance—he has a thousand and one things. His work is a need he has to fulfill. He enjoys it, but he is not obsessed with it.

A happy man is never a perfectionist. Only unhappy people are perfectionists, only unhappy people are obsessed with their work— because that is the only way they can avoid themselves, they can avoid facing themselves, they can avoid encountering themselves. They are continuously working; late hours they will go on working; unless they fall asleep they go on working. Why? because they are afraid. If they stop work, then what to do? Then they are left to themselves and they cannot face themselves.

Society is, of course, interested in specialists. And specialists, more or less, become inhuman—because they know too much about too little. Their whole vision becomes narrow, narrow, narrow.

I have heard—the story must belong to the twenty-first century:

One man knocked at a doctor's, an eye specialist's office, and he said, "My left eye is hurting very much, and I cannot see rightly, my vision is blurred."

The doctor said, "Excuse me, I am sorry, but I specialize only in right eyes. For the left eye you will have to go to some other specialist."

Narrower and narrower goes on the path of the specialist. He never sees the tree; he only can see the leaf. The whole is lost in the part. And, of course, the part cannot exist without the whole. In fact, all divisions are arbitrary. The leaf is not separate from the branch; the branch is not separate from the tree; the

213

tree is not separate from the roots; the roots are not separate from the earth. Everything is in organic unity. The specialist goes on dividing, and by and by those divisions, those demarcations, take on too much importance. A specialist becomes inhuman.

I have heard:

A doctor put an elderly man on a diet because of his weight problem. The man returned to his doctor in two months' time and he had lost dozens of pounds.

The doctor was very pleased with the result.

The patient said, "I feel so young, doctor. Only today I saw a girl's bare arm and I felt like biting it!"

The doctor said, "You could have done. It's only about forty calories."

A specialist is a specialist. All specialization becomes basically inhuman. It loses track of the whole. But the society is interested in efficiency. So beware of the society.

Society is not interested in your happiness, in your joy. The interest of the society is more production, efficiency, more work—and don't ask for what, because they don't know for what. If you work hard they will say to create better situations—for what?—to work still harder. It is just like a man who earns money and you ask him "For what?" He says, "To earn more money." "And then you earn more money, then what?" He says "To earn still more money." The thing seems to be vicious.

The individual has totally different interests from the society, because the society has no soul. The society is soulless. And if you become too much a part of the society, it will reduce your soul also to a non-entity.

Beware, before you have lost your whole opportunity. Don't be a slave. Follow society to the point you feel is needed, but always remain master of your own destiny.

It happened:

Abe Katz got a call from his stockbroker one day. "Abe, do I have a deal for you!" started the broker. "It's an Indian copper mine and the shares are selling for only fifty cents apiece."

214

"Buy a thousand," ordered Abe.

A few days later another call came in announcing the price had gone up to $1.00.

"Looks good," said Abe. "Buy another thousand."

A week went by before the broker was heard from.

"Well, Abe, I'm sorry to tell you the stocks are down to twenty-five cents . . . what to do?"

"Sell!" barked Abe.

"To whom?" answered the broker.

It is easy to purchase, it is difficult to sell. It is easy to become part of the society and get into the rut; it is difficult to get of it. And once you are in the rut, you start becoming afraid: What will happen if you get out of it? You will lose money, you will lose this, you will lose that. But you are losing your life all the time!

Life should be the supreme value. Nothing should be put above life. I call a man religious who puts life as the supreme value, and sacrifices everything to life, and never sacrifices his life to anything. Even if your country says, "The country is in difficulty— sacrifice your life! Become a martyr!" don't be foolish. Life is the supreme value. No country has any right to sacrifice a single life. It is *your* life, and it is only yours.

If your religion says you are a Mohammedan and says, "Fight Hindus! and sacrifice your life!" or you are a Hindu and Hinduism says, "Go and fight and kill the Mohammendans! Even if you are killed, don't be worried—in heaven you will be paid well"—don't listen to all that nonsense. Enough is enough! Much has happened on the earth, much suffering because of these people.

Never sacrifice your life for anything! Sacrifice everything for life! Life is the ultimate goal—greater than any country, greater than any religion, greater than any god, greater than any scripture.

But nobody is going to say that to you, no leader is going to say that to you, because then their whole business is gone. No priest is going to say that to you, because then their whole business is gone. That's why politicians and priests are very against me.

215

If you understand me well, then do, become part of the society—you *are* part of the society—but do only that which is needful, never get lost.

The fourth question: *How can I tell the difference between 'no-doing' and being lazy . . . and if 'floating'— how to make decisions?*

IT IS not difficult. Both have different tastes, and very clear-cut, very distinct. When you are lazy, it is a negative taste—you simply feel you have no energy, you simply feel dull; you simply feel sleepy, you simply feel dead. When you are in a state of non-doing then you are full of energy—it is a very positive taste. You have full energy, overflowing. You are radiant, bubbling, vibrating. You are not sleepy, you are perfectly aware. You are not dead—you are tremendously alive.

So there is not a problem. You can just check in, and always continue to check. There is a possibility the mind can deceive you: it can rationalize laziness as non-doing. It can say "I have become a Zen master" or "I believe in Tao"—but you are not deceiving anybody else. You will be deceiving only yourself. So be alert.

When you are lazy you will *know* it certainly. It is like a headache: how do you know when you have a headache? and when you don't have? You will say you simply know. It is self-evident. In the same way it is self-evident: if you are lazy you will feel sleepy, in a stupor—no energy to do anything, no energy to be creative, no energy to go anywhere. Remember: no energy is the basic taste.

When you are in a non-doing state, you are so full of energy that you want to go somewhere, but nowhere to go. The difference is not no energy but nowhere to go. You are *so* radiant, but what to do? You are sitting there overflowing. The energy goes on welling up, and goes on cleansing you, as if you are under a

216

shower of energy—fresh, you have taken a bath just now; sharp, intelligent, aware. The taste will tell you.

Let me tell you one anecdote—I loved it:

Two big mountain lions were stalking through the jungle single file. Suddenly the rear lion took a big swipe with his tongue across the ass of the front lion.

"Are you turning queer or something?" asked the front lion.

"No," answered the back lion. "I just ate a Jew and I'm trying to get the taste out of my mouth."

Now you know when you eat a Jew—then the taste. . . . The taste will show. And the taste is so clear-cut and distinct that there is no question of confusion.

The last question: *Through your lectures you have often undertaken the comparative study of different Enlightened persons or incarnations—of course, that of their personalities. How are you going to study the personalities of the two living Enlightened persons—Rajneesh and Krishnamurti?*

Don't waste your time on these people—they exist not!

CHAPTER 9

*I*N THE TANG DYNASTY *there was a stout fellow who was called the Happy Chinaman, or the Laughing Buddha.*

This Hotei had no desire to call himself a Zen master, or to gather disciples around him. Instead he walked the streets with a sack on his back full of candy, fruit and doughnuts—which he gave out to the children who gathered and played around him.

Whenever he met a Zen devotee he would extend his hand and say: "Give me one penny." And if anyone asked him to return to a temple to teach others, again he would reply: "Give me one penny."

Once when he was at his play-work another Zen master happened to along and inquired: "What is the significance of Zen?" Hotei immediately plopped his sack down on the ground in silent answer.

"Then," asked the other, "what is the actualization of Zen?" At once the Happy Chinaman swung the sack over his shoulder and continued on his way.

LAUGH YOUR WAY TO GOD!

nineteenth august 1976

LAUGHTER is the very essence of religion. Seriousness is never religious, cannot be religious. Seriousness is of the ego, part of the very disease. Laughter is ego-lessness.

Yes, there is a difference between when you laugh and when a religious man laughs. The difference is that you laugh always about others—the religious man laughs at himself, or at the whole ridiculousness of man's being.

Religion cannot be anything other than a celebration of life. And the serious person becomes handicapped: he creates barriers. He cannot dance, he cannot sing, he cannot celebrate. The very dimension of celebration disappears from his life. He becomes desertlike. And if you are a desert, you can go on thinking and pretending that you are religious but you are not.

You may be a sectarian, but not religious. You can be a Christian, a Hindu, a Buddhist, a Jain, a Mohammedan, but you cannot be religious. You believe in something, but you don't know anything. You believe in theories. A man too much burdened by theories becomes serious. A man who is unburdened, has no burden of theories over his being, starts laughing.

The whole play of existence is so beautiful that laughter can be the only response to it. Only laughter can be the real prayer, gratitude.

This Hotei is tremendously significant. Rarely has a man like Hotei walked on the earth. It is unfortunate—more people should be like Hotei; more temples should be full of laughter, dancing, singing. If seriousness is lost, nothing is lost—in fact, one becomes more healthy and whole. But if laughter is lost, everything is lost. Suddenly you lose the festivity of your being; you become colourless, monotonous, in a way dead. Then your energy is not streaming any more.

Laughter is a flowering. If Buddha was the seed, then Hotei is the flower on the same tree. If Buddha is the roots, then Hotei is the flower on the same tree. And if you want to understand Buddha, try to understand Hotei. And it is right that people used to call him the Laughing Buddha. Buddha has come of age in Hotei. Buddha has laughed in Hotei. Enlightenment has come to its very crescendo.

But it is difficult to understand Hotei. To understand him you will have to be in that festive dimension. If you are too much burdened with theories, concepts, notions, ideologies, theologies, philosophies, you will not be able to see what this Hotei is, what his significance is—because he will laugh looking at you. He will laugh because he will not be able to believe that a man can be so foolish and so ridiculous.

It is as if a man is just trying to live on a cookery book and has forgotten to cook food; just goes on studying books about food and how to prepare it and how not to prepare it, and argues this way and that—and is all the time hungry, all the time dying, and has forgotten completely that one cannot live on books. That's what has happened: people are living on Bibles, Korans, Dhammapadas, Gitas—they have completely forgotten that religion has to be *lived*. It is something that has to be digested.

It is something that has to circulate in your blood, become your bones, your very marrow. You cannot just think about it. Thinking is the most superficial part of your being. You have to absorb it!

This story has to be understood very deeply.

> *In the T'ang dynasty there was a stout fellow who was called the Happy China-man, or the Laughing Buddha.*

WHEN for the first time you hear the phrase 'Laughing Buddha' it looks a little contradictory, a contradiction in terms. A Buddha and laughing? Not a single statue exists, not a single painting, not a single description, of Buddha as laughing. But that is not because Buddha never laughed—that is because Indians are much too serious about religion.

Maybe that is one of the basic reasons why Buddhism disappeared from India. India was too serious, too intellectual, too full of theorizing. Buddha was very simple. His approach was not of the mind; his approach was of the existential being. And this country is the country of the pundits, the scholars, the learned men, the knowledgeable. If Buddha disappeared from this country, it seems natural.

He was bringing a totally different dimension—something very original; something very natural yet very original because man has forgotten it. He was doing a tremendous service to humanity. He was not a pundit, not a philosopher, not a metaphysician. He was a very simple being—silent, happy, fully alive, living moment-to-moment.

If you want to understand Buddha, go via Hotei. Hotei is his true disciple. It is very difficult, because whenever a man like Buddha happens immediately pundits and scholars gather around, because they get new material for their theorizing. Intellectuals immediately gather around. They have something new to philosophize about, to write about, to make scriptures of.

It is said—a very old story—that once it happened:

A man became Enlightened. The disciples of the Devil immediately went to the Devil, their master, and they said, "What are you doing sitting here? Run fast! Rush fast! One man has become Enlightened—and we have to destroy his truth before it reaches to people, otherwise Hell will become empty, nobody will be coming to Hell. Everybody will go to Heaven, to Paradise, or to Moksha!"

It is said that the Devil sitting there smiled silently. He said, "Don't be worried—there is no hurry and no worry. Scholars have already reached there. They will destroy the truth. They do our work so perfectly that we need not be worried."

Whenever a truth is born, a ray of light, suddenly scholars gather together—intellectuals, professors, philosophers, theoreticians—and they jump upon the truth, they crush it; they mould it into dead theories and scriptures. That which was alive becomes just a paper thing. The real rose disappears.

Once I was staying in a Christian friend's house. I started looking into his Bible: there was a rose. He must have kept it in the Bible. Many years old—dry, dead, crushed between the pages of the Bible. I started laughing. He came rushing from his bathroom. He said, "What! For what are you laughing? What has happened?"

I said, "The same has happened to truth as has happened to this rose. Between the pages of your Bible, the rose has died. Now it is just a memory of something which was alive one day. Just a remembrance. All fragrance gone, all aliveness gone. It is as dead as a plastic flower or a paper flower. It has a history but it has no future. It has a past but it has no possibility. And the same has happened to truth. In the pages of the scriptures it has died."

The Devil said, "Don't be worried. Take it easy—our people have already reached there: the scholars, the professors; they will immediately crush it."

When truth happens it is non-verbal, it is silent. It is so profound it cannot be expressed through words. Then sooner or

224

later people will come who will put it into words, who will systematize it. And in their very systematization it is killed.

Hotei lived a totally different life from an ordinary religious man. His whole life was nothing but a continuous laughter. It is said about Hotei that even sometimes in sleep he would start laughing. He had a big belly, and the belly would shake. Sardar Gurdayal Singh would have enjoyed meeting him, and Hotei would have enjoyed Sardar Gurdayal Singh. People would ask him, "Why are you laughing? and even in sleep!" Laughter was so natural to him that any and everything would help him to laugh. Then the whole life, awake or asleep, is a comedy.

You have turned life into a tragedy. You have made a tragic mess of your life. Even when you laugh, you don't laugh. Even when you pretend to laugh, the laughter is just forced, manipulated, managed. It is not coming from the heart, not at all from the belly. It is not something coming from your centre; it is just something painted on the periphery. You laugh for reasons—which have nothing to do with laughter.

I have heard: In a small office, the boss was telling some old stale anecdote, which he had told many times. And everybody was laughing—one has to laugh! They were all bored by it, but the boss is the boss, and when the boss tells a joke you have to laugh—it is part of duty. Just one woman typist was not laughing, was sitting straight, serious. The boss said, "What is the matter with you? Why are you not laughing?"

She said, "I am leaving this month"—then there is no point!

It happened:

Mulla Nasrudin listened very attentively while a stranger told a long story in the coffee-house. But the man spoke so indistinctly and muffed his punchline so badly that the story was not funny at all, and except for the Mulla no one laughed. But the Mulla laughed heartily.

"Why did you laugh, Nasrudin?" I asked him afterwards when the stranger had left.

"I always do," replied Nasrudin. "If you don't laugh, there is always the danger of their telling it over again."

225

People have their own reasons. Even laughter is businesslike; even laughter is economic, political. Even laughter is not just laughter. All purity is lost. You cannot even laugh in a pure way, in a simple way, childlike. And if you cannot laugh in a pure way, you are losing something tremendously valuable. You are losing your virginity, your purity, your innocence.

Watch a small child; watch his laughter—so profound, comes from the very centre. When a child is born, the first social activity that the child learns—or maybe it is not right to say 'learns', because he brings it with himself—is smiling. The *first* social activity. By smiling he becomes part of society. It seems very natural, spontaneous. Other things will come later on—that is his first spark of being in the world, when he smiles. When a mother sees her child smiling, she becomes tremendously happy—because that smile shows health, that smile shows intelligence, that smile shows that the child is not stupid, not retarded. That smile shows that the child is going to live, love, be happy. The mother is simply thrilled.

Smiling is the first social activity, and should remain the basic social activity. One should go on laughing the whole of one's life. If you can laugh in all sorts of situations, you will become so capable of encountering them—and that encounter will bring maturity to you. I am not saying don't weep. In fact, if you cannot laugh, you cannot weep. They go together; they are part of one phenomenon: of being true and authentic.

There are millions of people whose tears have dried; their eyes have lost lustre, depth; their eyes have lost water—because they cannot weep, they cannot cry; tears cannot flow naturally. If laughter is crippled, tears are also crippled. Only a person who laughs well can weep well. And if you can weep and laugh well, you are alive. The dead man cannot laugh and cannot weep. The dead man can be serious. Watch: go and look at a corpse — the dead man can be serious in a more skillful way than you can be. Only an alive man can laugh and weep and cry.

These are moods of your inner being, these are climates — enriching. But, by and by, everybody forgets. That which

226

was natural in the beginning becomes unnatural. You need somebody to poke you into laughter, tickle you into laughter— only then do you laugh. That's why so many jokes exist in the world.

You may not have observed, but Jews have the best jokes in the world. And the reason is because they have lived in deeper misery than any other race. They *had* to create jokes, otherwise they would have been dead long before. They have passed through so much misery, they have been tortured down the centuries so much, they have been crushed, murdered—they *had* to create a sense of the ridiculous. That has been a saving device. Hence, they have the most beautiful jokes, the funniest, the profoundest.

What I am trying to show you is this: that we laugh only when there is some reason which is forcing us to laugh. A joke is told, and you laugh—because a joke creates a certain excitement in you. The whole mechanism of a joke is: the story goes in one direction, and suddenly it takes a turn; the turn is so sudden, so drastic, that you could not have imagined it. Excitement grows and you are waiting for the punchline. And then suddenly, whatsoever you were expecting is never there— something absolutely different, something very absurd and ridiculous, never fulfilling your expectation.

A joke is never logical. If a joke is logical it will lose all its sense of laughter, the quality of laughter, because then you will be able to predict. Then by the time the joke is being said, you will have reached the punchline because it will be a syllogism, it will be simple arithmetic. But then it will not have any laughter. A joke takes a sudden turn, so sudden that it was almost impossible for you to imagine it, to infer it. It takes a jump, a leap, a quantum leap—and that's why it releases so much laughter. It is a subtle psychological way to tickle you.

I have to tell jokes because I am afraid—you are all religious people. You tend to be serious. I have to tickle you so sometimes you forget your religiousness, you forget all your philosophies, theories, systems, and you fall down to earth. I have to bring you back to the earth again and again, otherwise you

227

will tend to become serious, more and more serious. And seriousness is a canceric growth.

Much you can learn from Hotei.

> *In the T'ang dynasty there was a stout fel-*
> *low who was called the Happy Chinaman . . .*

HE MUST have been stout, he laughed so much. Laughter
brings strength. Now, even medical science says that
laughter is one of the most deep-going medicines nature has
provided man with. If you can laugh when you are ill you will
get your health back sooner. If you cannot laugh, even if you
are healthy, sooner or later you will lose your health and you
will become ill.

Laughter brings some energy from your inner source to
your surface. Energy starts flowing, follows laughter like a
shadow. Have you watched it? When you really laugh, for those
few moments you are in a deep meditative state. Thinking
stops. It is impossible to laugh and think together. They are
diametrically opposite: either you can laugh or you can think.
If you really laugh, thinking stops. If you are still thinking,
laughter will be just so-so, it will be *just* so-so, lagging behind.
It will be a crippled laughter.

When you really laugh, suddenly mind disappears. And the
whole Zen methodology is how to get into no-mind—laughter
is one of the beautiful doors to get to it.

As far as I know, dancing and laughter are the best, natural,
easily approachable doors. If you really dance, thinking stops.
You go on and on, you whirl and whirl, and you become a whirl-
pool—all boundaries, all divisions are lost. You don't even
know where your body ends and where the existence begins.
You melt into existence and the existence melts into you; there
is an overlapping of boundaries. And if you are really dancing—
not managing it but allowing it to manage you, allowing it to
possess you—if you are possessed by dance, thinking stops.

The same happens with laughter. If you are possessed by
laughter, thinking stops. And if you know a few moments of
no-mind, those glimpses will promise you many more rewards

that are going to come. You just have to become more and more
of the sort, of the quality, of no-mind. More and more, thinking
has to be dropped.

Laughter can be a beautiful introduction to a non-thinking
state. And the beauty is. . . . There are methods—for example,
you can concentrate on a flame or on a black dot, or you can
concentrate on a mantra, but the greater possibility is that by
the time the mind is disappearing you will start feeling sleepy,
you will fall asleep. Because before the mind disappears there
open two alternatives : sleep—*sushupti*—and samadhi; sleep and
satori.

When thinking disappears, these are the two alternatives
left: either you move into satori—a fully alert, no-thought
state; or a fully asleep, no-thought state—sleep. And sleep is
more natural, because you have practised it long. If you live
sixty years, twenty years you have been asleep. It is the greatest
activity that you have been doing; one third of your life is spent
in sleep. In no other exercise do you spend so much time and so
much energy.

So if you are doing TM-type meditations, repeating a mantra,
by the time the mantra helps you to become non-thinking,
immediately sleep will possess you. Hence, I call TM a sort
of tranquillizer. And that is the appeal in America for Maharishi
and his method, because America is the only country which is
suffering from sleeplessness so tremendously. Insomnia has
become almost common.

If after forty you have not started suffering from insomnia,
that simply means that you are a failure, that you could not
succeed—in business, in politics. In power you couldn't succeed; you are a failure. All successful people suffer from insomnia, have to suffer. They suffer from ulcers, have to suffer.
So remember: insomnia, ulcers and things like that are nothing
but certificates of success—that you have succeeded.

TM has an appeal for the American mind, because repeating
a mantra—monotonous, the same again and again—the mind
loses interest in it, starts falling asleep. That's the beauty of
laughter: you cannot fall asleep. Laughing, how can you fall

asleep? It brings a state of no-mind and no-thought, and does not allow you to fall asleep.

In a few Zen monasteries, every monk has to start his morning with laughter, and has to end his night with laughter—the first thing and the last thing! You try it. It is very beautiful. It will look a little crazy—mm?—because so many serious people are all around. They will not understand. If you are happy, they always ask why. The question is foolish! If you are sad, they never ask why. They take it for granted—if you are sad, it's okay. Everybody is sad. What is new in it? Even if you want to tell them, they are not interested because they know all about it, they themselves are sad. So what is the point of telling a long story? —cut it short!

But if you are laughing for no reason, then they become alert —something has gone wrong. This man seems to be a little crazy because only crazy people enjoy laughter; only in madhouses will you find crazy people laughing. This is unfortunate, but this is so.

It will be difficult, if you are a husband or a wife it will be difficult for you to suddenly laugh early in the morning. But try it—it pays tremendously. It is one of the most beautiful moods to get up with, to get out of the bed with. For *no* reason! because there is no reason. Simply, you are again there, still alive —it is a miracle! It seems ridiculous! Why are you alive? And again the world is there. Your wife is still snoring, and the same room, and the same house. In this constantly changing world— what Hindus call the 'maya'—at least for one night nothing has changed? Everything is there: you can hear the milkman and the traffic has started, and the same noises—it is worth laughing for!

One day you will not get into the morning. One day the milkman will knock at the door, the wife will be snoring, but you will not be there. One day, death will come. Before it knocks you down, have a good laugh—while there is time, have a good laugh.

And look at the whole ridiculousness: again the same day

starts; you have done the same things again and again for your whole life. Again you will get into your slippers, rush to the bathroom—for what? Brushing your teeth, taking a shower— for what? Where are you going? Getting ready and nowhere to go! Dressing, rushing to the office—for what? Just to do the same thing again tomorrow?

Look at the whole ridiculousness of it—and have a good laugh. Don't open your eyes. The moment you feel that sleep is gone, first start laughing, then open the eyes—and that will set a trend for the whole day. If you can laugh early in the morning you will laugh the whole day. You have created a chain effect; one thing leads to another. Laughter leads to more laughter.

And almost always I have seen people doing just the wrong thing. From the very early morning they get out of bed complaining, gloomy, sad, depressed, miserable. Then one thing leads to another—and for *nothing*. And they get angry . . . it is very bad because it will change your climate for the whole day, it will set a pattern for the whole day.

Zen people are more sane. In their insanity they are saner than you. They start with laughter . . . and then the whole day you will feel laughter bubbling, welling up. There are so many ridiculous things happening all over! God must be dying of His laughter—down the centuries, for eternity, seeing this ridiculousness of the world. The people that He has created, and all the absurdities—it is *really* a comedy. He must be laughing.

If you become silent after your laughter, one day you will hear God also laughing, you will hear the whole existence laughing— trees and stones and stars with you.

And the Zen monk goes to sleep in the night again with laughter. The day is over, the drama is closed again—with laughter he says "Goodbye, and if I survive again, tomorrow morning I will greet you again with laughter."

Try it! Start and finish your day with laughter, and you will see, by and by, in between these two more and more laughter starts happening. And the more laughing you become, the more religious.

There was a stout fellow who was called the
Happy Chinaman, or the Laughing Buddha.
This Hotei had no desire to call himself
a Zen master, or to gather disciples around
him.

E VERY master has his own unique way. Every master has
his unique method to express whatsoever he has attained —
it was laughter for Hotei. He went from one town to another,
travelling continuously all his life — laughing.

It is said that he would come to a town, stand in the middle
of the village, and start laughing. And then people would start
laughing at him, that a madman has come; then the crowd would
gather and by and by the laughter would spread. It would become infectious and the whole crowd would surge with laughter.
He would create waves of laughter: and in that laughter *satsang*
was happening — what in India we call 'satsang' — the presence
of the master.

Then, by and by, those who had eyes would start looking at
him: 'He is not a madman — in the garb of a madman a Buddha
is standing there.' Then those who had ears to hear, they would
start hearing that it was not just the laughter of a madman —
something of tremendous significance was transpiring between
them and Hotei.

This was his way of expressing his being. This was his way
of preaching — a beautiful way.

A clergyman was recently telling me a marvellous story
when his little girl said, "Now, pa, is that really true, or is
it just preaching?"

Even children understand that preaching is just preaching.
The old man was telling me a beautiful story and then his little
girl interfered and said, "Now, pa, is that really true, or is it
just preaching?" She knows! — her father is a preacher.

Preaching is not true — unless your whole life becomes your
preaching. Unless your whole activity becomes a message, unless

232

you become your message, preaching remains false. Hotei became his own message.

> *This Hotei had no desire to call himself a Zen master, or to gather disciples around him. Instead he walked the streets with a sack on his back full of candy, fruit and doughnuts—which he gave out to the children who gathered and played around him.*

Now, sometimes these children were really children, and sometimes these children were young people, and sometimes these children were old people—so don't be misguided by the word 'children'. Aged people, more aged than Hotei himself, they were also children for him. In fact, to make a contact with Hotei, you had to be a child, innocent. And he would distribute a few things : toys, candy, sweets. He is saying something symbolically : A religious man brings you this message — don't pay much attention to life, it is nothing but a toy. Don't pay much attention to life, it is nothing but a sweet. Taste it, but don't get obsessed by it. It has no nourishment in it. It has *no* truth in it. You cannot live upon it.

You have heard Jesus' saying: A man cannot live by bread alone. Can a man live by sweets alone? Bread at least has some nourishment in it; a sweet has nothing. Tastes good, but can be harmful in the long run.

Both children and the old, he would always treat everybody as children: he would give them toys—very indicative. A better way you cannot find to say that the world is just a toy thing. And the life that you think is life is nothing true—it is just a falsity, a dream, momentary. Don't cling to it.

> *Whenever he met a Zen devotee he would extend his hand and say: "Give me one penny."*

And whenever somebody was there whom he knew, who was a

devotee of Zen, Dhyan, and was meditative—mm?—just watch: to others he would give; to a person who has some leanings towards meditation he would say, "Give me one penny." He is saying, "Meditation is nothing but sharing—you give me one penny." If you are a meditative person, you give, you share— you don't hoard, you are not miserly. You don't possess. How can you possess in this world?

You were not here and the world was here; you will not be here one day and the world is going to be here. How can you possess you? How can you claim that 'I am the owner'? How can you own anything? And if you are meditative, your whole life will become a sharing. You will give whatsoever you can give— your love, your understanding, your compassion—whatsoever you can you will give—your energy, body, mind, soul—whatsoever. And you will enjoy it.

There is no greater enjoyment than that of sharing something. Have you given something to somebody? That's why people enjoy giving gifts so much. It is a sheer delight. When you give something to somebody—maybe valueless, may not be of much value—but just the way, just the gesture that you give, satisfies tremendously. Just think of a person whose whole life is a gift! whose every moment is a sharing—he lives in heaven. There is no other heaven than that.

> *Whenever he met a Zen devotee he would*
> *extend his hand and say: "Give me one*
> *penny."*

One of the greatest Indian poets, Rabindranath Tagore, has written a small poem: *What have you got for me?* The poem consists of a small story:

Once while I was begging from door to door, I suddenly saw a gleaming chariot pull up to me and stop. When I beheld its lordly driver step down and smile at me with searching eyes, I immediately envisioned the unsolicited charity that would surely be mine.

A beggar is relating this story. A beggar has come out of his house, and suddenly he sees a golden chariot stop and the King of kings gets out of the chariot. The beggar must have been thrilled by the very possibility that he could get something today.

> But to my everlasting chagrin, this King of kings suddenly thrust out his hand and asked, "What have you got for me?" Oh, Lord, torn with perplexity and indecision, I offered you a mere grain of wheat and on my carpet that very night I found a grain of gold. How sorry I was that I had not given you everything I had!

The beggar is, of course, accustomed to receiving, not accustomed to giving. He has never given anything. He has always been begging and begging. So suddenly the King of kings spreads his hands and says, "What have you got for me?" He was perplexed, bewildered, confused. He must have hesitated. He must have searched his bag. He could have given more, but he could not gather courage. He gave only one grain of wheat—just because he could not say no. How to say no to the King of the kings? And by the time he must have become conscious the chariot was gone, and there were only dust clouds on the road. And still, the whole day he must have worried about that one grain of wheat less in his bag today. He must have thought again and again; it must have been like a wound.

And in the night when he comes back home and drops on the floor all that he has begged in the whole day, he finds a grain of gold. Then he understands. Then he cries and weeps, but now it is too late—where can you find the King of kings again? Where? Now he wants to give everything that he has, now he has found the illogical logic of it: that which you give becomes golden, and that which you go on hoarding becomes dirt. If you hoard gold it becomes dust; if you give dust, dust becomes gold—that is the message of this beautiful anecdote. And I absolutely agree with it.

It is not just a parable: it is a true secret of life—give and you will get millionfold; share and in the very sharing you will become richer. Go on hoarding and you will become poorer and poorer. You cannot find a poorer man than a miser. He may have much, but he has nothing—because you can have only that which you have given. It is a paradox only in appearance.

Let me repeat it: You possess only that which you have given; you never possess that which you have hoarded—you become a master of something which you share. Share! unconditionally—because everything is going to be taken from you anyway; death is going to take everything from you.

And death will not beg—it simply snatches away, it robs. It doesn't ask your permission; it doesn't knock on your door and say, "Can I come in, sir." No. It simply comes. By the time you are aware, you are gone. By the time you can do something, everything has been taken away. Death is going to take everything.

Before death knocks on your door, share—whatsoever you have. You can sing a beautiful song?—sing it, share it. You can paint a picture?—paint, share it. You can dance?—go and dance, share it. Whatsoever you have—and I have never come across a man who has not much to share. If you want to share, you have too much to share. If you don't want to share, you may have enough, more than enough, but you are poor, you don't have anything.

It happened:

Mulla Nasrudin was fishing off a pier when he lost his balance and fell in.

"Help! Help!" Mrs Nasrudin started shouting. "My husband is drowning. Help! Help!"

Luckily, her cries were heard by two husky young men in the vicinity, and they dove into the water and pulled poor Nasrudin out.

As he lay on the pier drying out, Mrs Nasrudin leaned over him and whispered, "They saved you from drowning, man. Shouldn't we give them a rupee?"

Mulla opened one eye and whispered back, "I was only half-drowned. Half a rupee will do."

The miser's mind continues to the very end. Beware of it.

*Whenever he met a Zen devotee he would
extend his hand and say: "Give me one
penny." And if anyone asked him to return
to a temple to teach others, again he would
say: "Give me one penny."*

That was his whole preaching: Share! Give! What else can be
said, what else can be taught?

*Once when he was at his play-work another
Zen master happened along and inquired:
"What is the significance of Zen?" Hotei
immediately plopped his sack down on the
ground in silent answer.*

ZEN BELIEVES that truth cannot be expressed by words,
but it can be expressed by gestures, action. Something
can be done about it. You cannot say it, but you can show it.

When they ask a question, Zen masters don't expect an
answer verbally—they expect some gesture of spontaneous
understanding. And remember: verbal answers you can get
from scriptures, they can be borrowed, they can be second-hand
—and a second-hand answer is never true. A second-hand God
is never true. A second-hand truth is never true. Beware of
second-hand things.

Zen masters say: "*Show* your understanding, don't say! Show
in some gesture!" And you cannot deceive a Zen master, you
cannot deceive an Enlightened man. Yes, you can learn gestures
also. For example: now you know this story of Hotei—mm?—
you can have a sack on your back and you can move, and I
come across and I ask: "What is the significance of Zen?" And
you plop down the sack . . . I will hit your head! because it
is not a question of repeating the story. You will have to
show *your* understanding. It was Hotei's understanding—you
cannot copy it. When the question is there, you will have to
respond—out of your own heart, out of your own being, out
of that moment of understanding and awareness, you will have
to do something.

237

Hotei plopped his sack down on the ground in silent answer— what was he saying? The question was: "What is the significance of Zen?" He dropped his bag of doughnuts, toys, sweets. He is saying: "Zen is renunciation—like this!" Dropping the whole bag, all that you possess. That was all that he possessed at that moment, nothing else, just his bag.

That bag was the non-essential part; he had nothing else. Then only the essential is left. The bag was the only non-essential thing with him. He plopped it on the ground. He is saying in silent answer that Zen is a deep renunciation of the world. It is dropping all that is non-essential—like this bag! But it was not said: it was shown.

> *"Then," asked the other, "what is the actualization of Zen?* This may be the significance, but what is the actualization of Zen?" *At once the Happy Chinaman swung the sack over his shoulder and continued on his way.*

He is saying: "We renounce the world, yet we don't escape from the world. That is the actualization. We renounce the world, yet we live in the world." Again the bag is on his shoulder, again he is moving, but he is not a clinger. The bag is dropped!—deep down he is far away from the bag. He has no attachment to it. Still he will carry it; while he is alive he will carry it.

Zen says escaping is not renunciation—that's my message also. That's why I love this man Hotei: he really showed a deep, profound awareness. Be unattached, but be here—because there is nowhere else to be. This is the only world—there is no other world. So your monks and your *munis* and sadhus who are sitting in the temples and monasteries, in the Himalayan caves, are just escapists. Renounce!—but there is no need to escape. Renounce and still be here. Be in the world, but don't be of the world. Remain in the crowd and remain alone. Do a thousand and one things—whatsoever is needed, do it—but never be the doer. Don't gather the ego—that's all.

238

*"Then," asked the other, "what is the
actualization of Zen?"*

Essence is renunciation. Actualization, actual practice, is living
in the world and not being of it.

*At once the Happy Chinaman swung the
sack over his shoulder and continued on
his way.*

This is very difficult to understand, because centuries of escapists, centuries of these cowardly people who have been running
away from the world and condemning the world, have corrupted
your minds, have poisoned your being. It is difficult to understand, but if you can understand you will be benefited tremendously, great will be your benefit.

A person who escapes is not really a man of understanding.
His very escape shows his fear, not understanding. If you say,
"How can I be happy sitting in the marketplace? How can I be
silent sitting in the marketplace?" and you escape to the Himalayan silence, you are escaping from the very possibility of
ever becoming silent—because it is only in the marketplace
that the contrast exists; it is only in the marketplace that the
challenge exists; it is only in the marketplace that distractions
exist. And you have to overcome all those distractions.

If you escape to the Himalayas you will start feeling a little
still, but at the same time a little stupid also. You will start
feeling more silent, but that silence belongs to the Himalayas,
not to you. Come back and your silence will be left behind—
you will come alone. And back in the world you will be even
more disturbed than before, because you will have become
more vulnerable, soft. And you will come with a prejudice,
with this idea that you have attained to silence. You will have
become more egoistic.

That's why people who have escaped to the monasteries become afraid of coming back to the world. The world is the test.
The world is the criterion. And it is easier to be in the world
and, by and by, grow into a silence, then the Himalayan silence

comes into your being. You don't go to the Himalayas: the Himalayas themselves come to you. Then it is something of your own, then you are the master of it.

I don't teach escape. I also teach renunciation. Many people, orthodox, old people, come to me and they say, "What type of sannyas is this? People have taken sannyas—they are still living in their families, with their wife, with their children, going to the office, to the factory, to the shop—what *type* of sannyas is this?" They have only one conception of sannyas, a one dimensional conception—of escape. This is multi-dimensional. It is renouncing and yet living here, dropping and yet not dropping, changing and yet remaining ordinary, transforming one's being totally and yet remaining in the ordinary world like everybody else.

The Zen concept of renunciation is my concept of renunciation also. But it is difficult because the world has been condemned so much that it has become almost unconscious; it has become habitual to think in terms of condemnation. If somebody says you are worldly, you feel hurt, insulted. When you want to condemn somebody, you call him worldly—you have condemned him.

There is nothing wrong in being worldly. *Be* worldly, and yet remain unworldly—that is the very art, the art of living between two opposites, balancing oneself between two opposites. It is a very narrow path, like a razor's edge—but this is the only path. If you miss this balance, you miss truth.

> *"Then," asked the other, "what is the actualization of Zen?" At once the Happy Chinaman swung the sack over his shoulder and continued on his way.*

Remain herenow in this world, and continue on your way, and continue with deep laughter in your being. Dance your way to God! Laugh your way to God! Sing your way to God!

CHAPTER 10

I've developed a bad case of seeker's ego.

You have given initiation to sleeping babies!
What are you doing?

Aren't we being conditioned by you?

Give and share—to whom to give?

Are you holding my rope?

Did you ever feel: "The heck with Enlightenment—
I think I'll go out and drive a truck"?

TOWARDS NOTHINGNESS
twentieth august 1976

The first question: *I have developed a bad case of seeker's ego. It constantly tries to congratulate me on the great progress I have made. You hammer me, and it falls apart, but it comes back. Nothing to do but watch it — and yet it frightens me. Will you comment?*

IT'S NATURAL. When you are doing something and you are succeeding in it, a subtle pride arises. It is nothing unnatural, so don't be too much concerned with it. If you become serious about it, then it can become a permanent guest in the house. If you accept it as a natural thing — you walk, your shadow follows — if you accept the ego just like a shadow, then there is no problem.

The shadow has never created any problem for anybody, but if you start getting frightened about your own shadow then you will be in trouble. If you start fighting with your own shadow, you are doomed to fail. Never fight with the ego.

You can pretend to be humble, you can impose a sort of egolessness on your ego, but it will remain there, and it will go on disrupting and sabotaging your life. Just try to understand it. It is natural! You are succeeding, you feel good; you are progressing, you feel good; you are growing, you feel good!

It is said that when God created the world and He looked around, He said, "Very good! A beautiful thing I have done."

Nothing wrong about it! You paint a picture, then you look from many angles — you feel good; you have succeeded in materializing something which was immaterial. A vision, a dream, you have been able to bring to the world. When you compose a poem, you feel good! Nothing is wrong about it. Just remember that the shadow is not you.

This is *your* shadow, certainly — but the shadow is not you. The ego is a shadow. It is not you. This remembrance is enough — there is no need to fight because a shadow does not exist in the first place. It is a simple negativity, it is just absence. It has *no* positivity in it. So if you fight a negative thing, you will be defeated — because there is no way to defeat a negative thing. That which is not cannot be defeated. That's the problem.

That which is not *cannot* be defeated. And if you start fighting with it, *you* will be defeated. It is just like fighting darkness: there is no need! The problem is arising because you have an underlying notion that the ego should not be there. Why? Why not accept it also? Just remember it is not you. The problem arises only when you get identified with your shadow.

You are walking, the sun is there, and a shadow is falling. Somebody walks upon your shadow — do you fight with him? You know it is a shadow! He has not walked on you. Somebody walks on your ego: don't fight. He has not walked on you. Somebody insults you: it hurts because you get identified with the shadow — otherwise there is nothing. Somebody walks on your shadow : the hurt is imaginary and is a consequence of getting oneself identified with the shadow.

"I have developed a bad case of seeker's *shadow.*"

246

You are condemning it. You are creating the problem and anxiety for yourself. Accept it! It is part of a natural flow. But don't put the shadow ahead of you! *Don't* become a shadow of the shadow! — that's all. You remain yourself.

"It constantly tries to congratulate me . . ."

Accept its congratulation! and give a heartfelt thankyou to it.

"You hammer me and it falls apart . . ."

I don't hammer the ego, I never hammer the ego — I simply hammer the identification. I am not so foolish as to hammer your ego; that would be hammering your shadow. I simply hammer the bridge that you have created between the existential and the non-existential, between the essential and the non-essential, between the real and the unreal, between the fact and the fiction — between you and the shadow. I hammer only that bridge. And, of course, it falls apart, because it is just an idea. It has *no* reality : just an idea that 'this is me'.

If you want to do anything about the ego, the only thing that I feel can be helpful is: laugh at it. It is *ridiculous* to get identified with the shadow — simply ridiculous. But don't get serious. Accept it and you will be delivered from it.

I have heard:

It is said that a French prince visited a jail. In honour of the royal guest, the prison warden offered to release any prisoner the prince might designate. To pick out that prisoner, the prince began interviewing each of the men privately, asking, "Why are you here?"

"I'm innocent, my lord!" cried one. "I've been framed!" pleaded another. Perjury, prejudice, injustice and oppression were reasons given by the convicts for their being in prison.

Only one man told a different story. "Your highness," he replied, "I deserve to be here and I have no complaint. In my time I have been a wicked, desperate murderer. It is a great mercy, both to society and to myself, that I am here."

"You wicked wretch!" the prince replied. "What a pity

you should be confined among so many honest citizens. You admit yourself that you are evil enough to corrupt them all. I can't allow you to remain in their company another day. Guard! This is the man I wish released!"

Once you accept the reality, you are relieved, released; the prison exists no more. So don't try to be humble! Just know that ego arises. What can you do? *You* are not creating it.

It is just like when a wave moves: in the wake another wave follows it upside-down — that is the wake. It is natural. When there arises a big mountain, a valley follows it. The valley is nothing but the mountain upside-down. It is part of it. When you move, in the wake your shadow, your valley, follows. You simply accept it! Mountains are not crying tears that 'why do valleys exist?' And neither are waves worried.

The very idea that you have to get rid of the ego is wrong. Drop that very idea! When ego arises, simply note the fact that the shadow is falling — and remember not to get identified with it; remember that you are separate. This is enough. And the true humbleness is born out of this realization.

It is not an effort against the ego that brings humbleness. If you fight the ego, it can bring you a certain type of humbleness — but then there will be another ego arising and that will be the ego of the humble person. The pious ego: "I am the most humble person in the world. Nobody is humble in comparison to me. I am at the top." Again the ego has arisen. Ego will *always* arise whatsoever you do.

Doing brings ego. Ego is the shadow of action. And there is only one thing that is not doing and that is awareness, watchfulness. The *only* thing that is not part of the world of action is pure awareness. No shadow is created by pure awareness. It is so pure that light can pass through it — it is transparent and no shadow is created.

Shadow is created by solid things. The more solid a thing is, the more shadow it creates. Your body creates a shadow; your mind also creates a shadow — the ego is the shadow of the mind. If you become more aware, if you simply watch the mind, its functioning, its mechanism, then you are moving beyond the mind. You become just pure awareness, transparent. Then there is no shadow.

So just laugh at it. And if it tries to seduce you, have a good laugh! at your own absurdities. But don't become a warrior and don't start fighting with it.

The second question: *You say never to impose yourself on anyone else. Yet you give sannyas to children who can't possibly make up their minds to take it. You have even given initiation to sleeping babies! What are you doing?*

THE FIRST THING: I have never yet given sannyas to any-body who was awake—all are sleeping babies! Some are younger, some are older; that is immaterial. What does it matter — a baby of seven months, or an old man of seventy years? Sleep is the same.

Yes, I was also puzzled in the beginning when some mother would come with a sleeping baby. Then I pondered over it: why should I say no? because that would be unjust to the sleeping baby when I go on giving sannyas to so many sleeping people. So I decided to give sannyas to babies.

Another thing: they may be asleep, but they are more in-nocent. And innocence can receive sannyas in a deeper way than cunningness, cleverness. You are also asleep; the only difference is that you are more cunning. The children are more innocent.

You are asleep but you pretend that you are awake.

It happened: A friend came to see Albert Einstein; he had not seen him for two, three years. A baby had been born to the friend's wife and they brought the baby also. Just seeing Einstein, the baby started crying and became very much afraid and wanted to escape from there.

249

The father and the mother felt a little embarrassed, but Einstein said, "Don't be disturbed by it. In fact, he is the first person who has told his views about me so clearly. Others come; they may not like me but they smile — they are untrue. They talk against me outside, in my absence; and yet here they praise me. Your child is the first person I have met who has simply said whatsoever his opinion is. I am happy to meet such a true person. Don't be worried about it."

Children are simple, innocent. And sannyas is something which can be received only in deep innocence.

The more you grow in experience, the more cunning you become. Then even when you take sannyas, it is not a jump — it is a calculated step. You think about it. You ponder about it. You think for and against, pro and con. And then you think that it seems beneficial; or you think that it doesn't seem beneficial. Then you decide. Your sannyas is a conclusion.

A conclusion is always of the mind. There have only been a few people who have taken sannyas without thinking. I say to everybody, when people come to me I say to them: "Would you like to think about it? or are you ready?" A few people say they are ready; they don't want to think about it. Then it is reaching to a deeper level of your being.

When Maneesha came first, I asked her would she like to think about it. She said, "What — think? I am fed up with thinking! If you can accept me, I am ready." This is innocence. She is again behaving like a child. The sannyas will have a totally different meaning to her.

I have heard:

A backwoods preacher was exhorting his followers about sin and morality. Finally he demanded, "I want every virgin in this congregation to stand up!"

Nobody moved.

Again he shouted, "Every virgin in this congregation, rise!"

Finally a woman with an infant in her arms got up.

"Didn't you hear me, woman?" yelled the preacher. "I said the virgins!"

Replied the woman, "How do you expect a three-month-old baby to get up by herself?"

Now that baby was the only virgin in the whole church — but, of course, a baby cannot get up by herself.

When somebody brings a child to me for sannyas, many times I say no. I say wait a little. Unless I feel that the child is ready — of course, the child cannot come by himself — unless I feel the child has moved in his past lives closer and closer and closer in his search, and he is ready . . . otherwise, I say wait, let the child grow a little.

Not only to sleeping babies — sometimes I have given sannyas to babies in the womb. If I feel . . . and to feel a child is very simple. It is very difficult to feel you, because you are broadcasting such confusing statements about yourself — from your left side something else, from your right side something else, from your back something else, from your front something else. You *are* contradictory! You go on broadcasting contradictory vibes. It is very difficult to make certain of where you are, what you want. And the complexity is even doubled, because one moment you are one thing, another moment you are another thing. Like a chameleon you go on changing your colours.

A baby is simple, has one taste, has one colour. If I feel, if the vibes show me, that it will fit with his life pattern in the future, only then do I give sannyas.

And one thing more has to be understood: my sannyas is not in any way imposing something on you. It is simply conferring freedom on you. By giving you sannyas I am not giving you an ideology — I am just giving you courage to get free of all ideologies. By giving sannyas to you I am not giving you a certain religion — Hindu, Mohammedan, Christian — I am simply giving you courage to be an individual, to be a unique individual.

My sannyas is not a character that will confine you. My sannyas is an awareness that will give you more and more freedom. And if one day you feel that my sannyas is making a prison

for you, then drop out of it—that will be the true sannyas spirit.
But *never* allow it to become an imprisonment.

The child will grow. One day, if he feels that it is not for
him, he is free. There is no legal bondage in it. He can simply
drop out of it! If he feels in tune with it, he can go deeper into it.

I have no ideology to teach to you. I am not a teacher at all.
That's the difference between a teacher and a master. A teacher
has an ideology; he tries to condition your mind; he wants to
give you certain concepts. A master simply wants to uncondi-
tion your mind; he does not want to give you any concepts; he
wants to give you clarity of vision.

So if you are thinking that by becoming a sannyasin you have
attained to all the answers of life, you are completely missing
me. I have not given a single answer to you. I may have provok-
ed many questions in you, but I have not provided any answer.
I may have filled you with deep wonder about life; I may have
awakened you towards the grandeur of reality—but I have not
given you a philosophy.

I have not given you, in fact, anything. I may have taken
many things away from you. I am not giving you new clothes:
I am giving you nudity. I would like you to move towards truth
naked—naked of all theories, concepts, philosophies. A naked
human being with an innocent heart, with a deep courage.
Looking at life as it is. Not projecting any idea of one's own.

So my sannyas is not like a baptism where you become a
Christian, or the thread-ceremony where you become a Hindu.
You don't become part of any organization—I have none. By
becoming a sannyasin, you simply come in tune with me, you
simply start moving with me. You simply allow me to take you
to the truth that I have seen. You simply allow me to take you to
the open sky where I found something which satisfies *utterly*.

And a child is more capable of that than an old man.

The third question: *I am a professor of psychology. I have studied and taught conditioning. Can anybody avoid conditioning? Aren't we being conditioned by you?*

IT DEPENDS on you. You can be conditioned by me — but I am not conditioning you. Let that be absolutely clear!

You can be conditioned by me. If you are listening only through the mind you will be conditioned, because the mind goes on gathering knowledge. The mind is very suggestible, corruptible, vulnerable. If you are listening to me through your mind, through your reason, through your argumentative faculty, through your intellect, you will be conditioned. Even if you are not convinced by me, even if you go thinking that you are not convinced by me, still you will be conditioned. Maybe against me, but that too will condition you. For or against does not matter: if you listen through the mind you will be conditioned — because mind is the faculty of conditioning.

But there is another way to listen also — and it is not of the mind, it is of the heart. It is not through argumentativeness, through knowledge — it is through pure heart-trust. Then you listen to me not like a philosopher but like a poet. You are never conditioned by a poet.

You can enjoy poetry, but you are never conditioned by it. You are not conditioned by roseflowers — you can enjoy, you can celebrate, but you are not conditioned. A beautiful sunrise or a sunset, or a full moon in the night — are you being conditioned? These green trees all around, do they condition you? You can celebrate, you can enjoy, you can dance with them, you can sing with them, but you are not conditioned by them.

Think of me as a poet, a painter, a dancer; never think about me as a philosopher or a theologian. I am not. What I am doing here is poetry, sheer poetry. I am not giving you any ideology, so there is no question of being conditioned. But you have to look in the right way, otherwise there *is* every possibility of your being conditioned by me.

If you listen to me just to gather knowledge, you will be con-

253

ditioned. If you listen to me in such tremendous depth and profundity that it is not a question of gathering knowledge but a meeting of the hearts, a communion. . . . I am not here, the speaker is not here. Long ago the speaker disappeared. All that is coming out is coming out of a tremendous emptiness, nothingness. Look into my eyes and you can feel it! And if you are also empty while listening to me, who is going to be conditioned and by whom?

If you put aside your mind . . . in fact, if you are really intelligent you will always put your mind exactly where you have left your shoes—leave your mind also there. I would like Krishna to put a notice there: Shoes and Minds are to be Left Here at the Gate. If you bring your shoes it is not such a big thing, it is not so profane. But if you bring your minds here, then you never come to me.

Minds are conditioned, always conditioned; they are ready to be conditioned. Minds are bio-computers: they go on absorbing whatsoever is heard. It is a mechanical thing. Put the mind off while listening to me. Be a heart—love, trust. Listen to me in deep emptiness. Don't be there! I am not here—don't you be there. And then something will happen, something will transpire between me and you. Between two nothingnesses the river of truth starts flowing. And it is never conditioning: it is always unconditioning. It will *wash* your whole being, it will give you a shower; it will cleanse you, purify you.

The questioner says: "I am a professor of psychology."

That's a problem. It is really a great disease, psychology. It is almost pathological. I feel sorry for you. If you had had cancer that would not have been so bad, because the cancer can be treated. But a professor of psychology?—impossible! No treatment exists yet, because this disease called 'psychology' is so invisible and so subtle that it is very difficult to operate upon it.

'The professor of psychology' means one who has been conditioned so deeply that he does not believe that he exists. He believes only in body and mind. He does not believe in the soul; he does not believe that there is really anything transcendental to the mind. And I am saying leave your mind where you leave

254

your shoes—how can a professor of psychology do that? Because if he leaves the mind where he leaves his shoes, he will have to sit there, he cannot come here—because he believes only in the mind, nothing beyond it. He does not believe in anything transcending mind. Then, of course, he has no way to escape from conditioning.

Everything will condition him. Whatsoever he reads, whatsoever he hears, whatsoever he sees, will be a conditioning. Now he is caught in an imprisonment—because he does not know that there is something beyond also. The beyond within—he is not aware of that. He does not believe in awareness.

You can look into the books of psychology: you will see chapters on memory, you will see chapters on imagination, dream, instinct, sex, and a thousand other things, but you will never find a chapter on awareness. No—that doesn't exist. You will find everything calculated, only the calculator is not there. You will find all the observations categorized, only the observer is not there.

The psychologist does not believe in himself. This is absurd! He does not believe in the observer; he believes only in the observations. He says: "I have seen this"; but if you ask: "Is there a seer within you?" he says, "No." Then who has seen this?

The very name 'psychology' is a misnomer, because 'psyche', from where the word comes, means soul—and soul is not a part of psychology. The name should be changed. It is not the right name for it. Psychology either has to find a soul or has to drop the very name 'psychology'.

And if you are just a student, the disease is not very advanced; but if you are a professor then you have gone beyond the point of return. It is very difficult for a professor to relax back, to see things again as they are. He *knows* so much. He has accumulated so much knowledge, so many screens are there on his eyes. It is difficult to find more blind people than professors.

I have been a professor, that's why I say so—I know. I know from within. I have lived with professors for many years. They are the most unintelligent people in the world. Even a farmer in a village seems to be more intelligent, because he is more responsive to the reality. A professor never responds to reality. He is always reacting out of his knowledge.

So whatsoever I am saying, the professor will be interpreting it in his own ways. Right now, whatsoever I am saying, he will be interpreting and classifying and he will be saying yes or no. And he will be classifying me: to what school I belong, to what ideology, what I am talking about. He is not listening! It is very difficult for a professor to listen: he is so full of inner noise, inner chattering. The noise is so much that nothing ever enters in him.

It happened:

"Whisky and whisky alone is responsible for your deplorable condition!" the judge admonished the drunken prisoner, who was a professor — maybe a professor of psychology.

"Glad to hear you say that, judge," beamed the drunk. "My wife says it's all my fault!"

If you have a certain idea in the mind, that idea will function as a nucleus: it will gather things around it which are supportive to it; it will drop things which are not supportive to it. A man who wants to come closer to truth has to drop all ideas, otherwise his own prejudices will be confirmed again and again. You can move with a prejudice and you will always find evidence for it.

Now the drunk used to think that he alone was not responsible, and the judge says: "Whisky and whisky alone is responsible for your deplorable condition."

"Glad to hear you say that, judge," beamed the drunk. "My wife says it's all my fault!"

If you come with a mind, you will go with a bigger mind. If you come with a no-mind, you will go with a bigger no-mind. It depends on you: how you come to me, what you bring to me, what you are ready to offer to me — a mind? then there is no communication. You will gather a few bits from here and there, and you will collect them in your old ways. It will be addition to your knowledge; it will not be a revelation, it will not give you anything new. It will not be a breakthrough.

256

But if you can listen to me just listening, not thinking, not interpreting, not classifying — just listening as if you don't know anything; listening in deep silence with no knowledge interfering in between — you will not be conditioned at all.

Innocence can never be conditioned. Only cunningness can be conditioned. Innocence is such freedom! It listens, but it remains above. Innocence is like a lotus flower: it remains in the water, but untouched by it. Then you can move around the world, you can go and listen to many people, you can read a thousand and one books, you can study all that down the centuries the human mind has invented, discovered, systematized, and you will remain unconditioned, you will remain free. Something within you will remain above, distant.

A habitual drunk staggered up to the front door of a home late one night, and kept rapping loudly until a lady in pyjamas came to answer.

"Par'n me, ma'am," he lushed, "this is an emergency. Can you tell me where Mulla Nasrudin lives?"

"Why," she exclaimed, "you are Mulla Nasrudin yourself!"

"I know, I know," he replied, "but that still doesn't answer the question — where does he live?"

You are a soul — which can*not* be corrupted. Innocence is its very nature. It is just like the sky: you see clouds come and go, and the sky remains just the same; it is not corrupted by the clouds. Dust storms arise, and settle back; the sky is not corrupted by dust storms. How many things have not happened under the skies? Millions of things have happened — nothing has corrupted it. It remains pure.

The inner sky is also pure, just like the outer sky. Thousands of things go on happening, but the innermost core remains virgin. There is *no way* to corrupt it.

That's why I say: if you are too much addicted, drunk with psychology, then it will be difficult to understand what I am saying. But if you can put aside your head for a while, if you can behead yourself for a while, if you can approach towards me directly, immediately, then you will hear what I am saying, you

257

will understand what I am saying—but you will not be conditioned by it, you will remain free. That is the beauty!

A Buddha has not conditioned anybody, a Jesus has never conditioned anybody. If people are Christians and have become conditioned, that is their choice—you cannot throw the responsibility on Jesus. If people have become Buddhists and have completely forgotten about Buddha, and go on talking only about Buddhist doctrines and dogmas, that is their responsibility—otherwise, Buddha has not conditioned anybody.

These people come to free you. They bring freedom, they bring purity, they bring innocence. But the ultimate result depends on you.

The fourth question: *Give and share.*
 Renounce non-essential and be
 essential.
To whom to give—the poor and needy?—in general
 or relatives and friends?
 beggars—organized or individuals?
 institutions—political and religious?
 purchase institutional presents—
 books and other things?
 saints and mahatmas?
 etc?

I GIVE YOU POETRY—you immediately translate it into prose. I have been simply saying: Share! You ask: With whom? You have changed the subject.

Mulla Nasrudin was talking to a woman and saying great things, was getting very romantic. He was saying, "Your eyes— never, never have they happened before. And your face— it is just like the moon. And the glow that surrounds you,

258

and the vibe that you create — it is the most beautiful thing that has ever happened." And he went on and on.

And, of course, as women are very practical, the woman asked, "Are you going to marry me, Nasrudin?"

Nasrudin said, "Please, don't change the subject!"

I am talking about sharing and you immediately change the subject, You say: "With whom?" Your emphasis is not about yourself. You have not asked: "I am a miser and I cannot share. It is difficult for me to share." You have not asked how to share, how not to be miserly. You have immediately changed the subject — as if you are ready to share but it is very difficult to find the right persons. So with whom?

"The poor and needy? — in general or relatives and friends?"

You are going into details — without asking the basic and fundamental question: Are you ready to share? When the cloud is ready to shower, it doesn't ask: "Where to shower? — on the mountains? in a lake? on grounds? in the fields? in the gardens? Where to shower? — on good people? virtuous or sinners? on temples or on churches? on saintly people or on worldly people?" It doesn't bother — it simply showers. It is not a question of on whom to shower. The cloud is ready — it *has* to shower, to unburden itself.

When the flower blooms, it doesn't ask: "Towards whose nostril should I float now? Where should I send my fragrance? To saints and mahatmas? or to sinners?" No, it never asks. It goes on spreading its fragrance, it goes on unconcerned about whom; the fragrance moves unaddressed.

That's what I would like to say to you: Share! and let your sharing be spontaneous. When you have to give, give! Why bother? But people are very cunning — they say: "Give? First we have to see whether it is the right person or not." How is one going to decide who is a right person or not? What are the criteria? How are you going to decide who is the right person?

A person may be poor but may be a criminal — so whether to give to him or not? A person may be poor, needy, his wife may be suffering from illness, his children may be hungry, but he

259

may be a drunkard. If you give him money, he will simply go and drink—he is not going to purchase medicine with it. With whom to share?

In Jainism there is a sect called 'Terapanth'. It has gone to the very logical end; it has rationalized miserliness to the very extreme. This sect says: "Don't give because you don't know what the other person will do about it—you give money to somebody; he may go and purchase a gun and kill a few people. Then? Then you will be responsible! It will be part of your karma. If you had not given him the money he would not have purchased the gun and he would not have killed so many people. He has killed now—you are part, knowingly, unknowingly, and you will have to pay for it."

Now this is the businessman's mind, and all these Terapanthis are business people. "Don't give, because who knows what will be done, what will happen out of it?" They say if a person is dying by the side of the road, thirsty, crying and asking for water, you just go on your way, don't be distracted by him—because if you give him water and tomorrow he kills somebody, then? or goes and steals something from somebody, then? You will be part of it.

Humanity is very cunning. Human beings are very cunning. This is the end-result of Mahavir's teaching—who taught about love and sharing. This Terapanth is a sect of Jains. Mahavir says: "Share!" But how things can turn! even to the very opposites. And it is appealing—it is rational, it looks right. Then these Terapanthis say: "If somebody is poor, he is poor because of his past karmas—who are you to help him? He is suffering from his past karmas and you are becoming a distracting force. If you give him money and you help him not to suffer, he will have to suffer some day or other—so you simply postpone. Let him be whatsoever he is."

If you want to share you will never ask these questions. These questions come up out of miserliness.

If you ask me, I will say: Share! If I cannot say anything positively about with whom to share, at least I can say one thing negatively: Never share with saints and mahatmas!—because what can you share with them? What can you give to them? If

260

they are really saints and mahatmas they are in tremendous bliss—you cannot give them anything. You can beg something from them. You can ask them to shower what has happened to them. You can receive. You can be the receiving end—you cannot be the giver. They don't need.

Otherwise, keep it as a simple remembrance that whenever there is any situation in which you are asked to share and you can share, you have something to share—share! and don't be bothered who the person is with whom you are sharing. That is none of your business! You shared—that's all.

And it is always beautiful—whether you share with a sinner or you share with a pious man, whether you share with a criminal or you share with a very respectable citizen, it is always beautiful. It will always give you tremendous joy. It is not a question of what happens afterwards! In the very sharing you have enjoyed a climax of being.

A Jewish couple were honeymooning at Niagara Falls. The boy's money ran out after a week, but he and his bride were having such a good time they wanted to stay longer. So he wired his father for more money. His telegram read: "Dear Dad. It's great here. Want to stay longer. Please send money. Love, Son."

The father wired back: "Dear Son. It's great anywhere. Come home. Love, Dad."

It is great anywhere!—love is great. It is not a question of whether you are near Niagara Falls or in the Himalayas: love is great everywhere, yes, anywhere. Sharing is great: with whom you share is irrelevant.

I know your mind will always find ways not to share. Avoid those tricks of the mind. You have to share. You should be happy whenever you can find an opportunity to share.

Mulla Nasrudin lay on his deathbed for months, while flocks of relatives gathered like vultures waiting for the kill. At last the dear old man went to his peaceful reward and the lawyers announced the date of the reading of his will.

All the relatives assembled on the appointed day. The lawyer tore open the envelope, drew out a piece of paper and read: "Being of sound mind, I spent every dime before I died."

That is the golden rule: Before you die, share whatsoever you have. If you are of a sound mind you will share your whole life. Before you die, spend youself in love.

The fifth question: *Are you holding my rope? Does that scare you?*

I HAVE told you one story—the question is concerned with that story—about the botanist who lowered his son with a rope round his waist into a deep valley in the Himalayas. It was difficult to reach in any other way to the flowers that were flowering in the valley. The father was, of course, afraid, scared. The child was enjoying—mm?—it was a beautiful adventure. He was thrilled. But the father was afraid.

The child reached down, he plucked the flowers. The father shouted from the top, "Are you okay, little one? Are you not afraid?"

The child laughed—the whole valley echoed his laughter—and he said, "Why should I be afraid when you, my father, are holding the rope? Why should I be afraid?"

The questioner asks: "Are you holding my rope? Does that scare you?"

Now this is a totally different situation. In the first place, I am not holding any rope—because any rope will create a bondage for you. In the second place, I have not lowered you into the valley to pick flowers—I have lowered you into the valley to disappear. . . . You cannot look back, and you cannot look at the top and say, "You are holding the rope." Even if I managed to give you the notion that I am holding your rope, it is all false.

It is just a trick to lower you down—there is no rope! And once lowered you cannot come back, because there is no way. Why should I be scared?

And it is not a question of picking some flowers there—it is a question of disappearing completely. I am sending you towards nothingness. I am sending you towards ultimate death. Yes, in the beginning I pretend that I am binding a rope around your waist: this mala, etc. This is the rope! I have to persuade you. Once you are persuaded . . . gone.

My whole effort is to help you to disappear. My whole effort is to help you to be so empty: *anatta*—non-being. Because if you are, you will remain in trouble. If you are, you will remain limited. If you are, there will be a definition to your being—and you will never be overflowing. Only emptiness can be overflowing, only emptiness can be at ease. Only emptiness can be life abundant. To be, the way passes through non-being.

If you really want to be, you will have to drop all concepts of your being. You will have to disappear, by and by. You will have to melt into nothingness.

Yes, I am lowering you, and I convince you that the rope is in my hand—you don't be worried. I have to do that to give you courage. The rope is non-existential. You will come to know about it—that the rope is non-existential—but you will come to know only when there is no question of returning. You will not be able to return. And you will be happy that there is no rope. You will be happy that there is no way to return. You will be happy that I persuaded you to disappear. You will feel grateful, eternally grateful.

Right now it may be difficult to understand what I am saying. *You* are the trouble; you are the anxiety, the anguish; you are the disease. In total health, you will not find yourself: the total health is a zero experience. That zero experience is what religious people have called the God experience.

I am not scared at all—I am simply laughing. And the day you understand, you will also not be scared. You will also laugh from the valley, and the valley will re-echo your laughter.

263

A SUDDEN CLASH OF THUNDER

The last question: *Bhagwan, Did you ever wake up in the morning with the feeling "The heck with all this Enlightenment business. Today I think I'll just go out and drive a truck"?*

IT IS not a question of ever waking up in the morning and saying to myself and feeling: The heck with all this Enlightenment business—it is an everyday rule. Every morning I say to myself: The heck with all this Enlightenment business. Today I think I will just go out and drive a truck. But where can I find a better truck with so many school-children inside it? Then I decide finally, by the time it is eight I again decide that one day more . . .

This question is from Swami Deva Nartan, and he has a P.S. also to it. The P.S. is: "You told me not to be so serious. You see, I'm trying."

Now my P.S. to the answer: "Whatsoever I have said, please, don't take it seriously. I am saying it very seriously!"

264

INDIA

- SHREE RAJNEESH ASHRAM, 17, Koregaon Park, Poona 411 001 Tel: 28127
- SAGAR DEEP, 52 Ridge Road, Malabar Hill, Bombay 400 006 Tel: 364783

USA

- ANANDA, 29 East 28th Street, New York, N.Y. 10016 Tel: 212 686 3261
- DHYANATARU, 375a Huron Ave, Cambridge, Mass. 02138 Tel: 617 491 2671
- BODHITARU, 7231 SW 62nd Place, Miami, Florida 33143
- MAITREYA, 431 W 20th St, New York N.Y. 10011 Tel: 212 924 2069
- SARVAM, 6412 Luzon Ave., Washington D.C. 20012 Tel: 202 726 1712
- GEETAM, Box 576, Highway 18, Lucerne Valley, California 92356 Tel: 714 248 6163
- PARAS, P.O. Box 22174, San Francisco, California 94122 Tel: 415 664 6600
- DEVALAYAM, P.O. Box 592, G.P.O. Kansas City, Missouri 69141
- PREMSAGAR, P.O. Box 2862, Chapel Hill, North Carolina 27514

CANADA

- ARVIND, 1330 Renfrew St., Vancouver, B.C.
- PRATIBODHA, 208 Old Yonge St., Willowdale, Toronto, Ontario Tel: 225 2960

ENGLAND

- KALPTARU, Top Floor, 10a Belmont Street, London NW1, Postal Address: 28 Oak Village, London NW5 4QN, Tel: 01 267 8304
- NIRVANA, 82 Bell Street, London NW1 Tel: 01 262 0991

266

- PREMTARU, Church Farm House, Field Dalling, Holt, Norfolk
- SURYODAYA, The Old Rectory, Gislingham, by Diss, Nr Eye, Suffolk
- TUSHITA, North Moreton, Didcot, Oxfordshire 119BA
- ANURODHA, Flat, 1, 30 Church Road, Moseley, Birmingham 15

HOLLAND
- AMITABH, Pieter Paauwstr 6, Amsterdam

SCOTLAND
- GOURISHANKAR, 9 Ravensdean Gardens, Penicuik, Midtothian Tel: Penicuik 73034
- PRASTHAN, 21 Wilmot Road, Glasgow C13 IXI

FRANCE
- PREMPATH, 45-390 Desmonts
- SHANTIDWEEP, 25 Avenue Pierre Premier de Serbie, Paris XVIe Tel: 720 7930

SPAIN
- PALASH Can Bonet, Sta. Gertrudis, Ibiza, Baleares

DENMARK
- ANAND NIKETAN, Skindergade 3, DK — 1159, Copenhagen 4 Tel: 01 11 79 09

ITALY
- ARIHANT, Via Cacciatori delle Alpi 19, 20019 Settimo Milanese, Milan

SWITZERLAND
- SATYAM, 15b Route de Loex, 1213 Onex, 1200 Geneva Tel: 022 93 19 46

WEST GERMANY
- PURVODAYA, D-8051 Margaretenried, Fongi-Hof Tel: 08764 426
- SHREYAS, 8 Munich 60, Raucheneggerstr. 4/11
- ANANDLOK, 1 Berlin 61, Mehringdamm 61 Postal Address: Berlin 61, Luckenwalderstr. 11

JAPAN
- ASHEESH, 5-4-17 Kichijoji-Kitamachi, Musashino-shi, Tokyo
Tel: 0422 53 6483

EAST AFRICA
- ANAND NEED, P.O. Box 72424, Nairobi, Kenya

SOUTH AFRICA
- BODHISATTVA, P.O. Box 1, New Germany, Natal

BRAZIL
- PURNAM, Caixa Postale 1946, Porto Alegre, Rio G. do Sul
Tel: 425588

- SOMA, Rua Caraibas, 1179, Casa 9, 05020 Pompeia, Sao Paulo

NEW ZEALAND
- SHANTI NIKETAN, 10 Bayfield Road, Herne Bay, Auckland

AUSTRALIA
- SHANTI SADAN, Havelock Clinic, 1 Havelock St, West Perth,
Western Australia 6005

- The Ultimate Alchemy Vols I and II
  (discourses on the Atma Pooja Upanishad)
- The Book of the Secrets Vols I—V
  (discourses on Tantra)
- The Supreme Doctrine
  (discourses on the Kenopanishad)
- VEDANTA: Seven Steps to Samadhi
  (discourses on the Akshya Upanishad)
- YOGA: the alpha and the omega Vols I—VII
  (discourses on Patanjali's Yoga Sutras)
- Roots and Wings
  (talks based on questions)
- The Empty Boat
  (discourses on Chuang Tzu)
- No Water, No Moon
  (discourses on Zen)
- When the Shoe Fits
  (discourses on Chuang Tzu)
- Neither This Nor That
  (discourses on Sosan—Zen)
- . . .and the flowers showered
  (discourses on Zen stories)
- Returning to the Source
  (discourses on Zen stories)
- The Hidden Harmony
  (discourses on the fragments of Heraclitus)
- TANTRA: The Supreme Understanding
  (discourses on Tilopa's Song of Mahamudra)
- The Grass Grows by Itself
  (discourses on Zen stories)
- Until You Die
  (discourses on Sufi stories)

- Just Like That
  (discourses on Sufi Stories)
- TAO: The Three Treasures Vols I—IV
  (discourses on Lao Tzu)
- The True Sage
  (discourses on Hassidic stories)
- Nirvana: The Last Nightmare
  (discourses on Zen stories)

- Hammer on the Rock
  (darshan diary Vol I)
- Above All, Don't Wobble
  (darshan diary Vol II)
- Nothing to Lose But Your Head
  (darshan diary Vol III)
- Be Realistic: Plan For A Miracle
  (darshan diary Vol IV)

- The Search
  (discourses on The Ten Bulls of Zen)
- Come Follow Me Vols I—IV
  (discourses on the life of Jesus)
- Ancient Music in the Pines
  (discourses on Zen stories)
- Dang, Dang, Doko-Dang
  (discourses on Zen)

foreign editions

- The Book of the Secrets Vol I
  (Harper and Row, USA)
- The Book of the Secrets Vol I
  (Thames and Hudson, UK)
- No Water, No Moon
  (Sheldon Press, UK)

- Straight to Freedom
  (Indian edition: Until You Die)
  (Sheldon Press, UK)
- Only One Sky
  (Indian edition: TANTRA: The Supreme Understanding)
  (Dutton, USA)
- I am the Gate
  (Harper and Row, USA)
- Meditation: The Art of Ecstasy
  (Harper and Row, USA)
- Tantra, Spirituality and Sex
  (Rainbow Bridge, USA)

translations

- Tantra: Sonzai no Uta
  (Japanese—Merkmal Ltd, Tokyo)
- Tantra: Het Allerhoogste Inzicht
  (Dutch—Ankh-Hermes)
- Meditazione Dinamica
  (Italian—Edizioni Mediterranee, Rome)
- Yo Soy La Puerta
  (Spanish—Editorial Diana S.A., Mexico)
- Le Livre des Secrets Vol I
  (French—Les Editions A.T.P. Paris)
- La Rivoluzione Interiore
  (Italian—Armenia Editore)
- Hu Meditation og Kosmic Orgasme
  (Danish—Borgens Forlag A/S)
- Il Libro dei Segreti Vol I
  (Italian—Armenia Editore)
- Michi O Saguru
  (Japanese—Merkmal Ltd, Tokyo)